Race in the Shadow of Law

Race in the Shadow of Law offers a critical legal analysis of European responses to institutional racism. It draws connections between contemporary legal knowledge practices and colonial systems of thought, arguing that many people of colour experience the law as a part of a racial problem, rather than a solution, to racial injustice. Based on a critical legal ethnography of anti-racism work in Europe, and with an emphasis on the German context, the book positions Black and anti-racist perspectives at the centre, rather than the margins, of critically thinking through the intersection of race and law. Combining this ethnography with comparative legal analysis, discourse analysis and critical race theory, the book develops a critical discussion of the European legal frameworks aimed at regulating racism, and particularly institutional racism, in policy and policing. In linking this critique to the transformative potential of social movements, however, it goes on to examine the strategic and creative possibility of disrupting conventional modes of engaging, and resisting, law.

Eddie Bruce-Jones is based at Birkbeck School of Law, London, UK.

Race in the Shadow of Law

State violence in contemporary Europe

Eddie Bruce-Jones

Routledge
Taylor & Francis Group
LONDON AND NEW YORK

First published 2017
by Routledge
2 Park Square, Milton Park, Abingdon, Oxon, OX14 4RN

and by Routledge
711 Third Avenue, New York, NY 10017

First issued in paperback 2018

Routledge is an imprint of the Taylor & Francis Group, an informa business

British Library Cataloguing in Publication Data
A catalogue record for this book is available from the British Library

Library of Congress Cataloging-in-Publication Data
A catalog record for this book has been requested

ISBN 13: 978-1-138-62427-6 (pbk)
ISBN 13: 978-1-138-64936-1 (hbk)

Typeset in Baskerville by
by FiSH Books Ltd, Enfield

In memory of Oury Jalloh and Mariama Djombo Diallo.
For Mamadou Saliou Diallo, Mouctar Bah and the many others who have fought for something close to a truth.

Contents

List of abbreviations

ADEFRA	ADEFRA e.V., Schwarze Deutsche Frauen und Schwarze Frauen in Deutschland (Black German Women and Black Women in Germany)
AGG	Allgemeines Gleichbehandlungsgesetz (General Equal Treatment Law)
AsylbLG	Asylbewerberleistungsgesetz (Asylum Applicant Entitlement Law)
BGH	Bundesgerichtshof (German Supreme Court)
BPolG	Bundespolizeigesetz (Federal Police Act)
BVFG	Bundesvertriebenengesetz (German Law on Displaced Persons)
CRT	critical race theory
ECHR	European Convention on Human Rights
ECRI	European Commission against Racism and Intolerance
EU	European Union
GG	Grundgesetz (German Basic Law)
HJ	Hitler Jugend (Hitler Youth)
HPRC	Herero People's Reparation Corporation
ICCPR	International Covenant on Civil and Political Rights
IOJ	Initiative in Gedenken an Oury Jalloh, e.V. (Initiative in Remembrance of Oury Jalloh)
ISD	ISD e.V., Initiative Schwarze Deutsche und Schwarze Menschen in Deutschland (Initiative of Black Germans and Black People in Germany)
KZ	*Konzentrationslager* (concentration camp)
LG	Landgericht (regional court)
NGO	non-government organisation
NS	Nationalsozialismus (National Socialism)
NSU	National Socialist Underground
OLG	Oberlandesgericht (upper regional court)
OSI	Open Society Initiative
OVG	Oberverwaltungsgericht (upper administrative court)

SEK	Sondereinsatzkommando (special command unit)
SS	Schutzstaffel (security service during the Third Reich)
TFEU	Treaty on the Functioning of the European Union
VG	Verwaltungsgericht (administrative court)

Acknowledgements

This book began as a doctoral dissertation, successfully defended on 4 September 2013 at the Philosophische Fakultät I of the Humboldt-Universität zu Berlin, under the direction of Dekan Prof. Michael Seadle, in the Institut für Europäische Ethnologie. I would like to thank my doctoral thesis supervisors, Prof. Wolfgang Kaschuba and Prof. Beate Binder, for their patience and helpful suggestions throughout the writing of this book.

I would like to thank Mouctar Bah, Nadine Saeed, Thomas Ndindah, Komi Edzro, Anett Zeidler and the members of the Initiative in Remembrance of Oury Jalloh for sharing their reflections and thoughts with me over the years. Their tireless work is nothing short of astounding. I must thank Gabriele Heinecke and Philipp Napp, the lawyers for the Jalloh's family in the appellate trail, who generously gave their time, professional expertise and friendship to me during my time as a trial observer. I would like to thank my wonderful colleagues at Birkbeck School of Law, University of London, as well as colleagues at the law faculties of Humboldt-Universität zu Berlin, Westminster University, City University in London and the University of Bristol for allowing me to workshop various chapters of the book in research colloquia. A special thanks to Katharina Oguntoye and Amy Evans for their helpful insights. I owe a debt of gratitude to Prof. Prof. Grada Kilomba for her brilliant courses from 2003–2005 on Psychoanalysis of Race, Sexism and Racism from a Black Perspective, which were crucial in helping shape my thoughts on racism in Germany. Similarly, I would like to thank Prof. Kimberlé Crenshaw for her Columbia and UCLA course on Global Affirmative Action and for advising my first article on the subject of German anti-discrimination law. This work would have been difficult to imagine without the support of Jose de Pablo. This work would have been impossible were it not for intellectual superheroes like Kwesi Aikins, Jamie Schearer, Tahir Della, Prof. Peggy Piesche, Sharon Dodua Otoo, Noah Sow, Cengiz Barskanmaz, Biplap Basu, Mutlu Ergun, Philipp Khabo Koepsell, Prof. Carsten Junker, Prof. Kristin Kopp, Prof. Iyiola Solanke, RonAmber Deloney, Aretha Schwarzbach-Apithy, Dr.

Olumide Popoola and many others who have influenced my thinking over the last 15 years in Germany. I would not have undertaken this journey were it not for the intellectual impact that studying Afro-American Studies and Anthropology at Harvard had on me. I must thank my undergraduate academic advisor, Prof. Kwame Anthony Appiah, for suggesting I take up my graduate fellowship with the DAAD; Prof. Michael Herzfeld, Dr. Barrington Edwards and Prof. Werner Sollors for their support of my senior thesis work on Black Literature in Germany; Dr. Naomi Pabst for her course on Black Feminisms, and Professors Henry Louis Gates, Jr., Cornel West and Evelyn Higginbotham for taking the time to workshop our undergraduate senior theses – as a university lecturer, I am still grateful for that experience, 15 years later.

I am grateful to Ricky Watson, Jabez Williams, Todd Ford, Aïda Worku and Sasha Rossman for keeping me balanced; Roselyn Batino and Natural Sedova for the incredible music and Kirk Henry and Troy Lopez for keeping me fed.

This book would have been impossible without the support of my mother, my grandparents and my late father.

Preface

> Racism, specifically, is the state-sanctioned or extralegal production and exploitation of group-differentiated vulnerability to premature death.
>
> (Ruthie Wilson Gilmore, *The Golden Gulag*, 2007)

State violence cannot be understood as merely physical violence. However, I am indebted to Ruthie Wilson Gilmore for describing racism as a phenomenon that is authorised and empowered by the state, in a variety of structural ways, that has a negative material impact on the lives of those it affects. It shortens, contracts, squeezes our lives, and we spend a great deal of energy in the labour of struggling to remain whole. This conceptualisation of racism *as* state violence is the starting point of my investigation. The law encompasses prominent institutional logics of the state and provides important terrain for investigating racism in this regard.

This project is the result of quite a long period of investigation. In some ways, it is a continuation of research and themes I investigated during a research project on Black German literature and resistance in 1999–2002. It is also motivated by the years I lived in Germany (six years between 2001 and 2011) and my continual involvement in Black German communities during the same time period. Some of the people with whom I had the opportunity to engage for this project were friends or colleagues whom I have known for over a decade. This intimacy has allowed me not only to gain a deep understanding and empathy for the issues at stake, but it has also caused me to integrate a number of personal reflections in order to make the reader clear that I am positioned in this highly politicised set of circumstances. This is part and parcel of any reflexive description of participant observation and is to be expected in most modern critical ethnographic or social anthropological writing.

It should be made clear that the German context cannot be read to typify Europe, and the peculiarities of German cultural and social norms and values should be considered centrally in interpreting the confluence of racism, law and structural or state violence. However, part of the point of contextualising this examination within Europe is to counter the notion that Germany is exceptional. In fact, the complex relationship between law and colonial logics, the privilege of whiteness and the intra-institutional features of racial exclusion are all aspects shared across various European countries. The book, then, is an opening and an invitation to explore these connections in Europe by way of increased academic and social engagement on the topic of race, law and state violence.

This book does not attempt to explain the efficacy of public policy or effectiveness of legal provisions using the terms of law, but rather is an attempt to gain insights on the social reality of encountering legal institutions from the varied perspectives of Black activists in Germany. By using a range of sources from literature to interviews and public media campaigns, this project aims to reframe legal discussions as socially integrated features of daily life by using the point of encounter as impetus rather than using either legislative language or the logic of statutory interpretation on their own.

Prologue

Some remarks on ethnography, race and law

Legal rules, principles and discourses aim to regulate human behaviour. Law can be articulated, in a narrow sense, as the totality of binding rules, while politics can be seen as the discourses and contexts that surround the production and articulation of those rules. However, the usefulness of this narrow view of law is quite limited when analysing law's relationship with society. Such a view can be critiqued by examining the legal encounter – the experience of law and its operant logics. By this, I am not referring to encounter with the rules themselves, but rather with the *justificatory principles* underlying the rules and the *process of legitimation* upon which such justificatory principles are based when conceptualising justice and difference. First, legal rules are applied in ways that are open to influence by social dynamics and ideologies beyond the rules themselves, upsetting the intended alignment between formal and substantive notions of justice. Second, the pervasiveness of the legal concepts in our sensibilities about identity, authenticity, rights, moral expectations, racism and citizenship, to name but a few examples, colour our notions about what law is as a set of knowledge-producing institutions.

This book examines the ways in which Black people in Germany have struggled against certain legal ideologies concerning racism, citizenship and belonging. This struggle is not primarily in the form of direct litigation, but rather it reveals itself through poetry and essays, on the stage in plays and musical performances, in demonstrations and protests, in public debates and on online media platforms. This book presents a series of interventions that Black people have made in thinking about legal and political subjectivity in Germany that help reformulate how one might consider exclusion from the contemporary German *demos* (Balibar 2004).[1] The project also suggests an analytical framework for the idea of ethnographic space and integrates intervening disciplines of psychoanalysis and critical race

1 Balibar critically considers the existence of a European *demos* and the violence inherent in the European project.

theory (CRT) to mediate the encounter between legal doctrine and lived experience. In this context, it aims to describe Black German expectations and encounters with law, just as law reinforces ideas of Blackness, Germanness, European-ness and the significance of difference.

There is a great deal to be gained from examining Black experience-informed expectations of, affect towards, resistance to and critique of the legal knowledge produced in Germany. In analysing Black German encounters with law, this book aims to do two things: (1) explore more profoundly the epistemologies of knowledge production that Black Germans offer about belonging in Germany and Europe vis-à-vis the law (knowledge practices); and (2) identify the failures of certain legal rules and equality policies as conceptualised by Black people, exposing the need for approaches to law that integrate critical examination of the concept of race in Germany. To this end, the book employs a combination of discourse analysis, doctrinal interpretation, interviews and first-hand reflection.

Who are Black Germans?

There are a number of overlapping narratives that describe who Black Germans are. For instance, there is a migration narrative that recounts various periods of Black migration to Germany during the last century. There is a history of Blackness in the German imagination that can be traced back to the 13th century and seen through early German colonial thought (Oguntoye et al. 1986, Oguntoye 1997, Reed-Anderson 2000). There is the strong legacy of Wilhelm Amo, who in the 1700s became the first African to graduate from a European university when he earned his doctorate in philosophy from Wittenberg, later becoming a professor of philosophy in Halle.[2] There is also a very contemporary narrative of the development of a Black German political and social presence, mainly spanning from the post-World War II era until the present, but really beginning to take form in the 1980s with the writing of influential books and the founding of key organisations.[3] The different narratives that historicise the existence of Black people in the German context provide the basis for a discussion of Black German cultural participation and recognition. In Chapter 5, I describe the process by which Black people and other people of colour in Germany have reclaimed and recast dominant narratives and asserted new ones to describe and position Black people and Black thought in the German context.

Black Germans began a literary and political movement in the mid-1980s that has helped create the space for Black German cultural and

2 For more on Amo and other prominent Black Germans from past and contemporary times, see Initiative Schwarze Menschen in Deutschland 2011.

3 For further detail, see Chapter 5.

political production. During this time, many Black Germans and Black people living in Germany began to write and organise, recover and record stories, and reposition Black people within broader German historical narratives (Oguntoye et al. 1986, Oguntoye 1997, Hügel-Marshall 1998, Massaquoi 2001). This movement was comprised of political organisers, anti-racism activists, academics and artists who were committed to claiming vital cultural and social space for Black people to survive within the German context.

Today, there are a number of politically active Black-led organisations in Germany. Black German men and women, together with Black people who had been living in Germany but did not self-identify as German, organised in the mid-1980s to form a number of political organisations. Among these were the Initiative Schwarze Deutsche (later renamed the Initiative Schwarze Menschen in Deutschland)[4] and ADEFRA (Schwarze Deutsche Frauen und Schwarze Frauen in Deutschland).[5] These organisations continue to provide important spaces for organising Black activists, artists and professionals in Germany. Currently, there are other influential national organisations, such as media watch group Der Braune Mob,[6] as well as dozens of local, regional and national chapters of Black political,

4 See website of the Initiative Schwarze Menschen in Deutschland, e.V., http://neu.isdonline.de accessed 30 May 2016.

5 See website of ADEFRA, e V., http://adefra.de accessed 30 May 2016. As per the website, Adefra e.V. is *'ein Forum, in dem sich Schwarze Frauen mit unterschiedlichsten Themen wie Politik, Bildung, Lifestyle und Gesundheit beschäftigen. ADEFRA repräsentiert eine Vielfalt von Schwarzen Frauen: Töchter, Mütter, Frauen, die allein oder in Beziehung leben, Frauen aller sexuellen Orientierungen, alte und junge Frauen. Alle verbindet auf die eine oder andere Weise – unabhangig von Weltanschauung, Glauben, Nationalität, Beruf und Sozialisation – die Erfahrung Schwarz und eine Frau zu sein'*. Translation: 'a forum in which Black German women deal with very different themes, such as politics, education, lifestyle and health. ADEFRA represents a plurality of Black women: daughters, mothers, women living alone or in a relationship, women of all sexual orientations, old and young women. Everything connects, in one way or another – independent of world view, belief, nationality, occupation and upbringing – the experience of being Black and a woman'.

6 See Der Braune Mob, e.V. website, http://derbraunemob.de accessed 30 May 2016. As per the website, the underlying purpose for the organisation's media watch work can be summarised by the following: *'Vorsichtige Schätzungen beziffern die Anzahl Schwarzer Deutscher auf mehr als dreihunderttausend und die Zahl Schwarzer Menschen in Deutschland auf mehr als eine Million. Gemessen an diesem Umfang finden die Anliegen Schwarzer Menschen in Deutschland erstaunlich wenig Gehör. Nach wie vor werden Schwarze Menschen als Teil der deutschen Bevölkerung konsequent ignoriert und das gefährliche und gestrige Bild vom ausschließlich weißen Deutschland bewusst oder unbewusst transportiert'*. Translation: 'Careful estimates put the number of Black Germans at more than three-hundred thousand and the number of Black people in Germany at more than one million. Measured against this scope, the concerns of Black people in Germany receives astoundingly little attention. Black people continue to be consistently ignored as a part of German population and the dangerous and passé picture of an exclusively white Germany is consciously or unconsciously conveyed'.

cultural, artistic and media organisations, such as Afrika-Rat, Nigerian Community Germany,[7] Africa Positive,[8] CyberNomads and Joliba.[9]

While it is important to note that Blackness is a socially constructed category, it is equally important to realise that the falsity of biological 'race' thinking does not render the category useless when analysing social organisation or identity formation (AG gegen Rassismus in den Lebenswissenschaften 2009). The rest of this section examines Blackness as an analytical category, investigates ways in which the concept of diaspora is employed in Germany's Black community and, in the process, it attempts to define the concepts of community consciousness and political formation.

Blackness as an analytical category

'Black' is not a signifier that should be read or used without some critical understanding of the politics of identity. Blackness is a descriptive construct that has been used in the West as both a degrading and empowering term to describe those with African ancestry. It has been used as a racialised demarcation by those in power for the purpose of social stratification and domination (Haney-Lopez 2006, Mecheril 2007). This term has been re-signified by people of African ancestry (and others) as an affirmative political marker[10] and, in many contexts, a declaration of African heritage. In some contexts, it is more inclusive than just meaning African ancestry and can include any non-white identity. Because the term 'Black' and its various translations can carry with it various local meaning beyond this generalised meaning, it would be cumbersome and inaccurate to universally deploy this general concept of Blackness. Nonetheless, there is a broad context in which the notion of Blackness, as political and perhaps historical self-understanding, can be conceived. This takes the form, for example, of sharing common experiences of Blackness that transcend national borders, a recognition of the role of European colonialism in Africa as formative of contemporary global geopolitical issues, and the solidarity inherent in Black diaspora thinking.

In this relatively early moment of pan-European political and legal harmonisation, ethnographers are currently presented with the unique challenge of describing what is meant by Black European identity. It is challenging to position Black subjects and Black subjectivity within the project of ethnography. If Blackness matters as an analytical category, how the

7 See Nigerian Community Germany, e.V. website, http://nigeriancommunitygermany.com accessed 30 May 2016.

8 See Africa Positive, e.V. website, www.africa-positive.de accessed 30 May 2016.

9 See Joliba Interkulturelles Netzwerk in Berlin, e.V. website, http://joliba-online.de accessed 30 May 2016.

10 For a detailed discussion of the Negritude movement, see Cesaire and Kelley 2000.

ethnographer chooses to locate, identify and describe Blackness is absolutely essential to the resulting research. Even when the ethnographer chooses to allow her interlocutors in a given study to define Blackness for themselves, the ethnographer does select the interviewees. This means that the ethnographer makes decisions about who may inform the project of Black ethnography in advance of allowing interviewees to define Blackness from their own perspectives. Having a position on and making judgements with respect to the type of representations one is making is a constituent part of ethnographic research methodology. Given this, I had to make a decision at the beginning of my research about informants in this project. This would lead me to critically question the concept of Blackness in Germany.

In considering my interlocutors in this ethnographic study, with a pan-European Black presence in mind, I consider what it means to shape discourses around Blackness. 'Discourse setters' in the Black community, including writers, activists and academics engaged in public discussions around community issues, advocate for the epistemological terrain in Europe that renders coherent Black European subject positions. Epistemology in this context, and in the broader context of this book, means knowledge and the value system around how the knowledge is produced and where it comes from. The problematic element in conceiving the 'discourse setter' is that certain types of discourse, for example, academic discourse and other media with social prominence and acceptance, may only represent a certain type of Black European narrative of experience and may reify certain types of speech in power. This is a problem that much of anthropological study faces because theorising identity takes on a representational form, intentionally or serendipitously. In this case, it bears reiterating that the frame of the study concerns those structuring their narratives of self and space around the existence and the possibility of Black Germany and, by extension, Black Europe.

Many of the people who have informed this project consider themselves both Black and German, but this is not always a straightforward proposition, even in local terms. Being Black and European is discursively complex. It does not enjoy widespread ideological support and does not have a great deal of linguistic traction, though this is changing slowly. Aside from the tense discursive juxtaposition of Black and European identities, self-description as 'Black' also requires some unpacking. For instance, in the United Kingdom, 'Black' may include not only people of African descent, but also those who would elsewhere in Europe describe themselves as South Asian or Middle Eastern.[11] In a similar way, it is difficult to pin

11 See e.g., the website of the Southall Black Sisters http://southallblacksisters.org.uk accessed 30 May 2016. In the United Kingdom, particularly in the 1970s and 1980s, the term 'Black' has referred not only to people of African descent, but also to South Asians and other people of colour (non-white people).

down precisely what it means to be German or indeed European in the context of this study. A legalistic way to make a distinction between German and non-German would be to focus on German citizens, i.e., passport holders. However, given varying national conceptions of insider-outsider status in Germany, and given that non-white and certain white non-ethnic-Germans are often considered *Ausländer* or foreigners, European identity itself has to be carefully theorised if it is to be properly engaged in this project. White Europeans are, according to this mainstream public discourse, more readily understood as Germans, given the racialised understanding of German-ness. European means, in some respects, more than being a citizen of a European Union member state – whiteness is a central defining feature of belonging in and to Europe.

Black community in Germany

Community is a broad term that I use to describe coordinated social relations among people of African descent in Germany. Conventionally, when one thinks of a 'community', one likely imagines a group living in a geographically-circumscribed area or bound by a unifying cause, culture, ethnicity or nation (see Anderson 2006).[12] In this sense, there has been debate as to whether a Black community actually exists as a united network of people who communicate and coordinate with one another. Whether or not it fits into Benedict Anderson's particular model of the 'imagined community', many Black people in Germany experience community with one another. Not all Black people in Germany regard other Black people as connected to them in a profound way, and some affirmatively reject a sense of affiliation with other Black people for various reasons, sometimes related to upbringing in relative isolation from other Black people and had an uneasiness about approaching other Black people for fear of confronting one's own Blackness (see e.g. Hügel-Marshall 1998: 88–89).[13]

12 Anderson describes communities in his seminal work primarily in the context of national belonging. However, there are parallels between the types of religious, cultural and symbolic connections that people have as part of a nation and similar shared experiences that people have as part of a diasporic community. Though the national community recalls aspects of political borders and geographically circumscribed areas, one main feature of both types of imagined community, national and diasporic, is the people do not have to share the same physical space or daily practices, but relate to one another by way of cultural and social commonalities and experiences.

13 Hügel-Marshall describes her apprehension in the 1980s, after moving to Frankfurt, about attending a meeting of Black Germans. Her anxiety and 'un-readiness' was prompted by her fear of confronting the experience of being Black herself. She states: *'Eines Abends nach dem Training drückt sie mir einen Artikel über Afrodeutsche, die sich das erste Mal bundesweit, und zwar hier in der Nähe von Frankfurt, treffen wollen. Afro-deutsche – was für ein Wort? Was geht mich das an, denke ich und werfe den Zeitungsausschnitt in den Papierkorb. Was um alles in der Welt will ich mit "meinesgleichen"? Nein, ich will auf keinen Fall zu diesem Treffen. Ich bin nicht*

So, as with anywhere, sometimes diasporic relationships are simply not enough to constitute community for some people.

Community, in a basic sense, is also formed through communicating commonalities in experience and self-perception. Identity, including common histories and common experiences of exclusion, can form the basis of mutual identification. A community may share a base of knowledge and, with that knowledge base, it may filter the other information gained from society (for example, media and the 'official record').

The idea of a Black community or multiple Black communities brings to bear two important questions for this book. First, what is the relevance of 'community' in this context? The second is, what does community have to do with political formation? I use both of these two context-specific terms to describe unity and coalition among Black people living in Germany. Community is the broader of the two terms, and political formation picks up on a thread of community, comprising a specific (but relatively large) aspect of Black German social cohesion.

African diaspora politics as community consciousness

There are a number of ways in which one can conceive of the term 'diaspora'. These range from the conventional notion of diaspora as a group that has been dispersed by way of exile, to the modern examples that have come to help shape the term's contemporary application, such as the 'gay diaspora' and other forms of diaspora for which it is not necessarily the migration but rather the shared experiences that shape self-understanding as a group (see Cohen 2008: 8–10).[14] However, the main way in which I use the term 'diaspora' in this book is to describe people of African descent

bereit, aus meiner Anonymität herauszutreten, mich womöglich sichtbar zu machen, für wen? Nein, ich will nicht andere afrodeutsche Gesichter sehen und meinem Schmerz begegnen. Meine Angst ist zu groß, zu groß, um all dem Erlebten, das ich versuche hinter mir zu lassen, erneut zu begegnen. Der Haß auf meine Hautfarbe ist viel größer als der Wunsch, andere afrodeutsche Frauen und Männer kennenzulernen'. Translation: 'One evening after training she prints me an article about Afro-Germans want to meet up from across the country for the first time, right here near Frankfurt. Afro-German – what type of word [is that]? What does that have to do with me, I think and throw the newspaper clipping in the wastepaper basket. What in all the world do I want with "people like me"? No, I do not want to go to this meeting under any circumstances. I am not ready to step out of my anonymity, to make myself visible anywhere, for whom? No, I do not want to see other Afro-German faces and confront my pain. My fear is too big, too big, to confront anew all that I have experienced, which I am trying to leave behind me. The hate of my skin colour is much larger than the wish to meet other Afro-German women and men'.

14 Cohen mentions a 'gay diaspora' concept in the context of a growing discursive turn towards viewing a 'gay community', though the terminology and terms of connection are highly Western in this regard.

around the world who consider themselves to be affiliated or connected via a common history, a common present-day circumstance, or both.

The concept of the diaspora offers a ready alternative to the stern discipline of blood kinship on one hand and national belonging on the other. It rejects the popular image of self-evident nation-centric identities, tidily composed of uniform families. As an alternative to the metaphysics of race, nation and bounded culture coded into the body, diaspora is a concept that problematises the cultural and historical mechanics of belonging. It may well be conceptualised as a sort of call-and-response identity, coordinated with the dynamics of global migration and structural power relations. It disrupts the basic association of identity with geography by refashioning the simple sequence of explanatory links between place, location and consciousness.[15] It also disrupts the relationship of place and memory as a marker of identity in a similar fashion by drawing attention to the contingent political dynamics of commemoration and those stories and experiences that travel (Gilroy 2000: 123).

Here, it is vital to note the influence of James Clifford and his useful concept of self-location. Clifford, in his instructive text *Routes,* aims to address whether one can 'locate oneself historically to tell a coherent global story, when historical reality is understood to be an unfinished series of encounters' and whether one can investigate '[w]hat attitudes of tact, receptivity, and self-irony are conducive to non-reductive understandings' (1997: 13). He argues that a 'degree of self-location is possible and valuable, particularly when it points beyond the individual toward outgoing webs of relationship' (1997: 12) He makes this observation in the context of discussing the borders, what he refers to as the 'policed and transgressed edges' of anthropological areas of study, such as culture, and how these borders conflict with the disciplinary research techniques of self-reflective travel writing. He ultimately concludes that such scholarship is 'relational, negotiated and in process' (1997: 12).

Many people of African descent in Germany, in many ways, share a common alliance despite their diversity of ethnicity, nationality, religion and social status. A diasporic politics of affiliation for political and social purposes has become a very common mode of interaction, perhaps somewhere between cooperation and community formation, relying on shared social experiences and a common understanding of the position of Black people globally, with particular regard paid to global geopolitics of power, colonialism and racism. This translates in Germany to a variety of shared challenges based on a shared set of experiences, from countering everyday racism in the form of racial stereotypes to pushing for law reform or filing strategic litigation against public institutions and private parties.

15 By consciousness, I mean contextual self-perception of oneself, one's group or one's political formation.

James Clifford uses global self-location as the starting point for investigation in *Routes*, which explores migration and identity. By way of introductory remarks, he argues:

> The essays gathered here grapple with this predicament. Is it possible to locate oneself historically to be an unfinished series of encounters? What attitudes of tact, receptivity, and self-irony are conducive to nonreductive understandings? What are the conditions for serious translation between different routes in an interconnected but not homogenous modernity? Can we recognize viable alternatives to 'traveling West,' old and new paths?
>
> (Clifford 1997: 13)

Here, Clifford points to the possibility of existing in a state of perpetual historical incompleteness, which I read as contingency and multiplicity, inasmuch as the need to 'translat[e] between different routes' suggests an historical position that is multiply located. The idea of diaspora in general, and the Black German diaspora specifically, embodies this mode of historical self-positioning. Clifford indicates elsewhere in his introduction that travel is an interactive and constitutive process that shapes the world's 'cultural centers, discrete regions and territories' (1997: 3).[16] With this in mind, while mine is a project that examines Black thought and action in Germany, it is important to be aware that similar processes of communication and cooperation are presently occurring across Europe, and that these national projects connect in a variety of ways.

Field space

Given the focus of this book on mapping epistemology and gaining insight into Black experiences with certain German institutions, it has been necessary to critically engage with the concept of field space. Here, it is important to note that research on Black German political formations requires thinking of the 'space' in field space not only in terms of physical

16 Here, Clifford (1997) uses Europe as the example. He elucidates: 'Dwelling was understood to be the local ground of collective life, travel a supplement; roots always precede routes. But what would happen, I began to ask, if travel were untethered, seen as a complex and pervasive spectrum of human experiences? Practice of displacement might emerge as constitutive of cultural meanings rather than as their simple transfer or extension. The cultural effects of European expansionism, for example, could no longer be celebrated, or deplored, as simple diffusion outward – of civilization, industry, science, or capital. For the region called "Europe" has been constantly remade, and traversed, by influences beyond its borders. And is not this interactive process relevant, in varying degrees, to any local, national, or regional domain?'.

orientation but also in terms of political affiliation, the relationality of multi-issue social movements and transnational, transhistorical narratives. The discourses around this notion of 'space' operate through interpersonal relationships, at group meetings, on online platforms, as well as through news media, literature and songs. In this way, one must regard the written page and the digital world as extensions of the physical geographical field.

One of the first questions that an anthropologist confronts herself with is that of her interlocutors, the people about whom the anthropologist writes. As a researcher, one must decide from whose perspective she will adopt her analytical references and whose symbols and systems of meanings she will attempt to describe. With regard to the current project, the short answer is that I have spoken with self-identified Black Germans and Afro-Germans,[17] as well as people of African descent in Germany who do not identify as German. In either case, the people with whom I spoke had a stake in the project of Germany – those who had made their lives in Germany and sought some degree of social recognition and, as the case may be, legal protection in the country. The longer answer is that the specifics of what makes Black German identity possible are epistemological, rather than merely legal, national, ethnic, racial or regional. The project of describing Black German positionality, as an ethnography, has a chicken-and-egg issue at its core whereby, before one can locate Black German people as situated social actors, one must examine the knowledge that Black Germans produce about themselves. Researching this situated position, then, does not start by arriving at some physical place and observing what one encounters. It involves instead careful consideration of epistemologies produced in Black European communities and political formations, which guide the researcher along the contours of the structure and political orientations of social thought within these spaces. In the case study on Germany, then, the researcher must decide that the question of *who* Black German people *are* should follow rather than lead the question of uncovering the epistemological conditions necessary for Black German people to exist. This requires an overt political positioning that makes some anthropologists uncomfortable – in my estimation, political positioning in anthropological studies, including the decision *not* to focus on epistemology, has been conventional, though often inexplicit. However, it

17 While many people of African descent in the German context use both terms Afro-German (*Afro-Deutsch*) or Black/Black German (*Schwarz/schwarze Deutsche*) to describe themselves, some people prefer one over the other, and only very few people objected to the term Black. For the purpose of effective communication and to acknowledge that many people of African descent living in Germany do not consider themselves Afro-German and use the term Black exclusively, I am choosing to use the term Black in this work, but that is not a decision that is self-evident.

seems that the orthodoxy of such positioning practices is being taken up when applied to describing diasporas and global cultural flows.[18]

Diaspora politics and fieldwork

Audre Lorde, in her influential collection of essays *Sister/Outsider* remarked carefully on the importance of self-positioning in terms of identifying one's own social marginalisation or relation to systems of oppression, but also in building connections among other groups and connecting oneself to the others' stories and struggles (Lorde 1984). This double reflection on position also seems to articulate certain parameters contouring my experience as a person of the Black diaspora engaged in social, academic and activist endeavours for over the past 15 years in Germany. Global and comparative elements of Black experiences are productive components of a larger discussion and a larger archive of Black thought. On a certain level, although I am not German myself, I have felt a great deal of affiliation with the internally diverse Black German community, an extended family of sorts, and into it I have been generously welcomed. Within its intellectual, social and activist circles, I built a life and I continue to invest significant personal, political and intellectual commitments. The concept of diaspora precludes having to think of communities as discrete and allows me to focus on a politics of connectedness while celebrating and learning from the differences that we bring to this particular spatial and political situation of Blackness.

In a strict sense, my fieldwork in the context of this project has involved interviews and critical discussions with activists and litigants, as well as participation in activist campaigns and legal observances. However, in my daily life in Germany since 2001 (with absences), I have accumulated experiences that have led me to a deeper local understanding, and discussions over the years on issues of concern among Black people in Germany have contributed in no small way to the angles of reasoning that I take (for example, critical race theory), the examples that I use and the resources from which I draw (for example, literature).

Theoretical frameworks

This project is grounded in contemporary anthropological theory, but is situated at the disciplinary juncture of law and critical anthropology. There are three main theoretical pillars that I employ in this book. The first is a

18 The call for papers for the 2009 Annual American Anthropological Association Conference contemplates a phasing out of anthropological methods in favour of transdisciplinary methodology not so focused on territory, among other things. See American Anthropological Association 2009.

framework for understanding and interpreting racism, informed principally by the works of Philomena Essed and Grada Kilomba (Essed 1991, Kilomba 2008). The second is a commitment to writing with the theoretical position of what Norman Denzin calls 'standpoint epistemology' (Denzin 1997: 55–57) in mind. The third and final pillar is the use of CRT and, to a lesser extent, psychoanalysis as tools for interpreting both legal rules and social experiences in the project.

Theories of racism

This project relies on a number of ideas about race and racism both in terms of the content of the study as well as providing a framework for the methodological approaches engaged in this project. Beyond the basic idea of race as a social construct that is discursively still rooted in misrepresentations of profound biological difference,[19] this project seeks to investigate knowledge that is produced owing in part to experiences with racism. Examination of experiences of racial bias, oddly, does not require an in-depth inquiry as to what race *is*, but rather a focus on the articulations of the biases and other expressions of racism. For the purposes of this project, Blackness is the mode of differentiation that underscores people's experiences, and though it is read through the lens of racial differentiation, the observations are not dependent on a specific understanding of the category of race.

This book examines racism in light of several assumptions. The first is that racism is best understood as a set of ideologies, rather than an individual system of belief. Interpersonal racism must have a context, and it is this context that gives racism its coherence. The context, then, can be understood as societal racism – comprised of attitudes that are wide reaching and can manifest themselves in individual and institutional behaviour. One of the most appropriate frameworks for investigating racism on a structural level using the tools of ethnography (including interviews, observations and discourse analysis) is presented in Philomena Essed's seminal work on racism, *Understanding Everyday Racism*. Essed, who writes about racism in the Netherlands, suggests that experiences of 'everyday racism', including descriptions of 'vicarious experiences of racism' and reconstructing these experiences in an analytical sense provides the best window into understanding racial behaviour (1991: 3). The reasoning behind this is that those who experience racism in their daily lives notice patterns and are able to highlight 'micro manifestations' of racism are able to lend

19 The relationship between remnants of biological race thinking and the social experience of race has engendered a debate in its own right, namely over whether racial thinking has shifted to cultural forms of racism or whether culture is really used as a proxy for biological difference. For further discussion, see generally AG gegen Rassismus in den Lebenswissenschaften 2009.

considerable insight to those attempting to understand bigger structural patterns (Essed 1991).[20]

Relatedly, psychoanalyst Grada Kilomba explores racism in Germany through a series of episodes that she analyses using the lens of psychoanalysis. By describing structural racism as visible through the careful analysis of 'episodes' and by unpacking these episodes using the vernacular of psychoanalysis, including the descriptions of such techniques as dissociation, recognition, shame and denial, Kilomba makes a poignant and important contribution to the discussion of German racism, with respect to anti-black racism and the intersection of race and gender in particular (2008).

Lastly, and importantly, it must be noted that the term *race* in English is very different from the term *Rasse* in German. Race is popularly conceived in the English-speaking world as a socially constructed identity category that, while a scientific fiction, describes a mode of characterising difference that is very 'real' in terms of social experience. Similarly, *Rasse* is acknowledged as describing biological fiction in Germany, and the term appears in key legal texts, such as the German Basic Law.[21] However, *Rasse* is a term that was mobilised so centrally by the Third Reich that it is, for many Germans, difficult to say the word *Rasse* without conjuring images of Hitler and the violence of extermination.

Neo-colonial theory

This work is not centred around a particular school of postcolonial thought, as it draws from observations made by a number of thinkers who conceptualise colonial relations as continuous rather than fundamentally having ended. Such an approach explores neo-colonial relations, rather than post-colonial ones, and employs a social vision of decoloniality – confronting the persistent colonial logics and structures as they exist in the present day. First, Fanon's idea of the 'corporeal schema' of the world informs some of the ways in which Black lived experiences fit with notions of knowledge production and power. Fanon outlines this concept in *Black Skins, White Masks* (Fanon 1967, Bruce-Jones 2008). Though influential in the area of post-colonial studies, Fanon can also be considered a decolonial thinker. In her introduction to a collection of works by Fanon entitled *Postcolonial Fanonism*, Azzedine Haddour describes Fanon's ethics in his 1961 book *The Wretched of the Earth*:

20 Essed also notes that investigations that link experiences to structures 'require a truly interdisciplinary approach to the problem and creative use of concepts originating from different fields and paradigms'. For this reason, this study attempts to link the paradigms of legal analysis and anthropological enquiry.

21 Grundgesetz (German Basic Law). Germany. Art. 3(3). There is a debate as to whether the term *Rasse* should be replaced in the German Constitution by the phrase 'racial discrimination'. For a critical analysis of this debate, see Barskanmaz 2011.

> The dismantling of the Berlin Wall has been hailed by some critics as a movement towards the completion of the project of globalization, the advent of open society, the triumph of freedom in the world and the liberalization of the open market. Paradoxically, this movement has reinstated the Manichaeism that determined the politics of the old colonial regimes. Fanon's ethics of decolonialization calls for a different kind of globalization, for a new world order in which segregated economies must be abolished. Fanon envisages the emergence of a new humanism, freed from the weight of the colonial past and from the ideological conflict of the Cold War.
>
> (Fanon and Haddour 2006: xxi)

Here, Haddour, aptly citing Berlin as an example, describes a Fanonian ethical position – one that aimed to dismantle remnant colonial politics recognising that globalisation has not radically restructured the world order, but merely shifted around previously existing colonial relations. In his body of work, Fanon describes a racialised world and seeks to identify these colonial politics in everyday life in post-colonial France (and former French territories). His contemporaries offer similar analysis in other parts of the world. For example, Kilomba (2008) identifies continuities in colonial thinking in contemporary German society from a Black perspective, while Balibar (2001) examines spaces where certain people are unsafe in Europe, which he calls death zones. These authors, and others (for example, Grosfoguel 2008, Gordon 2015) identify the regimes that privilege national, cultural, racial and religious characteristics over a shared ethic of humanism.

Decoloniality has been a focus of the work of thinkers like Lewis Gordon and Ramón Grosfoguel, who trace the intellectual contours of Fanon's zones of being and non-being, in an overall attempt to complicate contemporary Western notions of human rights as a solution to the political inequality and historical oppression of various groups on the basis not only of nationality, but also of the strong social demarcations of race and ethnicity. It is from the perspective of decoloniality that this investigation views the trajectory of coloniality – indeed, the German colonial era is not the source of all racialised prejudice and institutional violence against racialised others in Germany. However, the era is underemphasised in both popular and academic accounts of German history, and it serves as an important marker not just on account of geopolitical relations vis-à-vis African countries (Friedrichsmeyer et al. 1998), but also for identifying some of the violence that takes place within the borders of Germany that can be seen as reflected in colonial politics.[22]

22 For further discussion on this point, see Chapter 5.

Standpoint epistemology

As a social scientist doing ethnographic research, I am employing methodologies that are also filtered through the lens of my experience as both a European ethnologist and legal academic, a Black person who has lived in Germany for a number of years, and as someone who is politically and personally committed to anti-racism. This does not mean that my production of analysis is invalid – on the contrary, it means that if I, as a researcher, integrate my own standpoint into my analysis in a direct way, particularly given the self-reflective pitch of anthropology and European Ethnology in recent decades, it adds to the validity of the work by reflecting on the position of the social scientist. Standpoint epistemology also extends to the subject of this project, as examining history and social structures from the perspectives of Black people is a unique contribution that this piece offers. I am guided in this use of the idea of a standpoint or perspective driven view by Adrienne Rich and Audre Lorde, who did not shy away from inhabiting space in the world and being open and honest about their positions, interests and points of contention (for example, Rich 1986).

I use Norman Denzin's term 'standpoint' only half-heartedly because, while the term is meant to emphasise that the positionality and experiences are a prominent part of the text, there is a danger that one may mistakenly take this to mean that it is possible for an ethnographic or any work to be 'free' from having a standpoint. I suggest that standpoint epistemology is a deliberate acknowledgment of the central role of experience in organising the way we describe experiences as informers and co-constitute and record experiences as anthropologists.

Denzin suggests two routes for addressing how to deal with the question of validity from within the framework of critical post-structuralism. One strand of reasoning that actively employs the concept of validity leads to what Professor Patti Lather calls 'catalytic validity', or the use of subject position, particularly the orientation around race, class and gender,[23] to draw on commitments to these groups for the purpose of mobilisation and emancipation (Denzin 1997: 10–12). The second strand is abandonment of the concept of validity in exchange for the concept of verisimilitude. Denzin describes the verisimilitude of texts in three ways: '(a) a collection of laws set by convention, (b) a mask that presents these laws as evidence of a text's submission to the rules of a particular genre, and (c) the production of a text that 'feels' truthful and real for the reader' (1997: 10). If verisimilitude is a function of one or all of these three components, then the application of verisimilitude that I wish to use here is the sense that different genres have their own verisimilitudes that regulate the production of validity.

23 I would extend this rationale to any oppressed or socially marginalised group.

Mediating interventions of critical race theory and psychoanalysis

Race in the Shadow of Law aspires to intertwine reflective anthropological and legal analysis, moving toward something resembling critical anthropology. This features an introspective approach to research, particularly with respect to the institutional conventions that may reinforce certain thinking regarding what kind of knowledge is valuable. This book investigates the lived realities and worldviews of a group of people connected by politics, history, and certain experience-based knowledge. It is important, then, to recognise the extent to which structures, including anthropological methods, might conventionally position the knowledge of my interlocutors as potentially unimportant, misguided and ungrounded because they are out of touch with the values advanced by the discipline. This would be an unfortunate mistake. Introspection of the methods and underpinning assumptions within the discipline that may perpetuate this positioning of certain knowledge forms should be taken together with standpoint epistemology to ensure that those speaking throughout this book are given ample opportunity to reconfigure the readers' values and modes of thinking about knowledge forms.

The tense space between legal doctrine and legal encounters is what this book seeks to explore. This tense area is rich and lends a great deal of insight to the assumptions that different communities have about their rights, duties and indeed, identities.[24] Conventional notions of legal subjectivity position the legal subject as a rights-bearing subject. However, this project is interested in the way that recasting and resignifying the aims and assumptions behind conventional rights impact upon one's legal subjectivity.

To best illuminate the strands of thought and action that Black people in Germany have engaged in dealing with this tension, this book takes theoretical cues from scholars from a range of disciplines. Along with contemporary critical anthropology, the book employs two specific and highly relevant fields of inquiry throughout. These fields are psychoanalysis and CRT.

Psychoanalysis occupies a relatively central space in the study of Blackness, racism and gender in Europe, particularly given that here, the work of Frantz Fanon is quite well known among academics, activists and other social thinkers invested in unpacking the issues of racism and neocoloniality. In this regard, the work of Grada Kilomba, a psychoanalyst and

24 By identity, I am referring to both personal and political forms of identity that broadly encompass various aspects of self-understanding within the context of social relations. The social relations that figure predominantly in this study are self-positioning vis-à-vis national discourses, a sense of community, as well as the shared experiences that inform these relations.

professor of gender studies in Berlin, is instructive. Her book *Plantation Memories* (2008) examines situations in which interpersonal interactions can be explored and revealed as structurally embedded continuities of colonial logics that have profound impacts on the ways people regard themselves vis-à-vis the nation. Kilomba's work helpfully uses accessible situational analysis within the context psychoanalytic readings, paying close attention to the racialised gendered relations. These interventions broadly include introducing the concepts of a fear–desire dialectic and triplicate representation (Fanon 1967: 112).[25] *Race in the Shadow of Law*, however, references Fanon and Kilomba to a limited extent and primarily as a guide for approaching the interaction of race, colonial and national discourses in the European context.

CRT is not a highly visible or widely read field, particularly in Europe and, particularly, among those outside of legal academia (Möschel 2007). However, the importance of using CRT in my analysis as an anthropologist is to use the most relevant critical legal lens to empower the narrative-based approach that ethnographic interviews are bound to take – legal storytelling. Legal storytelling is the descriptive narrative of how the law, an institution imbued with a great deal of power and cultural signification, affects people's lives. The common approach taken by legal positivists to such narrative-based legal knowledge is to indict the informants' understandings of the law – to judge experiential knowledge on the correctness of interpreting formal rules. Accordingly, within legal academia, interviewing people about how they feel about the law and how they experience their legal subjectivity can sometimes be a David attempting to slay the sturdier, older and far greater Goliath. In the world of ethnographic research, however, the storytelling concept in CRT analysis is a gem in the rugged research terrain of power and position.

Legal anthropology situated

A set of disciplinary approaches to the intersection of law and anthropology has been taken over the past few decades, constituting what has been termed as legal anthropology (Sack and Aleck 1992, Mundy 2002, Merry

25 Fanon describes triplicate representation of Black people in post-colonial France: 'I was responsible at the same time for my body, for my race, for my ancestors. I subjected myself to an objective examination, I discovered my blackness, my ethnic characteristics; and I was battered down by tom-toms, cannibalism, intellectual deficiency, fetishism, racial defects, slave ships, and above all else, above all: "Sho' good eatin"'. Fanon reflects on his experience having both representation of his own corporeal self, his ancestors and the historical legacy of colonialism, and the social fantasy of race. I include this here because this triple position takes energy to explain and negotiate, and learning to speak with others about the energy required in this negotiation is a part of what it means to be Black in Europe.

2003, Moore 2005). Legal anthropology can describe a broad range of approaches and projects, such as the treatment of law as culture, the conceiving of culture as an analytic lens for understanding law, a focus on culturally informed analysis of legal decision-making, and interrogating the possibility of legal pluralism. This book seeks to do something different from the aforementioned projects. Rather than to analyse the law through a culturally specific lens, it examines how a certain group discusses belonging, identity and power in dialogue with legal discourses and narratives. This project uses ethnographic information and relevant writing and art to highlight aspects of contention between Black voices and conventional approaches to the intersection between law, power and belonging.

Case study approach

This study deploys a number of ethnographic tools in order to best highlight and interpret the experiences, writings and actions of those engaged in anti-racism work who are challenging legal and political ideologies. The book relies centrally on a case study approach to highlight a set of thematically related encounters and experiences, which sets the discussion in the remainder of the book. The cases are not discrete legal cases, though legal cases are involved; rather the cases are constituted by specific events in context, best thought of as episodes.

In examining the various cases or episodes, three main modes of research and analysis are used. First, interviews were undertaken. The interviews carried out were predominantly semi-structured or open exchanges with self-defined Black and Afro-German or Afro-European activists, artists or academics who are involved as participants or campaigners in legal disputes or points of political contention. Some of the first-hand information and quotation gathered came not from structured interviews, but from interactions to which I was privy or in which I was participating. The second mode is discourse analysis. I analyse the language of legal cases, interpersonal exchanges, media coverage, academic writing and poetry in order to best interpret the substance and context of the study. The third mode I used is thick description. Thick description is a form of ethnographic writing that focuses on specific details, including body language, physical and spatial descriptions and descriptions of time and environment, in order to holistically describe and assign meaning to events and situations. In addition to these main modes, I support my analysis with sociological, legal and other scholarly secondary source material.

In light of the theoretical frameworks that guide this study, and considering its methodological approach, a feature that emerges as an important artifact of my investigation is the concept of 'knowledge practices' (Riles 2006). Legal anthropologist Annelise Riles refers to knowledge practices as the practices within an institution that produce knowledge. The practices are important not merely in terms of producing the substance of law, but also in terms of mapping out the institutional rubric, logics and value system, governed by institutional rules and standards that serve as the means of production of knowledge (Bruce-Jones 2009). The book aims to help reorient the regard for *legal knowledge* about race and law in Germany and the rest of Europe by extension, from legal rules and principles towards a contextualised set of legal-institutional, social and political practices.

Structure

The book is organised into six main chapters. Chapter 1, Structural Racism and the Law in Europe, briefly describes some basic features of the ways in which race is recognised by the law, including legal protections against racial discrimination on the European and on the national levels in various European countries. It then discusses the concepts of structural and institutional racism, focusing specifically on conceptual gaps left when we attempt to think about the social experiences of racism through a legal lens.

Chapter 2, Transgression, examines some of the ways in which Black people are policed, both figuratively and literally, in public spaces. The broad purpose of this chapter is to identify and analyse how racial difference is transposed by legal rules regarding discrimination into challenges for Black people. The chapter presents empirical instances of discrimination in public transport, publicly accessible cafés and housing, and employment. The main oppositional strands of legal argument that these examples highlight are the right to be free from discrimination on one hand and the right to freely decide one's contractual relationships on the other. It explores various expectations and outcomes with regard to the law's protection of certain notions of substantive equality. It examines legal discourses that indicate what types of legal subjects have and enjoy which protections. It looks at alternative policy approaches to the idea of difference and articulates what many Black people in Germany view as being at stake in these discussions. Ultimately, the chapter uses a Black German perspective to reflect on the freedom of contract and similar principles as mechanisms of exclusion that rely on certain national or regional ideologies that make determinations about difference, the ability to assimilate and levels of acceptability of exclusion.

Chapter 3, Smoke and Mirrors, examines a legal trial as a case study. It investigates legal framings of the nation, the citizen and the Black *other* in an appellate trial, regarding the death-in-custody of a man named Oury Jalloh. Here, I examine the experiences of those present at the trial and describe broad systems of police behaviour and institutional posturing at the level of language, public positioning and non-verbal gesturing in and right outside the courthouse. This chapter takes a singular legal investigation and sets up the analysis in later chapters, suggesting that this case provides a window for viewing the cumulative knowledge and experience of Black people in Germany and their relationship with racism and the law. It highlights resistance to conventional ideologies of citizenship and nation-state thinking. It ultimately reflects on how and whether Black people position themselves as (human) rights-bearing subjects in Germany.

Chapter 4, The Politics of Remembrance, explores the commitment by Black Germans to discussing and acting to clarify a string of cases of police brutality or inaction resulting in the deaths of Black civilians as an entry point for discussing questions of legal rights, authentic belonging and treatment by society. These cases address racial ideologies that underlie certain forms of state violence and identify ways in which the defence against accusations of racism reveals legal technologies that serve to protect aspects of national ideology. The last part of this chapter focuses on the idea of storytelling and alternative narrative which counterbalances legal narrative as a mode of understanding truth, justice and rights.

Chapter 5, Gender, Colonial History and Contemporary Social Movements, explores depictions of the ideologies and the aesthetics of state regulation of Black social and political life in literature, stories, poems and other contemporary works written by Black people in Germany since the mid-1980s. The purpose of this chapter is to highlight a trajectory of thinking through and describing legalistic forms as a part of the historical narrative of the presence and experience of Black people in Germany. This chapter helps locate this book in the wider context of contemporary writing by Black people in Germany. It also paints a narrative of Black political formations written by Black people since just before German Reunification, which sets the stage for the subsequent chapters, focusing on the years 2000–2012.

Chapter Six, Towards a European Anti-Racism, is a brief closing analysis of the importance of the concept of epistemology when viewing law in society. It looks inwards towards the disciplines of law and anthropology, drawing from the substance of the case examples while also positioning this project of disciplinary critique within the realm of producing specialist knowledge. It aims to orient the reader toward an ethic of introspectiveness in conceptualising difference and belonging in Germany and Europe, offering both reformative and transformative possibilities.

Reimagining knowledge in the field

> The crucial point, however, is that the United States is no longer the puppeteer of a world system of images but is only one node of a complex transnational construction of imaginary landscapes. The world we live in today is characterized by a new role for the imagination

> in social life. To grasp this new role, we need to bring together the old idea of images, especially mechanically produced images (in the Frankfurt School sense), the idea of imagined community (in Anderson's sense), and the French idea of the imaginary (*imaginaire*) as a constructed landscape of collective aspirations, which is no more and no less real than the collective representations of Emile Durkheim, now mediated through the complex prism of modern media.
>
> (Appadurai 1996: 31)[26]

Cultural critic and anthropologist Arjun Appadurai, in his volume *Modernity at Large* (1996), makes an invaluable contribution to the discipline of anthropology by pushing the limits of our willingness to integrate a conglomerate process of imagining into our view of global social reality. Appadurai points his ethnographic lens towards a broader understanding of the global imaginary, providing more creative space to imagine communities that are fragmented, geographically dispersed and locally entrenched. A pivotal issue for anthropologists and possibly for politicians and other social thinkers is the implication that Appadurai's vision of modernity and belonging has on the concept of authenticity vis-à-vis culture and citizenship.

At the heart of this issue is another more foundational one, which is the production and regulation of knowledge from 'within' culture or national projects, the arena where belonging refuses to be merely personal and self-identificatory. In this space, experiential modes of knowledge are subverted to conventional (racist and nationalist) assumptions that obliterate the possibility of an authentic unconventional (non-white, non-citizen) European. The conundrum for people of colour in Europe, then, is: being a non-white European does not mean that one can produce authentic and credible knowledge about Europe from a non-white perspective, but rather that non-whites are allowed an honorary status as Europeans by 'authentic' Europeans (Sow 2008).

26 Appadurai continues by describing in detail how imagination constitutes social practice: 'The image, the imagined, the imaginary – these are all terms that direct us to something critical and new in global cultural processes: the imagination as social practice. No longer mere fantasy (opium for the masses whose real work is elsewhere), no longer simple escape (from a world defined principally by more concrete purposes and structures), no longer elite pastime (thus not relevant to the lives of ordinary people), and no longer mere contemplation (irrelevant for new forms of desire and subjectivity), the imagination has become an organized field of social practices, a form of work (in the sense of both labor and culturally organized practice), and a form of negotiation between sites of agency (individuals) and globally defined fields of possibility. This unleashing of the imagination links the play of pastiche (in some settings) to the terror and coercion of states and their competitors. The imagination is now central to all forms of agency, is itself a social fact, and is the key component of the new global order'.

This work is inspired, in part, by the visionary work of Arjun Appadurai. Appadurai is particularly instructive for helping me describe the Black German community and organisation given his interventions with regard to his embrace and use of diaspora, deterritorialised ethnography and the concept of the 'ethnoscape' (Appadurai 1996).[27] I also use the thick description and discourse-analytic techniques employed by Sherene Razack as she analyses deaths in custody and interprets the discourse as connected to constructing the nation and its subjects (Razack 2011). In line with Appadurai's observations that imagination constitutes social practice, one may conclude that conceptions of Blackness in Europe are influenced and shaped by many different factors and converging systems of meaning, including images, historical narratives, conceptions of identity and migration, and conceptions of ethnic nation-state identity. In short, notions of both Blackness and European-ness are interwoven into the living practices, 'global cultural processes' that shape subjectivity.

27 Deterritorialised ethnography refers to ethnography that does not use territory as its central organising principle, though it does not ignore spatial aspects of identity formation and social structure. Appadurai argues that such ethnographic projects are valuable for studying societies in an age of globalisation.

Part I

Between the lines and at the margins

Chapter 1

Structural racism and the law in Europe

Race is not a singular concept in Europe. It does not occupy a singular social position and nor does it enjoy a central or stable definition across European countries. One might expect there to be more internal coherence to the legal concept of race in Europe than currently exists, due to the overlapping histories and legal jurisdictions among European countries. However, despite various common discussions about racism taking place in Europe, race remains highly contextually contingent, dynamic and contentious. One commonality across much of Europe, however, is that *race* as such is frequently framed in a language that minimises its importance as an analytical concept. This is not to deny the importance of other identity traits and status positions, such as citizenship status, gender, sexuality and religion as constituent co-valences of systemic marginalisation. The issue is that in various settings across Europe, race is discussed as something of an American relic, part of a clunky imported vernacular unfit to serve as framework for understanding the European context. With this undercurrent of thought as a backdrop, the work of self-identified anti-racism activism can be difficult to describe to a broad public. This difficulty is sharpened in the current times of growing nationalism, xenophobia and racism throughout Europe. Rising nationalism and overt racism is dangerous not only for the threat that it represents to immigrants and people of colour, but also for the ways it distracts us from seeing forms of structural and institutional racism. In other words, it is difficult to focus social energy on identifying and countering obscured structural exclusion when overt racism captivates and monopolises the public imagination. This form of distraction is not new, but it is certainly a dynamic that must be considered in contemporary Europe, particularly now.

Perhaps race, on its own, is a somewhat anachronistic as an organising analytical lens for examining social and political marginalisation in Europe, given intense interrelatedness between race and other social categories. But then again, this is not a problem peculiar to race; any single frame of marginalisation or oppression would be insufficient to describe systems, processes or indeed experiences of social exclusion. Moreover,

Europe is certainly not an exceptional sphere in which race cannot be identified among the existing hierarchies of domination. It is important to note, however, that even as we recognise that race features prominently in an operant set of logics of exclusion in Europe, and that Europe does not enjoy an exceptionalism marked by the absence of race, it would be unwise to limit the discussion of European forms of racism and anti-racist work to a doggedly local or specific set of issues. Attention must be paid to the colonial logics that continue to racialise people in Europe, from imperial legal and economic structures to border policies, nativist social ideologies and concepts of the public good vis-à-vis the foreign other. Additionally, anti-racism work in other parts of the world influences and exchanges with such work in Europe. Notably, in the context of Black-led anti-racism work in Germany, movements in the United States and the United Kingdom around police violence and decolonial projects from various places in the global south are in deep and sustained conversation with the German work (for example, Fanon 1967, Grosfoguel 2007, Nghi Ha 2007, Kilomba 2008).

While the interface of race and the law is vast and complex, it is helpful to distil a few concepts, legal provisions and criticisms that are persistently debated in Europe – a basic overview of terrain of the legal regulation of race.

The landscape of equal protection in Europe

When comparing the various legal regimes that exist in Europe for recognising and regulating racial discrimination, aside from analysing policy and case law, it is imperative to scrutinise two aspects. The first is the way in which race, as a category, is conceptualised legally and socially. Without doing this, it is difficult to understand the aims of the relevant legislation and policy. Second, a critical understanding of the application of the law is, of course, crucial to evaluating the laws' effects in society.

European countries vary widely in their approaches to the legal recognition and regulation of race. This range can be explained in a number of ways, including the historical place of race in society in each country, political circumstances that have shaped the debate around legal forms of protection, and the flexibility afforded the member states of the European Union when implementing the EU Race Directive.

National equality laws

There are several models of anti-discrimination and equality legislation in European countries, and one cannot generalise the form that anti-discrimination laws take across Europe without losing a great deal of nuance. There are some regional similarities and similar approaches, but there are also significant differences. The differences in legal approaches are, of course, contextualised within very different social understandings of racial difference and its relevance. It is perhaps helpful to outline several European approaches in order to demonstrate a bit of the range.

The French model

France takes a unique view on racial discrimination, and it is close to what can be described as a colour-blind approach. French law bans the use of the category of race, imposing a criminal sanction for its use in the employment context (Bruce-Jones 2008). This approach, of criminalising use of the category, is aligned with the ideals of French Republicanism, which asserts that the unifying prospect of French national identity is an important principle for counterbalancing the various other forms of group identification that exist within French identity. Differences, in this way, are seen as divisions in the first place, rather than richness, and are subverted within in the national ideology of *Liberté, egalité, fraternité.* The specific aim for criminalising the category is to send the message that race is a dangerous social fiction that should not be perpetuated. Rather than to name the categorical fiction and regulate the discrimination stemming from it, the French model bans the naming of race and attempts, in this way, to stem discriminatory behaviour.

There are some clear problems with the French model. First, on an ideological level, the criminalisation of the category of race on the basis that it is a scientific fiction does nothing to address race as a lived, social reality. In some ways, it creates a new fiction, one that denies the social experience of racialisation. It also suggests that the law can affect complex social phenomena by banning aspects of language, which may be only partially true. Simply because employers do not use the term race does not mean that they are not making what might otherwise be understood as racial distinctions. Second, because the categorical ban of race carries criminal sanctions, complaints against employers are handled by the Ministry of Labour. Complaints are filtered through a federal agency, removed from the ambit of individual legal claims. Because allegations of racism by the Ministry of Labour are of serious concern, they are not brought lightly. There is some indication that they are brought more as a last resort, which may mean that the legal mechanisms for dealing with discrimination claims are rarely utilised.[1] Third, the prohibition of the use of race means that statistics about race are not collected by official bodies, and there are only a few exceptions in which such statistics can be collected by private parties. This makes it difficult to collect evidence for identifying patterns of racism.

1 There were very few prosecutions in under the 1972 law against racism (criminalising use of the category of race) throughout the 1990s. For more information, see Hargreaves 2004 and Bleich 2004.

As most discrimination does not involve the declaratory admission of identity-based maltreatment, identifying the disparate impact of policies and practices on protected groups is extremely important to effectively combating discrimination.

The German model

The German model consists of a general constitutional provision on equal protection (Art 3 German Basic Law) and a statutory provision that covers the fields of employment, vocational training, education and social welfare (Sec. 2. AGG). The constitutional provision covers discrimination on the basis of '*Rasse*' which is translated into English as race but which recalls in the German language the biological race thinking of *Nationalsozialismus* or National Socialism (NS) rather than the social construct of race. For this reason, the continued use of the term '*Rasse*' in constitutional matters is controversial. The provision itself is a general one, informing the rest of German law (including the National Policing Law)[2] as well as Germany's compliance with European and international laws. The statute, the *Allgemeines Gleichbehandlungsgesetz* or General Law on Equal Treatment (AGG), which covers several grounds of prohibited discrimination aside from race, was adopted in 2006, but it has been used on only very few occasions to bring claims of racial discrimination.

Similar to in France, German officials do not collect or utilise racial statistics when assessing how public duties are conducted or for examining patterns of discrimination. There is not, as in France, an express prohibition on collecting these data. The lack of collecting racial statistics leaves civil society groups to do the work of tracking discrimination themselves.

The United Kingdom model

The United Kingdom has no written constitution but has enshrined its equality principles in statutes. In contrast to most other countries in Europe, the UK developed race-specific anti-discrimination protections as early as 1965, when it passed the Race Relations Act of 1965 (Solanke 2009, Fredman 2011). This act outlawed racial discrimination in public places. With subsequent amendments, the act was expanded in scope and the protections against racial discrimination became more nuanced. Having been developed alongside the US American Civil Rights Act, racial discrimination provisions in the UK are among the oldest in Europe.

Today, the UK has an integrated anti-discrimination statute, the Equality Act 2010, which includes racial discrimination. The provisions are among

2 Sec 22 para. 1(a) BPolG. See also Cremer 2013.

the most extensive in coverage in Europe. Anecdotally, one can also assume that the provisions are the most regularly utilised among national equality laws across Europe. Under UK law, individuals may rely directly on the Act, bringing employers, service providers or public bodies before tribunals when challenging their compliance with the Act.

European law provisions

On the European level, there are two main bodies of law that affect racial discrimination in European countries. The first is European Union law, which relates to the primary and secondary legislation and case law from the European Union. The second is the European Convention on Human Rights (ECHR), as adjudicated by the European Court of Human Rights, the judgments of which are binding on members of the Council of Europe. The main difference, other than the fact that the Council of Europe comprises almost twice the number of countries as the European Union, is that the discrimination provisions found in the ECHR are only applicable in relation to the provisions of the ECHR, rather than as stand-alone provisions on equality. In contrast, the scope of the anti-discrimination prohibitions in the treaties and directives of the European Union enjoy a much wider scope of applicability. For this reason, the laws of the European Union are most relevant when characterising equality law at the European level.[3]

The primary legislation of the European Union, its founding treaties, includes general prohibitions on racial discrimination. The Treaty on the Functioning of the European Union (TFEU) expressly covers racial discrimination in (Art. 19). Additionally, the EU Charter of Fundamental Rights and Freedoms expounds a principle of racial non-discrimination (Art. 20).

While the primary legislation states the EU principles of equality law, it is the secondary legislation, and more precisely, the Race Directive 2000/43/EC, that details the specific terms of identifying and combating racial discrimination. The Race Directive is one of a number of directives and regulations prohibiting discrimination, but it is the one dedicated specifically to racial discrimination and other similar grounds. The Race Directive has a broad scope of applicability, which includes the areas of

3 Racial discrimination under the European Convention on Human Rights, though it applies in relation to other aspects of the ECHR rather than to the broad areas of employment, goods and services and welfare (which describes the scope of the European Union Race Directive) is an area worth of study. See Barskanmaz 2015. Race is particularly relevant in ECtHR case law in the context of policing in Europe in cases where police have either mistreated someone in their custody or failed to properly investigate. See for example, Nachova and Others v. Bulgaria (ECtHR) 6 July 2005; Ribbitsch v. Austria (ECtHR) 4 Dec 1995; Borbola Kiss v. Hungary (ECtHR) 26 Sept 2012; Eduard Popa v. Maldova (ECtHR) 12 May 2013.

employment, vocational training, education, the acquisition of goods and services, and social welfare. The Directive defines both direct and indirect discrimination.

There is one very large area of discretion that states have when extending European Union directives on discrimination to the member states, and that is in the ways they choose to transpose the laws into their respective national legal frameworks. In the UK context, the structure and content of the Equality Act 2010 resembles equality directives considerably, in terms of structure, scope of coverage and, importantly, the explicit recognition of race as a category of protection. In other words, even if the United Kingdom withdraws from the European Union (which is a distinct possibility at the time of writing this book, given that membership was put to a controversial advisory public referendum, which returned a 51.9 per cent majority decision in favour of leaving the EU),[4] many of the principles and protections of discrimination law found in the Race Directive would still be available under UK law. However, in the French context, the supposition is that the French way of dealing with the mandates of the Race Directive are achieved through the ban on the category of race and without the monitoring of racial or ethnic data.[5] While France is obliged to respect and implement the Race Directive, the ability to readily identify, discuss and combat discrimination in France is very different to the UK or Germany. The European Union laws, meant to harmonise the laws and principles on this and other issues, have limited ability to mandate the exact ways in which the laws and principles are transposed. So while the European Union aims to balance between harmonising laws across Europe and allowing scope for its member states to implement EU law in locally appropriate ways, on the issue of racial discrimination, it leaves a significant gap between the articulation of common principles and the ways divergent mechanisms of implementation impact on the everyday lives of European citizens. This gap allows member states to sideline the discourse of racism, which has the consequence of obscuring the social effects of racism. It is important in this context to recognise that the principles at the European level, though perhaps symbolically valuable on their own, are only as good as their implementation by the member states and that the guise of a successful system may give the false impression that discrimination has been dealt with.

Directives, such as the Race Directive, have legal effect in EU member states, even if they have not been implemented or if they have been improperly implemented.[6] EU law also mandates that member states designate special bodies specifically to promote equality and combat

4 BBC News (24 June 2016).

5 For a comparative view of France's transposition of the Race Directive, as compared with that of other EU member states, see Hamman and Frank 2015.

6 See *Mangold v. Helm*, C144/04 (ECJ) 2005; see also de Mol 2011.

discrimination.

While the European Union system adds a layer of accountability and oversight to the ways in which we regulate racial discrimination in Europe, it is clear that the European Union as a concept and set of institutions is complicit in a set of discursive and legal practices that endanger people of colour. The concept of European citizenship underscores a transnational unity that does not, in itself, work towards reducing the racial or ethnic divisions between those living in Europe. In some ways, the concept exacerbates these divisions. For instance, there is a real fear that racial discrimination in the form of profiling is used to police and regulate immigration at and near the external borders of the European Union.[7]

Ultimately, the European Union is not the singular solution for sorting out the equality law regimes of its member states. Furthermore, there is no one model that seems to afford reliable or efficient responses to the various expressions of social racism. A wise orientation towards EU law, as with any body of law, is to view it as a set of tools that can be used strategically and, at the same time, constitute part of the problem.

Race and policing: exposing structural racism

Policing is an important area for analysing race and racism in Europe for a number of reasons. First, policing institutions enjoy a particular position of privilege. Police officers are generally less susceptible to the type of legal scrutiny that civilians encounter when they commit violent acts. They are also essentially less vulnerable to being disadvantaged by being characterised by violence than their civilian counterparts. Conversely, people of colour and non-Europeans are frequently characterised as unjustifiably violent or otherwise criminal and therefore deserving of sharpened police surveillance. So if one imagines a spectrum of vulnerability to being on the receiving end of violence, police would be at one end and civilians in marginalised communities, including racial minorities and others, would be at the other end. Second, the equality provisions discussed earlier in this chapter do not strictly regulate the behaviour of police when they are in the line of duty. Discriminatory practices, while they generally fall within the scope of equality laws, can be legally justified as important to safety and security or public welfare.

The policing context can be regarded as a window into examining the synchronicity of race and legal regulation, and policing practices can and should be examined in the context of contemporary state discursive responses to immigration and protest. The enforcement of immigration controls, counter-terrorism campaigns and anti-crime initiatives more

7 See for example, Privot 2016.

generally adopt approaches that are easily susceptible to racialisation and race-based practices. One need only look at the practices of immigration checks on regional trains in Germany or the UK government's counter-terrorism PREVENT strategy[8] and similar policies in France[9] to understand how these policies target various groups in what can be understood as racially and religiously discriminatory way. Can we identify racism in policing without using the lens of race?

National laws in European countries typically allow police a wide area of discretion when defending their actions in court and when using physical appearance as a means of assessing the criminality and corresponding treatment of civilians. While there are guidelines on police behaviour regarding racial and ethnic discrimination, there is not robust European legislation on race and policing. Racial and ethnic profiling is a widespread phenomenon across Europe. Police use disproportionate violence in Europe against people of colour and immigrants, and other precarious groups. The Fundamental Rights Agency of the European Union does provide general data on the number of racially-motivated crimes across Europe, but this does not include policing violence in a systematic way.[10]

The policing context illuminates other structural problems at the juncture of law and racism that are of vital importance in other areas of social life. The fact that only empirical studies exist that document the racial disparity of police violence is a testament to the lack of a systematic way of measuring and tracking discriminatory treatment by police, which is partly on account of a failure to collect racial data. This leaves the burden for proving discrimination in the hands of NGOs, civil society groups and people of colour, who provide experienced-based knowledge about policing. For example, profiling has been assessed by the Open Society Foundation in its empirical research report on policing in the European Union.[11]

There are numerous obstacles to being able to identify and combat discrimination across Europe. The difficulty in collecting meaningful demographic data and statistics that reflect patterns of racism pose one set of problems, while the legal and social culture of relegating complex claims of racism to the margins presents another.

Considering these challenges, activists and advocates must be creative when trying to gain traction for social change around racism.

8 See Batty 2015.

9 See Ragazzi 2016.

10 Fundamental Rights Agency 2012.

11 Open Society Institute2009. Also working on and producing information about profiling are community organisations, such as KOP in Germany and StopWatch in the UK.

Institutional and structural discrimination: between recognition and obscurity

Alongside the development of anti-discrimination provisions in the UK, there has been a lengthy discussion around institutional racism in England and Wales in the context of policing. In terms of policy change, this discussion has been conventionally regarded to have culminated in the 1999 Macpherson Report. The report was produced in the context of an inquiry into the quality of the police investigation into the 1993 racist killing of a teenager named Stephen Lawrence. The report, authored by Sir William Macpherson, articulated the following definition of institutional racism:

> The collective failure of an organisation to provide an appropriate and professional service to people because of their colour, culture, or ethnic origin. It can be seen or detected in processes, attitudes and behaviour which amount to discrimination through unwitting prejudice, ignorance, thoughtlessness and racist stereotyping which disadvantage minority ethnic people.
>
> (Macpherson Report, 1999: para 6.34)

This definition served a few purposes. It was a response to the logic of individual intentional racism, which foreclosed the possibility of institutional analysis of racism as in the Scarman Report (1981), which regarded racism in policing institutions as an issue of rogue individuals or 'bad apples', rather than the Macpherson language of 'collective failure' including 'unwitting prejudice or ignorance'. The shift to the institutional level with the Macpherson Report was quite significant in the UK, if only because it changed the sense of understanding that many people had about the ability to charge an institution with racism.

Research on police profiling, such as that commissioned by the Open Society Initiative (OSI), touches upon the issue of institutional racism. However, the language of 'institutional racism' has not been a central feature of the discourse of many European countries, even after the publication of the Macpherson Report in the UK.

In Germany, the phrase 'institutional racism' (*institutioneller Rassismus*) has been used in recent years by community organisations and campaigning groups. The term is also gaining traction, slowly, partly as a result of a very high-profile legal case, known as the NSU case. NSU stands for National Socialist Underground and refers to a group of neo-Nazis responsible for a series of murders of mostly Turkish people between 2000 and 2007. The claim of institutional racism was not made on the basis of the murders themselves, but on the ways in which the murders were investigated by police and treated by the media. Police interrogated the families of the deceased and signalled that the deaths may have been the result of organised criminal activity rather than racial motivation. The media labelled this murder spree the 'Kebap Murders' (*Döner-Morde*), playing on the racial stereotype of the victims as Döner Kebap shop owners (in spite of the fact that not all of those killed were Kebap shop owners). The case against an alleged member of the NSU, Beate Zschäpe, has been on-going since her surrender in 2011, and the investigation and subsequent denial of Macpherson-like failures to properly handle the case have been criticised as an 'institutional denial of institutional racism', bordering on collusion.[12]

While various cases have brought about a reckoning with ideas of institutional and structural racism in academic and activist discourses, the ideas have not been generally mainstreamed in Europe.

Benefits of a case study approach

This book uses series of issues that have been taking place in Germany at the fault lines of race and policing in order to expose and illuminate both the moment that we are in within Europe, regarding the treatment of race as a concept, as well as the strategic potential for using activist, academic and artistic approaches to intervening in legal discourse on race and policing. While comprehensive ethnographies must be done on this issue throughout Europe, close scrutiny of a specific case and context may help us to see the potential connections between similar cases. How might we connect protests around the police shooting of Mark Duggan in the UK with the killings of Rekia Boyd, Mike Brown or Freddie Gray in the USA, or Christy Schwundeck in Germany? Further, how do we make progress in responding to institutional forms of racism if the concept of race is, in some respects, off limits?

A case study on the German context is helpful in answering these questions. Activists in Germany are currently doing a great deal of work to connect the issues of racism, coloniality, history, language and law. Where legal academia is limited in the German context, as it tightly restricts interdisciplinary analysis, there is a need for these types of non-legal interventions; though they occur in practice, rather than in the classroom, they are no less theoretical or pedagogical in how they shift the discursive field around race and the law in Europe.

The absence of laws on race does not mean that race does not play an important organising role in anti-racism work; nor does it mean that racism is not a problem. The law should not be seen as a mirror for social experience. However, the law plays an important role in organising the ways in which activists, campaigners, advocates and researchers approach social

12 For more information on this aspect of the NSU case, see Fekete 2015.

change initiatives, and as such, the law constitutes an important discursive field. It is difficult to gain traction on issues of race and racism without contending with the state of legal regulation – indeed legal change is many times central to social change initiatives.

Chapter 2

Transgression

Law and the choreography of race and place

A young man is singled out by police and made to identify himself on a commuter train because he is Black. Another young Black man is refused entry to a nightclub because, according to the doorman, it has reached its quota of Black people. An Afro-German woman is evicted from her flat because her neighbours do not want to live near a Black single mother. A theatre manager states that instead of hiring Black actors, the troupe's white actors would have their faces painted black. Trains, clubs, rental flats and performance stages are all spaces regulated in various ways by the state. Whilst all of these spaces are clearly within the scope of the German constitutional non-discrimination clause, entry into clubs, the rental of dwellings and terms of employment also enjoy the more specific statutory protection of the General Equal Treatment Law. However, formal legal provisions are part of a larger scheme of regulatory structures. Unfortunately, the regulation of these spaces is lodged squarely within broader social practices of racial exclusion. Both law enforcement and private citizens use racial thinking in the policing of public spaces, and their guardianship of these spaces is supported to various degrees by the law. Black people who have resisted being excluded from these spaces have, in the process, helped expose the social and legal norms that maintain racial exclusion.

Black people living in Germany are in a constant process of identifying and critiquing conventional framings and logics of law, particularly as these logics pertain to racial exclusion from certain public and semi-public spaces. This chapter provides examples of the ways in which Black people are interpellated[1] by law enforcement as legal subjects. It also illustrates certain political and strategic responses of anti-racism activists to judicial rulings and administrative decisions. Ultimately, the chapter looks beyond the scope of strict judicial reasoning and examines the ideological and epistemological positions that Black people and anti-racism activists have

1 By interpellation, I am referring to the way in which a dominant ideology constructs and identifies the role of the individual in her social context. See Althusser 2001: 109.

adopted in their struggle against the substance and form of the institutional production of legal knowledge.

The first part this chapter examines racial profiling by the police in public spaces and identifies ways in which such profiling is justified or otherwise supported by law and public policy. It examines exclusionary practices, including verbal intimidation and physical violence, as well as legal principles that govern and attempt to regulate such practices. Such regulation operates through the public policy discourses of protection and safety, as well as popular understandings of national history, foreignness and belonging. These aspects, together, support a notion of the nation state that serve to legitimize forms of state violence and reconcile racial exclusion by putting forth a particular idea of the public good. The second part of this chapter examines racial exclusion in other areas of German society, focusing on public clubs and cafés, dwelling rental and employment. This part examines how Black Germans and Black people living in Germany attempt to combat social processes that seek to legitimise exclusion and violence. This analysis attempts to reach a deeper understanding of the racialisation of public and semi-public spaces, as well as the related violence and exclusion.

Profiling: juridical techniques of exclusion

The term 'racial profiling', in the English language, has been used in recent years to describe the use of race by police officers as an indicator of whether a person has committed an illegal offense. Popularly known incarnations of this law-enforcement technique include the singling-out of Black, Arab, Roma and Latino/a people in Europe and the United States, ensuring their close scrutiny and potential exclusion or detention for reasons of public safety or suspicion of criminality or terrorism.[2] In Germany, particularly in the last few years, activists and NGOs have adopted this term, in English, to describe similar actions by police (Schearer 2012, Buhe 2013). The issue has become public, owing especially to the case of a man in North Rhein Westphalia, where the police successfully defended the singling-out of a young Black German man for repeated identity checks on the grounds of efficiency in protecting the 'general public interest'.[3]

2 See Brown 2012. See also Tischbirek and Wihl 2013. For a legal analysis of European discrimination against Roma people, see *Nachova and others v. Bulgaria* (Grand Chamber) Judgement 6 July 2005 (European Court of Human Rights 2005).

3 Urteil v. 28.2.2012 – 5 K 1026/11.KO (Verwaltungsgericht Koblenz 2012) 6–7. The case was defended successfully by the police officers in the administrative court of first instance, but was overturned in 2012 by the upper administrative court. See Beschluss v. 29.10.2012 – 7 a 10532/ 12 (Oberverwaltungsgericht Rheinland-Pfalz 2012). It is worth noting that the court's determination at first instance that the repeated racial profiling of the young man was legal heightened public debate around profiling.

While profiling in the German context is generally associated with police administered identification checks, in a broader sense, the fundamental racial stereotypes around criminality that underlie profiling are applied in a variety of other contexts. These contexts include prominent cases that take place outside of Germany but are seen as relevant to the African diaspora in Germany. Such cases give anti-racism activists important points of structural comparative analysis when looking to legal protection on policing issues where racial bias has presented important procedural disadvantages. For example, in the early part of 2012, the fatal shooting of a Black teenager in the United States named Trayvon Martin attracted international press coverage, including in the German media.[4] Black Germans, among many people internationally, organised demonstrations and solidarity events to protest the failure of the Florida authorities to prosecute the man who shot Martin. The circumstances are important – the man who shot Martin was not a police officer but a volunteer neighbourhood watchman armed with a gun who saw him walking down the block, thought that he looked suspicious and confronted the teenager, shooting and killing him.[5] The three-week delay between the shooting and formal prosecution coincided with the rendering of a police-profiling verdict in the German city of Tübingen, which was also widely reported. Martin's death also occurred shortly after the *Staatsanwalt*[6] in Frankfurt decided not to prosecute police officers in the fiercely criticised fatal 2011 shooting of Christy Schwundeck, a Nigerian-German woman in a Frankfurt job centre.[7] The temporal coincidence of these events mobilised Black and anti-racism activists in Germany, locally and regionally, and ensured that the protests and solidarity campaigns organised in Germany were wrapped into a decidedly larger cross-contextual discursive response to racial profiling and the Black legal subject.

To best understand the phenomenon of racial profiling by police, one should also consider other types of profiling that Black people face in Germany, carried out by other institutions. This is because legal postures regarding the parameters of permissibility of certain types of discrimination are connected within broad-based social understandings of difference and moral dessert. For this reason, it is useful to imagine profiling in a broader sense – as a framing practice, important for understanding how legal decisions and policies make use of stereotypes of Black people.

4 Between 31 March 2012 and 7 December 2012, *Der Spiegel* published 27 online news articles on the Trayvon Martin shooting. The series is available online at www.spiegel.de/thema/trayvon_martin/ accessed 26 April 2013. Local and regional news sources in Germany also reported on the shooting. See for example, 'Tod Von Trayvon Martin: Weiß Gegen Schwarz' 2012.

5 'Affidavit Says Zimmerman "Profiled" Martin' 2012.

6 Translation: state prosecutor.

7 See Chapter 4.

The following section considers identity checks carried out by police officers. The chapter then examines profiling for entry to bars and cafés, and profiling in the rental market. Lastly, the chapter examines forms of racial exclusion in employment, based on various contemporary examples that have sparked public debate.

Police-administered identity checks

The popular 2001 music video for *Liebe und Verstand* (*Love and Understanding*), a song composed and performed by Sisters' Keepers, a group of Black German women artists, deals with everyday racism in Germany. The video is filmed in a way that attempts to expose a form of structural racism faced by Black people but appeal to a white audience by making the protagonist a white man. It depicts a white German man being targeted for an identity check by two Black police officers. With this clever inversion of the oft-rendered experience of many Black Germans who are targeted and stopped by police officers, the video attempts to do two main things. First, it allows the viewer to experience racial profiling – the man in the video is closely inspected, his identification checked and double-checked by two unsmiling officers, who scrutinise his face with an intimate closeness. This is a story of humiliation and criminalisation that is recounted in different ways not only by Black people in Germany, but by other non-white people as well. The second notable aspect of this video depiction, in inverting the roles in the story, is that it engages the viewer in an exercise of identification.[8] Many Black viewers and others targeted by police will immediately recognise this scene and its social commentary. White German viewers may also recognise the commentary, and it seems the aim is to get white viewers to think critically about the situation by giving them a way to empathise with the typical subjects of arbitrary police checks. It is important to notice in this scene that the white male subject of this identity check holds a German passport – here, it is not his nationality but his appearance that constitutes the primary reason for exclusion. His skin raises a question with the officers, like a suspicious signature. The scenario reveals that, despite holding the 'right' passport, he would have to routinely undergo scrutiny, interrogation and dismissal by the officers, a ritual of humiliation.[9]

8 The entire video is seen through the eyes of the white man. In his experience, Germany is populated only by Black people. As he walks through the supermarket, the cashier scowls at him. While on the U-Bahn platform, an older woman hides her purse from him. These experiences are meant to resonate with Black people while prompting white people to empathise.

9 The successful German hip-hop group Advanced Chemistry picked up on similar themes of racial profiling, nationality and belonging in the 1992 music video for the song *Fremd in eigenem Land* (*Foreign in One's Own Land*), which followed the famous neo-Nazi riots outside of refugee residencies in Rostock-Lichtenhagen.

Whenever I am in Germany, whether for research or leisure, I visit one of my best friends, who is a Berlin-based actor. He reminds me that police profiling is a current issue, not an artefact of a previous decade. He is a Black man in his forties who moved from North America to Germany 20 years ago and, as an actor, he frequently works in other German cities. He is routinely stopped by police officers on train platforms when arriving in and leaving Munich and asked to show his identification. 'I'm a permanent resident here and they always ask me, I'm so tired of that, it's just plain racist', he tells me, as he has numerous times before. He notes that he is rarely stopped in other large cities, but is nearly always stopped in Munich, and that he has come to expect being stopped.[10] This experience is not unique to Germany, and it echoes the central issue in a relatively recent legal decision that was reached by the United Nations International Covenant on Civil and Political Rights (ICCPR) Committee on Human Rights regarding officers in Spain, who consistently stopped a Black woman on a train platform and told her it was because she was Black, implying that she was particularly unlikely to have valid papers for residence in Spain.[11] The Committee decided that this did indeed legally constitute racism and should not be allowed; however, its decisions are not binding. In France, a recent court challenge has gathered the experiences of 14 men and women who claim to have been racially profiled by police (France24 2012). Racial profiling in the form of identity checks has become part of a European discussion, one that has recently culminated in a series of lawsuits and has intensified as a public issue.

There is a strong presumption by national law enforcement in various European countries that racial profiling can be justified on specific train routes because it facilitates effective immigration control. This is the very issue that was taken up in a prominent 2012 racial profiling judgment in Germany on the train route running from Kassel to Frankfurt.

Situation I: to be Black on the train from Kassel

> Most of them were shocked by the officers' conduct, and some audibly criticized them. At the next stop, I was forced to get off the train. The police officers pushed me in front of them, although I put up no resistance. On the train platform they called in backup from the state police and ransacked my backpack. There was a chocolate bar inside, and one of the officers asked me if I'd stolen it. At that point I decided not to speak to them again until we were at the police station.
>
> (Student targeted by police, *Der Spiegel* 2013)

10 There is an expectation of being checked in Munich, according to a number of informants, though this has not been verified statistically.

11 Communication No. 1493/2006, *Williams V. Spain.* UN Human Rights Committee. 17 August 2009.

In 2010, two federal police officers were carrying out identity spot checks of passengers on a regional express train travelling from Kassel to Frankfurt am Main. They approached a young Black German man who had been walking through the carriage back to his seat, having bought himself a cup of tea. They asked him to present his identification. The young man refused to show his identification, claiming that it was unjust that he should be asked when other passengers were left undisturbed.

Officers explained that they would need to see his personal identification, and they followed him to his seat and looked through his backpack in search of identity documents. During the exchange, the young man remarked that this interaction reminded him of something. One of the officers asked what it reminded him of, and the young man responded that it reminded him of activities carried out by SS troops. The officer asked whether the young man was calling him a Nazi, to which the young man responded, 'no, that is not what I am saying'.[12] The officers instructed the young man to disembark the train with them at the next stop, which was Treysa Railway Station in Schwalmstadt, and they brought the young man to the police station there. At the station, after being asked whether he spoke English and advised of the possibility of having to pay fingerprinting fees and being placed in a holding cell, the young man voluntarily showed the officers his driving license (*Der Spiegel* 2012). He was subsequently sued for slandering the officers with the comment about their acting like SS officers. He was granted a leap-frog appeal (*Sprungrevision*)[13] with regard to the slander charges and, alongside of that, he countersued the officers for discrimination on the grounds of race. The case was decided on 29 October 2012 by the appellate administrative court (*Oberverwaltungsgericht*),[14] which quashed the verdict from the administrative court of first instance (*Verwaltungsgericht*) on the basis that racial profiling of this kind and under these circumstances is prohibited, as it violates the victim's rights under the German Basic Law Article 3 provisions on equal protection. The plaintiff discussed his impressions the following day with a German newspaper and expressed concern that, while the judgment forbade racial profiling of this nature, police had been arguing that the judgment did not reflect practical experiences, which, in the plaintiff's estimation, could be related to the unawareness that Black Europeans are

12 Original: *„Nein, das sage ich nicht"*. Beschluss v. 27.3.2012 – 2 Ss 329/11 (Oberlandesgericht Frankfurt 2012).

13 A leap-frog appeal occurs when a case that is heard by a court of first instance is appealed directly to the highest appellate level court, rather than to be heard by an intermediate level appeals court.

14 Urteil v. 28.2.2012 – 5 K 1026/11.KO (Verwaltungsgericht Koblenz 2012).

no longer a rarity (*Der Spiegel* 2012).[15] One can understand his reasoning to suggest that, regardless of these policing practices, physical appearance is not a reliable or appropriate proxy for immigration status. He mentioned in the interview that he did not initiate the lawsuit for the promise of financial compensation, but rather in order not to be treated 'differently' any longer by the police (*Der Spiegel* 2012), which suggests that he had been interested in using the litigation not only as an individual remedy but as a tool for shaping institutional behaviour and affecting structural change.

Two aspects of these cases (the profiling case and the slander case taken together) stand out as particularly meaningful. First, there is a significant disconnect between the expectation for protection against discrimination as put forth by the judgment on one hand and the young man who was profiled on the other. These two positions employ a set of linguistic cues that suggest divergent value systems and expectations for balancing the various interests at stake. Investigating these value systems exposes the social discourse around the issues and indeed mirrors certain power dynamics between the state and its citizenry. Second, unpacking the scenario and contextualizing it within a larger discussion on space,

15 The young man was interviewed by a German newspaper a day after the verdict was announced. 'Polizeikontrolle Wegen Der Hautfarbe' 2012):

> Spiegel Online: *Das Oberverwaltungsgericht kam nun in zweiter Instanz zu der Auffassung, dass Sie aufgrund Ihrer Hautfarbe kontrolliert wurden, und gab der Klage statt. Die Polizisten haben sich daraufhin entschuldigt, das Verfahren ist beendet. Haben Sie die Entschuldigung angenommen?*
>
> Student: *Ja, angenommen schon, aber ich fühle sie nicht. Die Entschuldigung war förmlich, ohne Reue und nicht auf einer menschlichen Ebene. Und an der negativen Reaktion der Deutschen Polizeigewerkschaft sieht man, dass einige eigentlich so weitermachen wollen.*
>
> Spiegel Online: *Die Gewerkschaft kritisiert, die Gerichtsentscheidung sei praxisfern, sie erschwere die Arbeit der Polizei.*
>
> Student: *Polizeikontrollen ohne Verdachtsmoment sind nicht erlaubt. Aber offenbar fällt es einigen Polizisten schwer zu akzeptieren, dass schwarze Europäer keine Seltenheit mehr sind.*

Spiegel Online also published an English version of the same interview. See 'Defying Racial Profiling in Germany' 2012:

> Spiegel Online: But the Higher Administrative Court for the state of Rhineland-Palatinate ruled that you were checked based on your skin colour, and allowed your appeal. The police then apologized, effectively putting the case to rest. Did you accept the apology?
>
> Student: Yes, I accepted it, but I don't feel it. The apology was formal, without remorse and not on a human level. The negative reaction of the police union (DPolG) shows that some will continue to act the same way.
>
> Spiegel Online: The union's criticism was that the ruling did not reflect the realities of law enforcement and would make police work more difficult.
>
> Student: Police checks are not allowed without grounds for suspicion. But apparently it is difficult for some police to accept that black Europeans are no longer a rarity'.

belonging and exclusion enables one to look beyond the doctrinal analysis of the judgments and appreciate the weight that the judgments have within the social lives of Germany's Black community.

Divergent expectations of temporality

When did this incident start, and who 'started it'? Did it start when the young man refused to show the officers his identification papers? Did it start when the officers targeted the young man for inspection based solely on his appearance? Or did it start before that, considering that such profiling is based on past police practice? For the answers to these questions, it matters to whom the questions are posed. In legal terms, the beginning of an incident concerning personal rights violations is conventionally regarded as the first interaction between the individuals involved *relevant to that incident*. However, in a broader context, where one seeks not the source of an incident for the purpose of articulating a legal remedy but an explanation of the incident for gaining a clear determination of the social phenomenon of profiling, the more accurate beginning is difficult to discern. This broader idea of the beginning is not a singular occurrence, but rather one that is rooted in a temporally ambiguous set of ideologies and patterns of practice.

The young man's actions reveal that he had different expectations of how the beginning of the situation should be framed than the officers and the lower court had. While this difference was treated as a centrally important feature of the slander case, it was left out as a matter of course in the racial profiling case, owing to public policy reasoning. The importance of temporality as a substantive value relevant to identifying and describing structural racism beyond these particular cases, and this instance provides a poignant example.

The young man in question had been stopped on this train line, one which he used regularly in his commute to work, about ten times over the previous two years (*Der Speigel* 2012). Thus, for him, this instance of profiling was not the beginning of his experience of profiling and his response was not motivated by a singular occurrence but by a pattern. During the course of the trials, the officer who had performed the identity check testified openly that he had performed the check on the basis of the young man's skin colour. According to the officer's testimony,[16] generally if he:

16 See Urteil v. 28.2.2012 – 5 K 1026/11.KO (Verwaltungsgericht Koblenz 2012): 3–4 (citing to the slander claim, originally filed in the administrative court in Kassel but was sent to the administrative court in Koblenz for lack of jurisdiction in Kassel; see Beschluss v. 31.11.2011 – 4 K 1163/11.KS (Verwaltungsgericht Kassel 2011)).

> guessed that a passenger was not from a Schengen country, and thus was possibly staying [in Germany] illegally, he asked where the passenger was travelling to and, in certain circumstances, he asked for identification papers ... The plaintiff, here, fell within this pattern on account of his skin colour.[17]

The young man was outwardly frustrated by this treatment, in the context of what can be described as systematic profiling, as he had been singled out on multiple occasions in the preceding two years.

The officers and the judge presiding in the lower court regarded the law as protecting the dignity of the young man only to the extent that the infringement of his dignity was sufficiently large and there was not a significant outweighing public interest. However, in this balancing of interests, the systematic nature of the circumstances facing the young man were not considered persuasive enough to alter the outcome of the decision declaring the profiling to be legally permissible. The presiding judge even went so far as to assert that the young man would potentially be profiled in the future under similar circumstances. This not only legally justifies the individual act, but the pattern of profiling. The outcome is at odds with the young man's assumption of the pattern as relevant to deciding the justifiability of this singular occurrence, which indicates that he views the pattern as central to understanding this particular episode of state behaviour.

What is interesting in the *Verwaltungsgericht* judgment in this regard, however, is that whereas the passenger's previous experience of being profiled was not considered relevant, the previous experience of the police was relied upon as a justification for singling out suspicious actors. In fact, previous police experience is used as an explicit means of determining whose identification is checked, which makes the practice of profiling a self-legitimating one (*Der Speigel* 2012: 7). The officers argued that profiling is necessary in order to most efficiently use their time while on board the train. This ultimately means that the efficiency of resource allocation, based on the understanding of policing as a public good, is judged in these cases to have outweighed the individual concern of discrimination.

While this judgment has been reversed on the merits (*Der Speigel* 2012), it remains to be seen how and whether the reversal will affect policing practice in practical terms in the future. This is because the type of precedent that the case provides is to be read narrowly, and it is not seen as a broad ban on the use of physical appearance in police identity checks. Indeed there have been subsequent lawsuits regarding racial profiling under

17 Urteil v. 28.2.2012 – 5 K 1026/11.KO (Verwaltungsgericht Koblenz 2012). Original: "*Wenn er die Vermutung habe, ein Reisender komme nicht aus einem Schengen-Staat, er sich also möglicherweise illegal aufhalte, frage er, wohin der Reisender fahre und unter Umständen nach Ausweispapieren ... Der Kläger sei hierbei aufgrund seiner Hautfarbe ins Raster gefallen*".

similar circumstances, which suggests that the practice is still on-going.[18] However, a more recent case suggests that there is at least some movement in the right direction. The upper administrative court of Rheinland-Pfalz ruled in April 2016 that the singling out of a family with dark skin (the language of the judgment is *dunkle Hautfarbe*, or dark skin colour) aboard a train from Mainz to Koblenz for the purpose of identity checks constituted a violation of the family's constitutional rights to freedom from discrimination on the basis of race under Article 3(3) of the German Basic Law. The reasoning for this judgment is that the police could not prove, given the train route that was in question and the circumstances of the identity check, that as per section 22 of the BPolG (Federal Police Act) there would have been such a high degree of protection of the public interest so as to justify unequal treatment on the grounds of race.[19]

In contrast to the human dignity violation charge against police for conducting the identity check, the slander charge against the young passenger relied on slightly different configurations of temporality from the perspectives of the young man and the court. The judge, in deciding whether the comparison of the officers with SS troops (which he had already decided was insulting generally) would be assessed as a purposeful social critique, he examined the temporal proximity and applicability of the comment to the situation. In this context, the previous experience of the passenger was taken into account and, accordingly, recounting the systematic disproportionate application of personal identity checks to him owing to his appearance rendered a legitimate comparison with NS practices.[20] By this logic, the critique holds up precisely because the practice of profiling against this young man was systematic; had this been a singular instance of profiling, the critique may have been far less persuasive.[21]

Ultimately, the conflicting expectations around temporal scope help to frame the discursive tension between racial profiling and the SS-analogy comment that plays itself out in this situation. It is to this discursive tension that I now turn.

18 See for example, the 2012 campaign set up by the ISD and other groups around further instances of racial profiling in trains and on platforms. Stop Racial Profiling website www.stoppt-racial-profiling.de. accessed 30 May 2016.

19 Urteil v. 21.04.2016, 7 A 11108/14 (Oberverwaltungsgericht Rheinland-Pfalz 2016).

20 The judge did not expound on this, but one can reasonably assume that biological race-thinking as a basis for differences in treatment would explain the link.

21 From the language of the judgment, it does appear as though had the comparison been made with slightly different words, there would have been a chance that the passenger's comment would have been deemed to have been less of a social critique and more of an insult. The presumption here is that, had the student focused on the identification of the person as a Nazi rather than on the SS-like methods of identity check, it would have been more difficult to distinguish between social critique and name-calling.

Talking back: slander and the limits of social critique

Slander cases do not infrequently accompany formal accusations of racism against police.[22] Verbal claims that police are acting in a racist manner are speech acts, and they are considered double-edged swords – insults on one side and valuable social critique on the other side. There is a trend of police using slander claims to rebut claims of racial discrimination and this trend helps illuminate broader aspects of how racial discrimination is discussed in Germany. I will discuss technical and wider social issues in turn.

The young passenger told the officer that his behaviour reminded him of SS practices. The police officer asked the passenger if that comment meant that he was calling him a Nazi, to which the passenger replied that it did not. The court agreed that this comment was insulting, but that the defence for such an insult would be allowed in this case for two reasons: because it was meant as a critique of constant profiling and the critique, as judged by the court, was understandable. This process of legitimising the speech act on the basis of the motive rather than the effect on the individual seems to seriously consider the passenger's view of the power structures that enable police to use racial markers to determine difference in treatment for citizens. However, taken together with the discrimination claim, the judiciary did not go so far as to condemn the actual treatment at the court of first instance. So on balance, the judgments as articulated in the courts of first instance legitimate both the treatment and its critique, sending quite an odd message: racial profiling is efficient and permissible, even if it can be legitimately critiqued as resembling law enforcement under fascist rule.

22 See for example 'Ausschreitungen: Fußballer Reagiert Auf Schmähungen Mit Hitlergruß' 2006; 'Rassistische Attacke Beim Fußball Nigerianer Wehrt Sich Und Zeigt Hitlergruß' 2006. In 2006, football player Adebowale Ogungbure showed the Hitler greeting in response to audience members, who heckled him racially. The Hitler greeting is formally illegal and Ogungbure was charged by the state prosecutor. However, the prosecutor dropped the charges, agreeing that Ogungbure was provoked when audience members made ape noises at him. See also Fekete 2010). In relation to the reporting of the death of al-Sherbini, Fekete writes, 'In Germany, an anti-racist academic faces prosecution for questioning whether court negligence could have been a contributory factor in the case of Marwa al-Sherbini, who was stabbed to death in a Dresden courtroom in July 2009.

Some of Germany's foremost academics, journalists, peace campaigners, trades unionists and politicians have formed the Action Group Against Racism and for Freedom of Expression and Academic Freedom (Aktionsbündnis gegen Rassismus und für Meinungs-und Wissenschaftsfreiheit). The Alliance is concerned about the implications for academic freedom posed by the prosecution of Dr Sabine Schiffer, director of the Institute for Media Responsibility in Erlangen. Dr Schiffer is accused of slandering a police officer; she was summonsed to appear before Erlangen Municipal Court on 24 March and, if convicted, could face a EU€6000 fine or two months imprisonment'.

It is clear that personal dignity issues were involved in both the discrimination claim (the passenger's dignity) and the slander claim (the police officer's dignity), and both were lost. The discrimination claim was lost to concerns of administrative efficiency of law enforcement practices, and the slander claim was lost to the critical social analysis of those systematic practices. In both cases, then, the behaviour that was legitimised was done so because of its relation to institutions and their practices. While this observation does not apply to every set of circumstances, it does reveal certain understandings of both personal and institutional interests in these cases.

A different outcome might have been reached in the administrative court in February 2012, had it interpreted the officers' behaviour as structurally embedded and rather than merely affecting the integrity of one individual. In other jurisdictions, this may have been done by viewing patterns of treatment of a number of individuals on the basis of a protected characteristic. Here, structural racism was not a part of the decision-making calculus – indeed, the judge mentions that this is an incident that could very well happen again. Patterns of treatment are, by virtue of the way this case was decided, not conceptualised as patterns that matter, but rather as isolatable and justifiable instances of individual treatment. This conflicts fundamentally with the experience and arguments put forth by the young passenger, who felt that the recurrence and systematic nature of this treatment was of central importance.

There are likely reasons that slander cases follow certain types of discrimination claims in Germany. On a certain level, it can be seen as a sort of offensive defence against discrimination claims, the charge stemming usually from a verbal response to or identification of potentially racist acts.

I call the use of prohibited speech acts a strategy of offensive defence because, as it is clear that certain specific words constitute legally prohibited speech acts, there is a sense in which the weight of such prohibition can distract from and even overshadow the initial racial discrimination. This happened in 2006 when Nigerian footballer Adebowale Ogungbure, who played for the German team of FC Sachsen Leipzig, was heckled with racial slurs by dozens of fans from the opposing team all throughout the game.[23] The footballer's response to this insult was to retort by showing the raised-arm 'Hitler salute' when leaving the infield, which is classified as a prohibited speech act in Germany.[24] The Hitler salute became an issue of equal or more importance in the way this episode was addressed by police than the slurs, ape noises and spit hurled at Ogungbure by the crowd.[25]

23 'Rassistische Attacke Beim Fußball Nigerianer Wehrt Sich Und Zeigt Hitlergruß' 2006.

24 Strafgestzbuch [StGB] (German Criminal Code). (BGBl. I S. 3322). Germany. Arts. 86a and 130.

25 'Affe, Bimbo, Nigger' 2007.

Although the context was clearly a gesture of critique, the footballer was issued a formal police complaint. The charge was later set aside, but in this situation, his speech act was most heavily scrutinised by the law, whereas the acts of the football fans were not treated as important or perhaps egregious or clear enough to warrant serious municipal or administrative inquiry.[26]

A claim of slander, similar to criminally prohibited speech in the context described above, provides a mirror effect for claims of racism. The two types of claims are structured similarly inasmuch as they each attempt to evidence a violation of personal dignity. However, the slander claim seems to have the proverbial 'last word', not only because it counters the accusation of racism, but precisely because the insult that the slander claim identifies *is* the naming of the racism. The claim, then, can potentially lead to a somewhat absurd result – the person who has experienced racist treatment can end up spending a great deal of time and energy digging herself out of a legal quagmire as a result of an otherwise legitimate complaint of racism.[27] To render the very naming of racism a potentially illegal speech act can have the effect of thwarting an open public discussion about racism under law and racism in society more generally.

From public spaces, I now shift to a discussion of semi-private spaces – bars, cafés and establishments that are privately owned but open to members of the general public.

Cafés, clubs and bars

The next aspect of racial profiling addressed in this chapter is exclusion from publically accessible cafés, clubs and bars on the basis of race. Cafés, clubs and bars are private establishments that are public-facing in their provision of services, a characterisation that I term 'semi-public'.

In general, certain nightclub events in Germany and elsewhere seek to appeal to specific partygoers, which suggests that there is a degree to which the event organisers, including club owners, wish to select the attendees for the social event based on characteristics that support the specific type of party that is being planned. Doormen in this context can be referred to as 'selectors', selecting the clientele (Kosnick 2005). This type of selection can be viewed as one of the privileges of an event planner – to decide who enters a private event, discriminating on certain bases legitimately for the purpose of the ethos of the party. The extent to which this is legally permissible is determined, then, by the counterbalancing legal principle of equality. While discrimination is, under some circumstances, legally

26 'Ausschreitungen: Fußballer Reagiert Auf Schmähungen Mit Hitlergruß' 2006.

27 In all four cases described, the allegations of racism have been largely recognised as having legitimate grounds.

permissible, it is generally only allowed when carried out on grounds that are not 'protected grounds', or those grounds enumerated or otherwise covered by law; if it is allowed, it must be carried out under only a strictly limited set of circumstances. These grounds include race, religion and sex, among others.[28] Ultimately, the permissibility of turning people away from private clubs that are otherwise open to members of the general public depends on balancing the right to discriminate against the right not to be discriminated against. This may seem straightforward at first, given that certain grounds are covered and indeed enumerated in the German Basic Law,[29] but in practice, it can be very difficult to enforce the rights of those who are impermissibly turned away from clubs.

Some cases are easier to prove than others. The more explicit the reasons for discrimination, the easier it is, generally, to formulate a *prima facie* discrimination claim. Direct discrimination is generally impermissible, though there are examples in which exceptions have been called upon. An example of this situation is one that Black males faced with the 2005 entry policy of a café called Einen Sonntag in August, which aimed to prevent drug sales on its premises (Bruce-Jones 2008: 445). This policy explicitly referred to Black males, and at the time, it was not clearly illegal, as the General Equal Treatment Law had not yet entered into force. Today, such practice is illegal because it directly discriminates against people on the basis of race. A related example of an exception to direct discrimination is the exclusion of people of a certain background into a bar or club in the interest of public safety.[30] This is also impermissible discrimination, but there is a provision of German law that allows small café, restaurant and bar owners to judge whether or not safety concerns should preclude the entry of specific individuals,[31] which leaves open the possibility that exclusion can simply be reasoned using racially neutral characteristics.

In 2014, a popular online media outlet, Vice, published a short piece about a bar on the edge of Görlitzer Park in Kreuzberg after its owner had

28 Grundgesetz [GG] (German Basic Law) Federal Republic of Germany. 1949. Article 3(3).

29 Ibid. Art. 3(3). "Niemand darf wegen seines Geschlechtes, seiner Abstammung, seiner Rasse, seiner Sprache, seiner Heimat und Herkunft, seines Glaubens, seiner religiösen oder politischen Anschauungen benachteiligt oder bevorzugt werden. Niemand darf wegen seiner Behinderung benachteiligt warden". Translation: 'No one can, on account of his sex, his ancestry, his race, his language, his country and origin, his beliefs, his religious or political views, be disadvantaged or preferred. No one can be disadvantaged on account of his disability'.

30 Allgemeines Gleichbehandlungsgesetz [AGG] (German General Equal Treatment Law). (BGBl. I S. 1897). Germany. Art. 20(1). Every ground covered under Art 3(3) of the German Basic Law, with the exception of race, is listed here as relating to a characteristic that can be used as grounds for exclusion to protect safety and security.

31 Ibid.

publicly stated that Black people were no longer allowed to enter the bar. By way of providing context, Görlizter Park, in particular, has been identified by some as a place where illicit substances are bought and sold, which has resulted in a zero-tolerance drug policy in the park and a noticeable increase in racial profiling, pat downs and identity checks of people of African descent. According to the bar owner, the drug dealers who were operating in or around the park were Black, and so the only way to ensure that drug dealers did not enter and operate on his premises was to institute an entry ban (*Hausverbot*) on Black people. Similarly, in May 2016 in Berlin-Neukölln, the owner of a small shop hung a notice in the shop window, forbidding Roma from entering. She argued that this was the only way for her to prevent thieves from entering.[32] These instances of invoking a ban on people entering a shop and preventing their access to goods and services solely on the basis of their race constitute impermissible direct discrimination under the General Equal Treatment Law as well as the corresponding EU Race Directive. However, these issues rarely result in litigation in Germany. Interestingly, the owners of the pubs are not ashamed to admit what they have done, even in the sometimes paralysing shadow of the history of fascism in Germany, which indicates that social discussions about the problematic use of race and ethnicity as features of social policy has not been reflected upon.

Indirect discrimination is typically far more difficult to prove than direct discrimination. This type of discrimination occurs when the reason given for exclusion is based on a characteristic that is not, itself, the race of the individual.[33] For instance, one prevalent reason offered for excluding some guests is inappropriate dress. Under such circumstances, certain guests argue that the issue of dress is merely a pretext for race- or ethnicity-based exclusion. For illustrative purposes, and to draw on cases that were widely reported and talked about in Germany, we can look to instances that took place in Tübingen and Leipzig, in which young Black men were turned away from nightclubs in cases of direct and indirect discrimination.

Situation II: a club in Tübingen

In 2010 in Tübingen, a former West German city of about 85,000 inhabitants in the state of Baden-Württemburg, David G., a young Black man, was refused entry to a discotheque. According to his statements, the doorman gave him the following explanation: 'There are already enough Blacks

32 'Rassismus aus Selbstschutz: Ladenbesitzerin erteilt allen Roma Hausverbot' 2016.

33 Race is an example, this would be true for other protected grounds, absent a legal exception, such as cultural or religious preservation, providing safe spaces for a certain gender, etc.

inside …'.[34] David sued the nightclub for refusing him entry on the basis of race.

The regional court in Stuttgart ruled in David's favour on the basis that he had indeed been excluded because of his physical appearance.[35] The court awarded him damages in the amount of €900 instead of the maximum of €5000 for two reasons. The first is because €900 was the price of approximately 150 entrance tickets to the club, which was deemed to be enough of a deterrent to prevent such behaviour from the club management in the future.[36] The second was because the club had let other Black men in on different nights, which suggests that there was not a complete ban on Black people as a group, which would have justified a higher penalty.

Indirect discrimination

Indirect discrimination (*mittelbare Diskriminierung*) is disadvantageous treatment based on a neutral criteria that disparately affects a group covered by discrimination provisions (Sacksofsky 2010: 2–3). In contrast, direct discrimination (*unmittelbare Diskriminerung*) is a situation in which race or ethnicity (or any protected ground) is offered as the reason for the exclusion. Indirect discrimination is much more difficult to prove in litigation than direct discrimination. Indirect discrimination relies on proving that there is a disparate impact on a certain group that is legally protected under the relevant discrimination laws – in this case, an ethnic or racial group, which would be covered under the German Basic Law and the German Equal Treatment Law. This requires convincing a court that, for instance, an employer's hiring practices or a nightclub's admissions policy or practices, though not explicitly discriminatory on the basis of race, effectively exclude people on the basis of race. As of 30 June 2010, according to a report commissioned by the Federal Anti-discrimination Agency (*Antidiskriminierungsstelle des Bundes*), there had been no cases of indirect racial discrimination brought and tried to completion under the German Equal Treatment Law (Sacksofsky 2010: 7). The dearth in cases is likely due to the difficulty not only in proving these cases in court but also the difficulty in gathering the relevant statistical information to track potential indirect discrimination claims. This book does not focus on indirect discrimination, but rather identifies it as an area that requires further empirical research – a need that lawyers and anti-racism activists in Germany know all too well.

34 This was the reason given by a doorman that a young man was refused entry to a nightclub in Tübingen in 2010. *See* Urteil v. 12.12.2011 – 10U 106/11 (OLG Stuttgart, 2011). Original: 'Es sind schon genug Schwarze drin … '.

35 Urteil v. 12.12.2011 – 10U 106/11 (OLG Stuttgart, 2011)

36 Ibid.

There are some indirect discrimination cases that are being brought in an effort to fight patterns of racial exclusion from bars and clubs, for example in Leipzig. One such case was brought by Hussein Eid, a young man excluded from a club called Club Velvet in October 2011, whereby the club proprietor insisted that he was not allowed in for reasons other than his appearance. He was awarded €500 by a local municipal court in Leipzig in May 2012.[37] Eid was pleased at the result of the litigation, and stated 'I am satisfied with the outcome. Discrimination is prohibited and, if no other solution is possible, it will be handled in the courts. I feel strengthened through the judgment – a good feeling'.[38] In Leipzig, there are other similar claims already pending, including a number of test cases that seek to gather statistical evidence of patterns of racial discrimination in club entry practices (Greiner 2013). Eid's remark about litigation being available if other solutions do not work suggests a way to think about law in these types of cases – that it may be used to push for remedy or reform rather than as a first response in addressing issues of discrimination. In this way, law can be seen as a part of a broad strategy for change, rather than a singular instrument or solution.

While the cases in Leipzig have had some success, one of the critiques that has been levied against the German General Equal Treatment Law is that it provides little remedy for those seeking relief having been excluded or discriminated against on the basis of indirect discrimination.[39] The typical experience that friends and colleagues have consistently discussed with me regarding exclusion from bars and clubs, particularly Afro-German and Turkish-German male colleagues, is that they are told at the door that they may not enter because they are dressed inappropriately or cannot enter on account of some other facially neutral characteristic. Some of those excluded understand the neutral reason as a pretext to exclude the men, and the actual reason for exclusion was race or ethnicity, since they experience the exclusion on many occasions. Those who experience recurring discrimination are in a good position to articulate legally valuable knowledge about impermissible practices; the difficulty is getting legal structures to acknowledge these forms of knowledge.

37 'Pressemitteilung: Klage Gegen Diskriminierende Einlasskontrolle Erfolgreich' 2012.

38 Ibid. Hussein Eid notes: "Ich bin zufrieden mit dem Ergebnis. Diskriminierung ist verboten und wird, wenn keine andere Lösung möglich ist, auch vor Gericht durchgesetzt. Ich fühle mich durch das Urteil gestärkt – ein gutes Gefühl". Translation: 'I am satisfied with the result. Discrimination is prohibited and, if no other solution is possible, that will be enforced before the court. I feel empowered through the judgment – a good feeling'.

39 For a critical perspective, see Sacksofsky 2010: 7. Sacksofsky offers that there have been no claims brought under the AGG for 'race' discrimination, and those brought under 'ethnic origin' discrimination were misinterpreted by the court to require a racial motivation rather than a racially disparate impact. Sacksofsky concludes that courts are not properly employing the concept of indirect discrimination in their judgments; See also Bruce-Jones 2008.

Residential housing

Racial discrimination affects people attempting to rent or remain living in privately owned residential properties. In 2004, before the introduction of the German General Equal Treatment Law in 2006,[40] Sebastian Edathy, a German parliamentarian of Indian descent, gave an impassioned speech in parliament in support of passing equal treatment legislation. He described the humiliating experience of having nearly been rejected as a prospective tenant because of the owner's fears that if a person of Indian origin were to move in, the flat would smell strongly of spiced food.[41] In a speech to the parliament, Edathy notes that had he not been a member of the German parliament, he would likely not have secured this particular tenancy agreement because of his ethnicity.[42]

The vague constitutional protections against discrimination based on 'race' and other characteristics was made more specific in 2006 with the new Act, and the type of discrimination that Edathy faced is theoretically no longer legal today.[43] However, this does not mean that housing discrimination has been resolved as a social phenomenon. After the adoption of the AGG, some private owners and housing associations were concerned that their ability to choose tenants using a full range of considerations would be limited by the law, and they expressed relief that there were still ways to legally justify selecting Germans – for the purpose of maintaining balanced neighbourhoods.[44] There are legal gaps in the protection that

40 Allgemeines Gleichbehandlungsgesetz [AGG] (German General Equal Treatment Law). (BGBl. I S. 1897). Germany. Art. 3(3).

41 Edathy website 2005.

42 Ibid. Spiced food, in this case, would have been the reason for exclusion, but that was attributed to his ethnicity as a stereotype, so this would have been direct discrimination.

43 *See* Allgemeines Gleichbehandlungsgesetz [AGG] (German General Equal Treatment Law). (BGBl. I S. 1897). Germany. Art. 19.

44 See for example, Leiß 2006. The Renters' Association reports: *"Die Folge: Kleine Vermieter müssen lediglich darauf achten, dass sie hinsichtlich der Merkmale Rasse und ethnische Herkunft keine Diskriminierung begehen. Wohnen Mieter und Vermieter auf einem Grundstück, greift das Gesetz ohnehin nicht.*

Zur großen Erleichterung der Wohnungsunternehmen steht es einem Vermieter zudem auch künftig frei, ausländische Bewerber mit dem Hinweis auf sozial ausgewogene Nachbarschaften abzulehnen. Der 'Bundesverband deutscher Wohnungs- und Immobilienunternehmen' (GdW) begrüßt daher die jetzt gültige Regelung, für die man sich drei Jahre lang eingesetzt habe. 'Es wäre absurd gewesen, eine verantwortungsvolle Mieterauswahl zu unterbinden und damit die Sicherung funktionierender Nachbarschaften zu gefährden', meint der GdW-Präsident Lutz Freitag".

Translation: 'The consequence: small renters must only pay attention, that they do not discriminate on the basis of race characteristics and ethnic background. If renters and tenants live on the same land, the law does not apply anyway.

To the great relief of the rental companies, in the future renters will also be able to reject foreign applicants by referring to the socially balanced neighbourhood. The "National union of German apartment and property companies" (GdW), in light of this, welcomes the law that has come into force, for which it was fought for three long years.

some people expect should exist on the basis of racial and ethnic exclusion from housing, including the inability to identify patterns of unfair treatment based on the failure to record and survey certain data by housing authorities, the difficulties in proving pre-textual discrimination or indirect discrimination, and the lack of litigation under the AGG.

Beyond the challenges that exist, given the legal parameters of protection under the AGG, a more personal look at one of the few cases of housing discrimination brought under the AGG on the grounds of race illustrates some of the less visible considerations that stifle open public discussion on the issue.

Situation III: an eviction in a small German town

'Some of the other tenants are unhappy about the colour of your skin and your personal situation as a single mother. Some of the elderly ones have been here for 40 years and I cannot ask them to leave'.[45] A doctoral student, Beate Z.,[46] living in a small town in Northern Germany, was evicted from her flat in 2008. Her landlord first delivered her notice of eviction verbally, whereby he explained that the neighbours would likely not 'warm up' to her because of her skin colour and because she had been raising a child on her own. He also confirmed these as the reasons for her eviction in the formal notice of eviction.[47] The landlord was clear about his reasoning in a letter written to Beate. Beate sued her landlord under the German General Equal Treatment Law, passed in 2006, which covers racial discrimination as a protected ground.

"It would have been absurd to prevent a responsible selection of tenants and, thereby, prevent the securing of a functional neighbourhood" said the GdW President, Lutz Freitag'. The language of this exception can be found in AGG Art. 19(3).

45 This was the reason cited by the landlord of an apartment complex for the eviction of Beate, an Afro-German woman living in a Northern German town. Interview on file with author.

46 Beate is a pseudonym.

47 Article on file with author, to maintain anonymity. "'*Mit Wirkung zum 1. 2. 2008 kündige ich Ihnen hiermit schriftlich die Wohnung, 'heißt es in dem Dokument, das auf den 18. Dezember 2007 datiert ist. In der Begründung wird ausgeführt, ,dass einige Mitmieter des Wohnhauses mit Ihrer Herkunft und Hautfarbe und mit Ihrer persönlichen Situation als Alleinerziehende nicht einverstanden sind.' Das Schreiben endet mit dem Hinweis: ,Wir wünschen Ihnen und Ihrer Tochter für Ihr weiteres Leben viel Glück' und trägt die Unterschrift des Vermieters*".

Translation: '"Effective 1.2.2008 I hereby terminate your rental of the flat", reads the document, dated 18 December 2007. The reason is explained thusly, "that some other tenants of the block of flats are not okay with your background and skin colour and with your situation as a single mother". The letter ends with the note, "We wish you and your daughter much happiness in life" and bears the signature of the landlord'.

When I read about Beate's case in the popular German news magazine *Die Stern*,[48] I had had immediate doubts as to whether the eviction had been legal. Could it be that a person could be evicted from her flat on the basis of race, alone or in combination with other factors, particularly after the adoption of the new Equal Treatment Law? It seemed to me and interested colleagues then that Beate had a good chance of winning her case, not least of all because the landlord had been so explicit in his racially motivated decision-making.[49]

A year after hearing about her case, I met Beate at an annual meeting of the Initiative Schwarze Deutsche, where we spoke briefly, albeit not about her case. After another year passed, I gathered the courage to write to her to ask to speak with her about her experience bringing her case. Beate agreed and weeks later, she and I met. We decided to talk over dinner in my old neighbourhood, the Bergmannkiez in Kreuzberg, Berlin, at a small Thai restaurant. After catching up on each other's lives, we discussed her experience with the ordeal.

We spoke about the background of her case, after which Beate cut to the heart of what was important to her in the whole experience of coming forth with her story and bringing the lawsuit, which was covered in local and regional news sources. It seemed from her description that even more painful and trying than having been evicted from her flat on the basis of racism was the way in which certain people characterised her intentions and values for having filed a discrimination lawsuit. Beate had clearly been mulling this over for some time,[50] and she concisely recounted some of the issues that were most important, painful and frustrating to her about the discrimination case and its treatment in the media.

First, she mentioned that one of the most unsettling of her experiences was that some people accused her of opportunistically bringing the claim for financial gain. She described the perception that her claim was shameless[51] because she could ostensibly recover up to €10,000 if she were to win her legal case. She said that people said things like 'the poor student needs cash',[52] which suggests that her central motivation was financial. In

48 Article on file with author to maintain anonymity.

49 This is an important point to recognise because most discrimination is not accompanied by a frank explanation describing the basis for discrimination, but is rather justified with an explanation that does not relate to a protected category. The effects of treatment that follows this pattern can be described as discriminatory, albeit indirectly, and this type of treatment, termed indirect discrimination (German: *mittelbare Ungleichbehandlung*), is much more difficult to protect against since it is more difficult to identify and prove.

50 She mentioned to me that this was the first semi-structured discussion that she was having about the incident since immediately after it happened. She had not wanted to discuss the story in the preceding years, in light of her experiences with the media.

51 Beate Z. Interview on file with author. Original: '*eine Unverschämtheit*'.

52 Ibid. Original: '*die arme Studentin braucht Kohle*'. Z., B. Interview by author.

response, Beate thought, 'how much does human dignity cost?'.[53] She mentioned that she felt affronted by these accusations, which essentially made her out to be a conniving student with a frivolous lawsuit. After the eviction and after filing the legal claim, a prominent newspaper offered Beate €2000 for an exclusive interview regarding her story, but she rejected the offer, unwilling to feed rumours that she was motivated by financial gain.[54] The second painful aspect of bringing a lawsuit was another accusation, related to the first – it had to do with Beate's news magazine. Some people suggested that Beate wanted publicity from bringing her story to light that she could use for her magazine. The third aspect of bringing the lawsuit that frustrated Beate was the procedural hiccup that made the case stumble at the beginning stages. The claim was brought before the regional court (*Landgericht*), which then refused the case on the basis that it should have been brought as a rental issue and not an issue under the General Equal Treatment Law. Therefore, Beate and her lawyers had to bring the case on a new basis before the local municipal court (*Amtsgericht*). The fifth issue that upset Beate was that, in her estimation, and given the totality of circumstances in her experience of bringing forward her claim, the meaning of the *Grundgesetz* had not been taken seriously. Beate recalls having been told things like 'you just want attention, such things do not happen in our city'[55] by local people and the mayor.[56] 'Everyone listened to the press', Beate told me.[57] Beate's concerns, though they had legal merit, were socially criticised. Unfortunately, later that same year, the property owner and defendant in the case passed away, and Beate's claim could not be heard.

Perhaps the most notable aspect of Beate's observations is that none of them relate directly to the substantive aspect of the lawsuit – proving or disproving impermissible discrimination. The two observations that she makes about the legal trial itself refer to procedural issues. One of those issues is the lack of a defendant, which nullifies the proceedings. The second was the filing of the lawsuit in the wrong court, which can also be seen as quite a central issue, given that many non-lawyers (and potentially some lawyers) could potentially rely on the notion that the AGG should apply in this context as it would in an analogous initial renting situation. The other three issues related to media and public perception of her in the context of the trial, which is clearly what affected her the most. This suggests that the letter of law, in her situation, was merely one part of a

53 Ibid. Original: '*wie viel kostet der Menschenwurde?*'.

54 Ibid.

55 Ibid. Original: '*Du willst nur Aufmerksamkeit, so was passiert nicht in unserer Stadt*'.

56 Ibid.

57 Original: '*Der Presse hat jeder hingehört*'.

much broader set of social experiences around reporting and addressing racial discrimination.

Given that this was such a clear case of direct discrimination, the presumption that Beate had been bringing a lawsuit for economic gain in an improper way suggests that perhaps her critics did not recognise the circumstances as socially impermissible, arguing that she should literally just 'stop complaining'. Perhaps they thought that, even if the discrimination was legally impermissible, the slight was understandable and a claim for financial recovery would be disproportionate or undeserved. This type of reasoning highlights a debate that has been taking place in Germany, both in legal circles and in public policy forums, about the relationship between the freedom to contract and the principle of equal treatment.[58] There is a balancing act that occurs between these two legal principles in any given situation where a contract or potential contract is involved, since the legally governed freedom to select one's contractual partner for a tenancy or for public services theoretically incorporates preclusion of discrimination on grounds of race or gender, with some exceptions.[59] This tension is one that relates to the interference of the state in private commercial relations, but it extends beyond the realm of service contracts to private enterprises, including restaurants, bars and clubs (Aino Schleusener 2011).[60] Considering that exclusion from public places on the basis of appearance can reinforce social segregation, it is easy to see why there is a resistance to allowing discrimination on the basis of constitutionally protected characteristics from becoming the norm. However, in contracts that are more private, perhaps not involving public-facing service provision, the tension between freedom to contract and discrimination prohibitions is more pronounced, because the balancing of these interests ostensibly involves more personal decisions and warrants, for many, less state intrusion (Aino Schleusener 2011). At the same time, employment is the area most squarely and thoroughly covered by German anti-discrimination law provisions.

Employment

The German Equal Treatment Law was established primarily to regulate discrimination in employment and the public sector. There is a general presumption among people of colour in Germany that racial bias is

58 See for example, Schöbener and Stork 2004: 61–62. Schöbener and Stork describe the legal duty to balance societal freedom to discriminate proportionally with the principle of equal treatment.

59 See Allgemeines Gleichbehandlungsgesetz [AGG] (German General Equal Treatment Law). (BGBl. I S. 1897). Germany. Arts. 8–10, 20.

60 Protection under the AGG extends to provision of goods and services that are available to the public under AGG art 2 Section 1, Nr. 5-8.

widespread among employers, and that decisions related to applicants' backgrounds are made in relation to applicants' names, perceived language skills or cultural proclivities. The typical resume is expected to bear a photo of the applicant, and there is a presumption among people of colour that stereotypes about performance and suitability will be attached to the Black face in the photo or the Turkish-sounding name at the top of the page.

While the AGG was seen as a step in the right direction, increasing protection against discrimination, there have been a number of important criticisms rendered against it by Black people and anti-racism activists. In June 2010, I attended an non-government organisation (NGO)-feedback session of the European Committee against Racism and Intolerance (ECRI) in Berlin at which aspects of the AGG were discussed. One of the harshest criticisms that Black delegates and other representatives of NGOs levied against the AGG was in regard to its very short statute of limitations. If a person wishes to bring a claim under the AGG, that person must do so within two months the incident.[61] This timeframe is extremely short, and while it may seem to be a procedural issue, it likely functions as a highly significant restriction on the number of claims that are brought, though perhaps it is rarely the sole reason that claims are not brought. In the ECRI feedback session, someone illustrated the dilemma thus: 'by the time one realises that one's rights may have been formally compromised, one must still figure out what to do, hire a lawyer, and gather the resources to see the litigation through to its conclusion'. Discussion of this tight timeframe was followed by another problem – the maximum damage award available for each claim is €5000. This means that, after the time and effort spent bringing a claim, not to mention the potential mental anguish and humiliation, the compensation may amount to little more than a token gesture, in comparison, for instance, with the missed opportunity of employment.

Given the frame of reference of this chapter, which renders racial inclusion or exclusion as part of a choreography of bodies, it is useful to look at some of the strategies that anti-racism activists, and Black people in particular, have employed to push back against the forms of exclusion from a particular area of employment from which there is a wide scope for justification of discrimination under anti-discrimination provisions – the theatre.

Situation IV: Black faces in the theatre

In 2012, a debate that had already been brewing between Germany's Black community and a number of theatres, including the Deutsches Theater,

61 Allgemeines Gleichbehandlungsgesetz [AGG] (German General Equal Treatment Law). (BGBl. I S. 1897). Germany. Art. 21(5).

reached its height. In late 2011, a group of Black German actors walked out of the production of a play called *Unschuld* to protest the use of blackface in the production.[62] The directors of the play had decided to use back paint to darken the faces of two white cast members who were playing Black characters. Their lips were painted red and the effect was a look quite the same as the blackface caricatures used in the American Jim-Crow era. Similar images are also found in German minstrel performances and children's books.[63]

Members of an organisation called Bühnenwatch (translation: Stage Watch) attended one of the showings of *Unschuld* and distributed flyers that explained the history and offensiveness of blackface. After the action, the head of the theatre approached them to discuss the issue. The members of Bühnenwatch remarked on their website that they would welcome the chance to discuss the issue, and that the purpose for their action was not purely to protest, nor to attack individuals, but to highlight a widespread problem of structural discrimination in German theatres.[64] The practical result of the discussion was that the actors who had been painted in blackface were subsequently painted white for the rest of the play's run (Seidler 2012).

In a different case, which made international news, the Schlosspark Theater in Berlin put on a production of the play *I am not Rappaport,* using black makeup on a white actor to play a Black man.[65] Members of the Black community in Berlin and elsewhere wrote to the theatre, demanding an explanation for the use of blackface, pointing to its historical significance as a degrading practice, and asking why they did not, instead, attempt to hire Black actors to play the Black figures. The argued that it was necessary to use blackface because Black actors could not be hired for the main troupe, due to the limited roles that they could play in any given season, presumably on account of appearance or other perceived deficiency.[66] A petition was circulated to protest the use of blackface at the theatre.[67]

62 A protest actions was launched against the play *Unschuld,* whereby members of the organisation Bühnenwatch (Stage Watch) distributed flyers explaining the significance of using blackface. The action is described on the Bühnenwatch website 2012.

63 For discussion of a recent debate in Germany about the use of derogatory words and images in children's books, see Topcu 2013. For a discussion of the use of colonial images in German children's books, see Bowersox 2013.

64 Bühnenwatch website 2012.

65 'Germany's Schlosspark Theatre Defends "Blackface" Actor' 2012.

66 Schlosspark Theatre, personal communication to Kristin Lein, (4.1.2012), on file with author. Original: "*Allein deswegen, weil das Stückrepertoire ihnen zu wenige Rollen in einer Spielzeit bieten könnte, die ein Festengagement rechtfertigen*". Translation: 'Alone because the core repertoire can offer them too few roles during the season to justify permanent hire.'

67 A petition was signed by approximately 1500 people in protest of another play, held by the Schlosspark Theatre in Berlin called *Ich bin nicht Rappaport* (I am not Rappaport) for dressing characters in blackface. See 'Against Black-Face Roles in German Theatre

What is at stake in this issue has multiple dimensions. First, and perhaps easiest to appreciate, many Black people take offense to this stereotype-laden depiction of people of African descent. Black people are corporeally represented on stage by white people with face paint, rather than, for example, verbal or situational cues and signifiers. Blackface is a degrading trope in which an oily mask is smeared on the actor's face, one that does not approximate human complexion. It is applied thickly, but not on the neck or hairline, so the mask does resemble a mask rather than stage makeup. It is clear that such face paint is not meant to convince an audience that the actor wearing it is actually of African descent, but rather to serve as a physical signifier of Blackness. If this is the case, the choice to reproduce a divisive and offensive signifier, laden with historical meaning, is careless at best.

Second, the policy of not hiring Black actors in permanent troupes suggests that potential employment in some theatres may be severely, or even absolutely limited for Black German people. Racially based hiring policies are generally impermissible, but in cases like this one, theatres rely legally on the courts' broad discretion in the form of an exception called a 'genuine occupational requirement'. This exception allows the theatres to deem race to be an important criteria for them to consider when casting performers. This is permissible under German law, and under European law, but must be clearly articulated, necessary and proportionate.[68] The argument by the ISD (Initiative Schwarze Deutsche und Schwarze Menschen in Deutschland or Initiative of Black Germans and Black People

(Petition)' Aavaz website. The text of this petition, addressed to the Dramatists Guild of America, reads: 'Last January Schlosspark Theatre in Berlin opened *I'm Not Rappaport* by Herb Gardner. The production featured a white actor in black-face in the role of Midge Carter, portrayed in New York by Ossie Davis. When concerned theatre professionals complained on the website of Schlosspark, they were blocked; yet neo-Nazis, who charged that the "niggers should go back to Africa," were allowed access. Schlosspark insisted the production was not "racist," that they cast a white actor because they could not find a "qualified black actor." The widow of Herb Gardner has deflected inquiries about the rights to *Rapport* to the agent in Germany. And she points to a 1986 conversation in which Gardner agreed to black-face "if a suitable black actor could not be found." That time and circumstance have passed. I am asking Actors Equity and the Dramatists Guild to decline participation in productions featuring black-face and condemn its use in Germany'.

68 Allgemeines Gleichbehandlungsgesetz [AGG] (German General Equal Treatment Law). (BGBl. I S. 1897). Germany. Art. 8. See also Aino Schleusener et al 2011: 184: „Unproblematisch ist eine Differenzierung nach Rasse oder ethnischer Herkunft, wenn dies der Authentizitätswahrung dient. So ist bei der Besetzung von Theater-, Film- und Fernsehrollen eine Differenzierung entsprechend der Vorgaben, die die Rolle mit sich bringt, zulässig". Translation: 'It is unproblematic to make a distinction based on race or ethnic origin if it serves to preserve authenticity. Thus, in hiring for theatre, film and television roles, selection of those who fit the part, is permissible'. For European provisions, see EU Race Directive, 2000/43/EC, Art. 5.

in Germany) and others is that the proposition that Black actors cannot play diverse roles, but white actors (with enough paint) can, is offensive and simply untrue. The debate reveals a painful double standard that prevents Black artists from representing white ones while allowing white artists to represent Black ones, which communicates a deficiency in the skills of Black actors, a discomfort with using white face-paint, or perhaps the simple impossibility of representing whiteness.

Third, there is a tension that reveals itself in the technical discussion about whether or not legal provisions should prevent artistic license from being an excuse for socially inappropriate and offensive speech and acts. The 2003 production of a play in at the Volksbühne in Berlin, by way of comparative example, caused a great deal of controversy (Wiedenroth-Coulibaly 2007: 411). At the centre of the controversy was the way that the play's name was presented on the billboard of the theatre. The play was titled *Der Kampf des Negers und der Hund*, from the original French *Combat de nègre et de chiens*. The German word *Neger* and the French word *nègre* are similar inasmuch as they can be wielded as epithets but are present, though controversially, in some social parlance.[69] Their use is generally viewed with disdain, but the disdain for many in both contexts seems to stem from reluctance to being politically incorrect rather than reluctance to do emotional harm to others by using an epithet. The play was advertised with the single word *Neger* set in large letters onto the billboard of the Volksbühne. This was meant to provoke discussion and presumably a buzz around the play, but members of the Black community in Berlin, as well as others, found that it did so at the expense of causing extreme offense to Black people.[70] The ISD referred to the use of this word as colonially-racist linguistic usage.[71] The ordeal brought into clear relief a tension in the public discourses around Blackness that, much like black face-paint, Black people find deeply offensive but are generally unable to prohibit.

Contesting normative conceptions of 'the public'

The four situations offered in this chapter produce a sketch of some of the ways in which Black people in Germany confront discriminatory practices, including how both legal and non-legal modes of countering such discrimination are employed. Important to recognise in viewing these situations

69 For the French context, see Jake Lamar 2010.

70 See Zöllner 2003. Freie Radios also interviewed members of the Initiative Schwarze Deutsche about their demonstration in relation to the Theatre's show. See 'Kolonial-Rassistischer Sprachgebrauch in Einem Theaterstück an Der Volksbühne Berlin (Interview mit Mitglieder der ISD)' 2004.

71 'Kolonial-Rassistischer Sprachgebrauch in Einem Theaterstück an Der Volksbühne Berlin (Interview mit Mitglieder der ISD)' 2004.

are the discursive methods used to justify race-based exclusion in the interest of a greater good. This dynamic is, in practice, a balancing of the legal principle of equal treatment on one hand and legal principles that are seen to protect society at large on the other, including safety and security in the context of policing and freedom of contract or freedom of association, in the cases of private establishments. While protection against racial discrimination is portrayed as an issue of individual dignity as connected to a group identity, freedom to discriminate (or to choose with whom to associate) is portrayed as a general societal interest. While these principles are not mutually exclusive, they do limit each other to some extent, and the tension between them has been explored both in specialist literature as well as in public debates.[72] Considering insights that this study offers for legal thinkers, it is worth discussing the situations with this tension in mind, as it reveals a dimension that may not be easily recognisable if one relies only on statutory interpretation. This dimension is related to the construction of the individual, the community or the public, and their interests.

In all four scenarios of race-based exclusion, the exclusion is attempted for the purpose of securing some societal benefit. In the first situation, the young man is profiled on a train in an effort to prevent illegal immigration, itself cast broadly as a public good issue, and to do so in a way that optimises the use of public funds, a second public good issue. In the second situation of profiling at the nightclub, exclusion is justified on the basis of maintaining what the management deem an appropriate balance of Black people among the party's guests, at the expense of the Black would-be-guests. In the third situation, the exclusion is justified on the basis of making the residents in the surrounding flats feel comfortable, which meant that Beate should leave. And in the fourth and final situation, exclusion was supported on the basis that theatres should be able to employ whomever they wish, and because white Germans more easily represented the majority of characters the theatre would portray, there would be no permanent places for Black Germans in the troupes. All four of these situations put forth a certain white-normative view of the 'public' or 'community' interest that is at stake, and in all four situations, the main argument in support of the race-based exclusion is not that there is no discrimination, but that the discrimination is justified on the basis of the larger public good principle.

In all four situations, each exclusionary policy or action is combated with a discrimination claim that, while articulated in the language of individual rights, reflects a competing value assessment with respect to the idea of community. The idea incorporates the statistical-demographical and economic arguments for race-based exclusion. This discord compels one to

72 See for example, Schöbener and Stork 2004.

critically examine the construction of 'public good' and 'community interest' in these situations.

On the train to Koblenz, the young man articulates the discriminatory treatment as persistent targeting and checking, which white passengers on the train were not made subject to. The defence against his claim was that the discrimination is necessary to optimise the use of public resources dedicated for this task, and the defence survived the scrutiny of the court at first instance. This means that the young man was meant to carry the burden of persistent police checks in order to fulfil the social interest of immigration control. He was put in the position of a body that is potentially out of place, a precarious body[73] that needs to be checked and verified while other bodies go without suspicion (Linke 1999: 94–95). The commuter train, with its particular route being already a space of suspicion, became a space that made him more legible as suspicious to German authorities, even more out of place than in other places or on other trains.

In the second situation, the young man is made to remain outside the club in Tübingen so as not to tip the balance of Black people in the club, although there is a question as to whether there were any Black people in the club to begin with. This could have been a whim of the bouncer or of the club proprietor, but to view this exclusion as a personal vendetta against Black people would ignore the systematic pattern of exclusion from other similar bars and clubs. If the young Black man was excluded to improve the experience of the white club-goers, it was probably done with the economic incentive of viewing the club-goers as clients that must be kept happy in order to continue their patronage.

In the third situation, Beate is excluded from her flat in order to appease her neighbours. Her neighbours, the landlord argues, would never come to like her because of her race and parental status, so it would be best if she left. This line of reasoning forces Beate to bear the burden of making the broader constituency of residents comfortable, at the expense of her own comfort in the ability to continue residing at her place of residence. It places her outside of the constituency whose opinion matters and allows the larger group's preference to define the spaces that Beate can and cannot inhabit. Her opinion does not factor in this process, owing perhaps to being demographically outnumbered or perhaps to the normative conception of who counts as a stakeholder in this residential community of renters. Beate's legal claim, based on the idea that such discrimination is impermissible because of the extent to which it infringes on her individual rights, is premised not only on the rights to housing, but the right to be treated equally based on being a part of a protected group.

73 I borrow the language of precariousness with respect to embodiment and state violence from Judith Butler. See Butler 2006: 1–21.

The idea of the *protected* group here is related, some would argue, to the very type of concern expressed by the neighbours in this scenario – it is very probable that Beate would have won her claim, as this is a quintessential direct discrimination claim, including explicit reference to the protected ground as a basis for exclusion, drastic curtailments of her rights with no foreseeable legal justification beyond the racial preference of the residents. It is important to recognise this here because this case, a real anomaly in the sense that few landlords would actually admit that a tenant is being evicted on the grounds of race, exposes a rationale that may be an undercurrent of this pattern of treatment in housing more generally. The explicit reference to race underlies the construction of the community interest and the marginalisation of Black people as individuals with *specific* interests that are subordinate to those purportedly of the larger community.

The fourth and final situation, concerning the use of blackface in lieu of hiring Black people to the permanent troupe at the *Deutsches Theater* and potentially other theatre groups, involves an industry-specific conceptualisation of community that seems to rely on a certain sensibility about what can be convincingly portrayed as German. In the discussions that members of the Black community have had with the theatre, it becomes clear that for the purpose of their artistic message and vision, Black people would be excluded to a large extent from the theatre's main troupe, and if Black characters were to be portrayed, they could be portrayed by white people. This rationale, of course, relies on the assumption that Black people cannot as appropriately be cast if they are to play white people. Given this set of issues, the community that matters for the theatre seems to be one that is white and German, or at least one that understands Black people as marginal and thereby limited in their ability to even depict normative (white German) characters on stage.

Conclusion

This chapter aims to demonstrate that when Black people enter and inhabit certain public and semi-public spaces in Germany, they are racially interpellated by white Germans and treated differently on that basis. One should acknowledge that the movement into or the occupation of these multi-layered and complex spaces constitutes a type of transgression, which requires one to put oneself at some risk. However, failure to take such risks and remaining obediently within certain steps of the dance may serve to reinforce social stereotypes and legal justifications that compose the current choreography of social and spatial life in Germany.

The prospect for legal regulation alone to protect Black people when inhabiting public and semi-public spaces cannot stand in for changing societal attitudes on race and belonging in general, and Blackness or whiteness in particular. It is important, however, to understand the law, given that it helps to structure and institutionally legitimise the arrangements of inclusion and exclusion in these spaces, including the checks, stops and scrutiny that take place, on both the interpersonal and institutional levels. Laws on or affecting how race is considered in contemporary Germany are inextricably linked to social thought about the place of racial difference and how protections against discrimination interlink with other societal values. The next chapter extends this link between social racism and institutional racism in the context of a case study on policing and a death-in-custody.

Part II

Colouring out of bounds

Thinking beyond law

Chapter 3

Smoke and mirrors

Performing in the theatre of the court

The trial had been referred to as a '*Scheinprozess*',[1] a farce[2] and 'Haribos for the press'.[3] It would become clear that many of the activists involved in pushing the Oury Jalloh litigation forward were not doing so because they believed in the ability of the trial to transform the conditions that resulted in Jalloh's death. Indeed, few had faith that the court would even see the same set of facts that the activists saw. It was clear to many that the court was not going to attempt to uncover the layers of involvement, investment and complicity in the structures that obscured the details of Jalloh's death, as the police had seemed to have closed ranks in collectively forgetting what had happened, and the prosecutorial and court system seemed not to be able to do anything about it. The prosecution had not even engaged the possibility that the death could have been a direct result of third-party actors, relying on a suicide thesis that could not be substantiated. Instead, the case would become a dialogic interaction among activists, lawyers, judges, prosecutorial services and the media, all vying for the unique ability to narrate a version of the events in their own terms and, thereby, to educate and influence those in a position to listen. In this way, the discussions that occurred outside of the courtroom were virtually as important to the activists working on this case as the discussions and episodes that occurred inside of the courtroom. The main point of the litigation was not to fight for a guilty verdict, but to have an effect on the way that this and similar issues were handled in the broader context of institutional racism and police brutality in Germany. With this in mind, it is important to recog-

1 At meetings of the Initiative in Remembrance of Oury Jalloh, the Oury Jalloh litigation was sometimes referred to as a *Scheinprozess* or a mock or fake trial. See also 'Pressemitteilung: The Voice Jena on Oury Jalloh – Prozessfarce Statt Rechtsstaatlichkeit' 2012.

2 See for example, 'Pressemitteilung: Initiative Oury Jalloh out of the Court Back on the Street' 2008. See also 'Pressemitteilung: The Voice Jena on Oury Jalloh – Prozessfarce Statt Rechtsstaatlichkeit' 2012.

3 This is a quote from an interview with Dirk and Marta (pseudonyms), members of the Initiative in Remembrance of Oury Jalloh, e.V.

nise that the critique of the police, judiciary and, to a certain extent, mainstream media *as institutions* was a primary mode of voicing dissent to institutional racism and police brutality, rather than focusing on the legal claims to justice as framed by the state prosecutor.

This chapter presents a case study that highlights aspects of the ideological work carried out in the service of dissenting against forms of institutional racism. It investigates a number of face-to-face interactions that position and contextualise litigation within the larger project of social change in Germany. It demonstrates that, even within the context of a so-called *Scheinprozess*, there are small battles wherein recognition of everyday racism and structural exclusion is at issue. Interventions by activists on seemingly small issues, as compared to the relative enormity of the Oury Jalloh case as a public spectacle, actually require a great deal of thought, attention and energy. As I argue in this chapter, this is because the smaller issues more acutely challenge structural racial violence as they threaten to reveal the processes that obscure racism and violence in a way that the litigation itself does not.

An important aspect of the unmasking of structural racial violence and the processes that seek to obscure it is the construction of a narrative of historical context.[4] A view toward the historical is important because it can make apparent the institutional and ideological continuities that underpin patterns of racial violence in the present. The discussion, however, does not confine itself to contemporary German history, but also evokes transnational modes of thinking, reaching well beyond the borders of Germany to call upon experiences from other parts of the Black diaspora, as well as reflections on the legacy of German and European colonialism in Africa, looking back to well before the NS era, which has come to largely define and indeed restrict Germany's use of the socially constructed phenomenon of race (Barskanmaz 2011).[5] Critique, informed by transnational and colonial analysis, is levied by activists upon the institutions of media, law enforcement and the judiciary.

My involvement in the Oury Jalloh case

It was not until 2009, four years after he was burned to death in a holding cell in the Dessau police precinct, that I got involved in forming an independent commission tasked with following the case of Oury Jalloh. I had not lived in Germany, full-time that is, for a few years, but after living in Germany for the better part of a decade, I considered this community my

4 This is discussed in Chapter 5.

5 In this article, Barskanmaz critically analyses the efforts by NGOs and some advocates to remove the phrase '*auf Grund seiner Rasse*' (on the grounds of one's race) from the German Basic Law and replace it with '*rassistisch*' ('in a racist manner').

own. The Oury Jalloh death had become a *case* in the broadest sense of the word, a recognisable instance of a social phenomenon no longer defined by legal proceedings but rather by a sense of injustice and both material and symbolic importance.

ISD is a registered organisation in Germany dedicated to addressing the political and cultural interests of Germany's Black community. It is important to note that Black people do not legally constitute a national minority in Germany[6] for the purposes of international legal treaty protection, such as coverage under the Council of Europe's Framework Convention on the Protection of National Minorities.[7] The ISD is one of few Black empowerment organisations and, with its regional chapters and national board, it is the largest, most influential and most widely recognised of such organisations. I had attended the annual national meetings of the ISD in the past, the first time in August 2001, where I made a number of close friends. In 2009, I attended the annual national meeting and gave a talk about German and French anti-discrimination law, after which the ISD's chair, Tahir Della, asked me to join a small group of people who were forming an independent commission aimed at securing a sense of truth and justice around Oury Jalloh's death. I cautioned Tahir that I was not qualified to practice law in Germany and that I was, rather, a legal academic. He and others reassured me that litigation would not be the direct aim of the commission, and that I would be helpful because I knew how to think through the legal issues in a European-comparative context. Besides, rather than participating in direct advocacy, the commission would be shadowing the trail. Earlier in the year, he had asked me to attend a meeting on international law and racial discrimination in Berlin on behalf of the ISD with the same reassurance. These prompts signalled two things to me: that certain socially and politically networked members within the Black German community were looking to have a broader social discussion about legal issues not necessarily restricted to litigation, and they welcomed a non-German, who spoke German and possessed local experiential knowledge about being Black in Germany into the intimacy of that discussion. This was an important and fascinating turning point for me, as I would be acting in a position of leadership, speaking on behalf of the Black German community, which I felt uneasy about but also proud of and obliged to follow through on.

The legal narrative: of facts

There are many ways to narrate an event or incident. In the legal arena, particularly in a courtroom environment where the *incident* is the

6 Bundesministerium des Innern website.

7 Council of Europe Framework Convention for the Protection of National Minorities. Council of Europe, Strasbourg, 1.2.1995.

foundational act or occurrence from which an adversarial legal claim stems, the narration of facts is expected to have a number of basic characteristics in order to sound clear, legitimate and fit for the purpose of helping the court to fairly adjudicate the matter. First, the narration is expected to be chronological. This is important for the purpose of allowing both experienced lawyers and non-lawyers to understand the event in a simple story format. Second, the narration is expected to include only those facts deemed relevant to understanding what happened in an effort to decide the case. This means that the narrative should not contain material that is wholly extraneous to the incident under scrutiny, but it should also not leave out details that, while in themselves are not determinative to the outcome of the case, may allow the listener to understand the situation better in order to proper weigh the sometimes very complex sides of the claim. Third, the language of the narration is expected to sound as 'objective' as possible, particularly with respect to implications of guilt, innocence, character and intentions of the parties.[8] In other words, the narrative, to sound legitimate must not contain arguments that imply the guilt or innocence of the parties. It is important to note with this third expectation that establishing and agreeing to a set of facts is a very important part of litigation, and the final content of the facts can be contentious. It is equally important to know that the presumption that there are objective facts 'to be found' rather than a constitution of facts during the process of legal inquiry is a problematic ideological position that undergirds the legitimacy of legal knowledge (Bruce-Jones 2009).

There is a ritualistic aspect to the statement of facts in certain court trials, and there certainly was one in the trial on the death of Oury Jalloh. In this trial, the facts of the case were read aloud at the beginning of the trial by one of the three judges. He read them from the documents, at a quick and even pace, page after page. He could have summarised them to a similar effect, but was required to read them aloud, ostensibly to put everyone on the proverbial exact same page and to have marked this understanding with a long and ritualistic recitation of the facts in their official articulation, he was performing a speech act that would ground the case, setting out its parameters for analysis.

The facts to which he referred were those as stated in the notice granting the appeal from the trial court's acquittal of the defendants from the negligence charge. Some of the relevant facts set out in the legal proceedings are the following. Oury, originally from Sierra Leone, had been in Germany for a number of years, having applied for asylum and received a

8 Of course an anthropological perspective would insist that an objective narration is not possible, but a legal frame relies on the appearance of an unbiased account in order to preserve its own legitimacy. For more on this in the context of evidence and expert testimony, see Good 2009.

rejection and a temporary stay.[9] On the evening of 6 January 2005, Oury was apprehended by police officers after two women complained that he had been harassing them. He was intoxicated and the police arrested and examined him before shackling his hands and feet to the bed of a holding cell. The next day, at around midday, Oury, still affixed to the bed, died of heat shock when he burned in the fire set on his mattress.[10]

The community's narrative: of questions and truths

By 'community', I am actually referring in this instance to various groups that may be described as having an interest in pursuing more thoroughgoing discussions about racism and state violence. These groups form a composite voice, one that diverges from the legal narrative in telling Oury's story. This larger 'community' is made not only of Black Germans, but also people of various backgrounds responding not only to the legal issues, but also to broader questions about what happened to Oury and how his situation fits into a pattern of violence against Black people, people of colour, asylum applicants and others in precarious positions in relation to the nation and the state.

For these communities, in light of a number of interventions they make in the course of Oury's trial, it is difficult to exact a 'beginning' of his story as such. Oury's death is legible as part of a pattern of violence that was in place long before his unfortunate situation, so the facts of this 'case' begin before the facts of the legal narrative. Whereas the legal narrative begins with Oury asking the women working for the city's sanitation department to use their telephone, the community's narrative has no definitive beginning. Rather, it has historical locus points that construct a framework for understanding Oury's encounter with the police – one that informs both the questions that the community asks as well as the urgency with which it asks them. These questions are posed not only to the lawyers and judges involved in the trial, but also for anyone who may be watching the events, as a way to inform and educate a wider audience of this instance and of the framework for understanding it.

It is difficult to speak of multiple communities without reinforcing the somewhat false distinctions among what may otherwise be seen an internally diverse segment of society that commonly opposes aspects of state

9 In Germany, a temporary under the law at the time was called a *Duldung* (this status designation has since been eliminated) and was not equivalent to 'temporary leave to remain' status, but rather served as an acknowledgement that the failed applicant was still in Germany and is expected to leave. A *Duldung* was able to be turned into valid immigration status in the form of 'leave to remain' (*Aufenhaltserlaubnis*) after 18 months under certain circumstances. See Deutsches Ausländerrecht (German Aliens Law). AuslR. 1 § 60a. 2005.

10 Urteil v. 7.1.2010 – 4 Str 413/09 (Bundesgerichtshof 2010) 4.

violence. Therefore, I will speak of interests and attention paid to certain social positions. This project examines, for example, those interested in racial justice, acknowledging disparaging treatment towards Black residents in Germany. Another social position that people have been concerned with is that of asylum applicants in Germany, who also bear a disproportionate load of state and administrative violence in contemporary Germany.[11] Particularly for the case of Oury Jalloh, but also in response to a range of other instances of police brutality and custodial deaths, asylum applicants and activists for asylum policy reform have been prominent among calls for justice. There are a number of reasons for this, not least of which is the persistent presence of police and administrative controls in the everyday lives of asylum applicants – from the conditions of housing and financial allowance to restrictions on work and travel and ultimately what many experience as targeting by police. Aspects of targeting by police on the basis of appearance (including racial and religious stereotypes) coupled with the distance that asylum applicants experience from both material and administrative support both shape the daily lives of asylum applicants, and forge a clear relationship between those fighting for asylum and immigration reforms and racial justice, respectively. Indeed while policy positions regarding specific law reforms may seem separate and discreet, ideologically these struggles are fought on an interconnected basis and activism around them is a shared endeavour to a significant extent.

Basic concerns: a room and twin elephants

The legal narrative of how the police encountered Oury Jalloh, characterised therein as an intoxicated person who was bothering sanitation workers early in the morning, leaves a number of questions and assumptions open. The elephants in the room, in this sense, are the seemingly common-sense presumptions that rebut a straightforward interpretation of the facts on which the legal narrative is based. Recognising that these elephants exist, however, is partially based on having a requisite understanding of structural racism and the criminalisation and targeting of certain groups.

Jalloh lived in an asylum residence on the outskirts of Dessau. Asylum applicants in most places in Germany are legally bound to remain within

11 The challenges faced by asylum applicants in Germany, the basis for much of the work of organisations such as Die Karawane and The Voice for many years, gained a great deal of public attention in 2012 and 2013, when a group of asylum applicants marched from Bayern to Berlin, alongside numerous demonstrations and a high-profile hunger strike about conditions and residence and movement restrictions. See Guyton 2012. See 'Flüchtlinge Verlängern Protest Am Brandenburger Tor' 2012.

the borders of the states to which they have been assigned, are given a certain amount of money to spend and have no right to work.[12] The asylum residence in which Jalloh lived was a long walk from the centre of town.

By the time Jalloh encountered police in the pre-dawn hours of 7 January 2005, one can imagine that a set of social understandings and administrative machinery were already in place, enabling a type of violence to be rendered upon him that may not have been so easy to render upon another individual – one perhaps with white skin, German citizenship and a more robust social status. Familiarity with some of the technologies of structural racism elucidates a range of the potential course of events on the morning of Jalloh's death based on quite a different understanding of the events than the legal framing of the issues suggest.

The legal trial formally begins with the state prosecutor's charge against the police of wrongful death with fatal consequence, but from the perspective of various members of the Black community and allied activist communities, there was a wider set of circumstances that prevented murder charges from being brought. This may not have been down to an individual prosecutor, although there have been criticisms of his reluctance to bring such charges, but rather the totality of circumstances. These other circumstances include the status of the victim and the defendants, the nature of state liability in issues of prosecuting law enforcement agents, and the filling in of the proverbial 'blanks' in the chronology of occurrences, given that the victim was dead and those officers interrogated either did not speak, gave conflicting responses or 'could not remember' what had occurred. One must note that the failure of the state to comprehensively identify and address forms of structural racism makes telling the story of Jalloh's encounter with the police somehow incoherent or flamboyant when read to the state in a legal forum. There is a slippery quality to the language available for reciting the events through a lens of racial recognition – paying attention to a pattern of treatment that affects people of colour disproportionately makes one sound unwarrantedly dramatic in Germany. This erasure of knowledge of institutional racism can be, itself, viewed as a type of violence, a denial of a painful lived experience.[13] In

12 Asylbewerberleistungsgesetz. AsylbLG. Germany, BGBl. I S. 2022. § 61 Abs. 1, 5.8.1997, though there are certain exceptional jobs paying €1.05 per hour under § 5 Arbeitsgelegenheiten, Abs. 1–4.

13 See Kilomba 2008: 32. Kilomba notes, with reference to the regulation of marginalised discourses: 'As Black writers and scholars, we are transforming configurations of both the margin and the centre. This transformation is mirrored in our discourses. When we produce knowledge, argues bell hooks, our discourses embody not only words of struggle, but also of pain – the pain of oppression. And when hearing our discourses, one can also hear the pain and emotion contained within its brokenness: the brokenness, she argues, of still being excluded from places which we have just "arrived," but can hardly "stay."'

order to counter this type of epistemological erasure, communities of colour and asylum applicants approach situations that resemble interpersonal violence with the added question – how have institutions been complicit in such violence?

From a different angle, the community of activists concerned with the Oury Jalloh trial mobilise within a climate of policing that they recognise is relatively heavy handed with certain types of demonstrations. The activists in the Jalloh trial were viewed by law enforcement as trouble makers during various parts of the trial, which is aligned with a more general thinking of certain types of social mobilisation as inappropriate or even extreme.[14]

One might describe the unspoken issues in the court, from the very inception of the trial, in general terms as the status of the defendant on one hand and the status of the victim on the other. The first is perhaps the feeling that the trial was not balanced from its beginning because of the nature of the defendant police officers. The police as an institution enjoy a privileged position with respect to the gathering of evidence and the presumption of legitimacy. The second is the sense that there was an undertone of bias in the events that unfolded and ultimately lead to the death of Jalloh – a Black African asylum seeker living in what could be described as a generally hostile environment given his precarious position in German society.

These unspoken issues, the elephants in the room, only grew larger and more apparent from year to year and from first instance trial to appeal proceedings. The counter-discourse that emerged among activists on the web and at demonstrations as a result of the failure of legal explanations to account for these questions provides insight as to the affect and scepticism that Black people in different parts of Germany have regarding the law's protection against police violence. Here, it is important to note that, while concerned members of the Black community held demonstrations in Dessau following Jalloh's death, a great deal of political mobilisation occurred in Berlin, as it is a natural place for anti-racism, refugee rights and anti-fascist activists to network, exchange strategies and organise.

The court as theatre

To scrutinise the language of the trial in its totality, which could be helpful in illuminating particular codes of communication, may provide only limited insight in the scope of this wider project. It is more effective here

14 See 'Linksextremistische Medien' ('Left Radical Media') website 2014. The website characterises left radical media sources as those that are 'not objective … pursue political goals and confront political opposition.' It characterises the newspaper *Junge Welt* as left radical extremist, and on the opposite side of the webpage there is a link to right-wing extremists.

to consider other discursive and spatial aspects of the trial proceedings as a window into the framework within which activists have found themselves confronted with the process of litigation.

What was the goal of the trial, the content of persuasion? In the case of a play it is to reflect some human story, to learn a moral, to be entertained, to hear a perspective – but it is also to take part in the social aspect of going to the theatre, to stay in-step with social discussions, to be culturally informed and to be convinced of the inherent value in these ideas. A trial is similar. One hears legal arguments, listens to a reasoned opinion and leaves with a sense not only of the substantive issues, but an impression of the system that has rendered the judgment. At stake in the persuasive capabilities of the institutions is the credibility and integrity of the institutions themselves.

The next sections, on the courtroom and its processes, use the *Leitmotif* of courtroom-as-theatre to discuss the interactions between activists and legal actors, who broke character, stuck stubbornly to character and at times, were heckled and kicked off stage as the delicate control of this particular staging threatened to crumble under the maddening silence written into the script.

The people and positions

> Actors had to become proficient at expressing physically the meanings that the poet had expressed textually – especially the emotions, mental states, thought processes, and character traits of the *dramatis personae*. To assist the actors in obliterating their bodily being-in-the-world on stage, this reconceived art of acting would transform their bodies into a 'text' consisting of signs for the emotions and mental states that build a character. The aim was to eliminate the tension between the actors' phenomenal bodies and their portrayal of the dramatic characters in favor of representation.
>
> (Fischer-Lichte 2008: 77–78)

In the preceding selection, professor of theatre studies, Erika Fischer-Lichte, describes the eighteenth-century shift in German theatre referred to as embodiment (2008: 77–78).[15] She continues on to deconstruct the representative aspects of actors in performance, asserting that the art of

15 Fischer-Lichte describes the shift to 'embodiment': 'The actors were no longer to be guided by their whims and fancies, their talent of improvisation, sense of humor, genius, or vanity. Rather, their function would be limited to communicating to the audience meanings expressed by the poets in their texts. The art of acting in its particular performativity would serve as a vessel for expressing only the meanings contained in the poetic text'.

performing in a theatre after the dramatic turn towards this notion of embodiment is actually a form of disembodiment, since there is a degree to which acting or representing through performance already relies on 'exorcising' reference to the actor's corporeal 'being-in-the-world' to produce an 'entirely semiotic body' (2008). This paradox is inherent not only to the theatre performances, but also other types of ritual performances that communicate on the two levels – the story itself and the manner in which it is presented, including the corporeal 'bodies-in-the-world' that essentially communicate another layer of information through their contextual relationship with the political and material world.

While theatre performance confronts an audience with the express presumption of representation, the experience of being in a courtroom and beholding its 'actors' is similar, though it is not meant to be. The court, as an institution, is meant to represent legal reason, a balanced and appropriate application of the rule of law, and the fact that there are living, breathing human beings that interpret and apply the laws is meant to be of relatively marginal relevance in the context of court proceedings (Fischer-Lichte 2008: 78).[16] However, the banal relations between individuals and the modes of communicating ideas beyond the technical legal case is an essential part of understanding what is happening in a courtroom. It is, thus, important for my approach to analysing the Jalloh trial, that one regard the tension between embodiment and disembodiment specifically, as regards individuals, but also the reality of power relations in the structure of communication, beyond the 'four corners' of the legal rule book.

The Oury Jalloh trial was a public trial, held in the largest courtroom in the Regional Court of Magdeburg. The public was thought to have enough interest in the trial to be considered in the choice of courtroom and was allowed to attend quietly. As a trial observer registered with the Court, each time I attended a trial day in the case, I sat in the press section, a balcony above the main audience with a clear view of the parties, experts and judges. Members of the public seated in the gallery and the press in the balcony were not able to see the faces of witnesses as they testified, but had full view of their body posture from the back, the tilts of their heads. We could try to imagine the expressions on their faces as they spoke confidently or tentatively or in exasperation from the questioning.

From above the courtroom, where I often sat alone or with one or two police officers, the court felt like a theatre seen from a mezzanine. The courtroom is, of course, designed to function, in very crucial ways, as a theatre – there is a cast of characters that have parts to play, and one becomes familiar with their names during the course of a sitting. The

16 This recognition of the actors in the court as playing roles as bodies-in-the-world that goes beyond the content of the application of laws can be compared to the turn to embodiment in the history of German theatre.

characters have a script to follow – not verbatim, but a set of guidelines that leads and shapes their choices of verb, distinguish appropriate sentences from inappropriate ones and only reasonable improvisation is permissible. Like the actors in a play, the parties and participants in the courtroom have opinions and lived experiences beyond their roles in the litigation, and these opinions and experiences inform the performance in various ways, some obvious and some nearly imperceptible. The art of persuasion and the integrity of the institutions of theatre and courts of justice rely on sticking closely to character.

The comparison to theatre makes sense as an analytical lens. While the aesthetic form of theatrical performance is quite different to the staging of a courtroom trial, both in the ways that theatre has been theorised as art and the court as a social-institutional expression of state power, certain similarities aid in understanding the human aspects of participating in a court trial, particularly as an observer. The trial has been reflected on as a performance (show trial) by some observing members of the public, when one engages in the experiment of understanding the trial as a performance, perhaps one draws parallels to the staging of a play that is useful in highlighting the participants' roles, various levels of messaging and communication, institutional rules and boundaries, and the potential co-construction of the trial.

Similar to in contemporary theatre performances, there is some degree of interaction that is expected in the courtroom between the parties, their lawyers, the judges, witnesses, experts, lay judges, stenographer, police guards, media and general audience. Everyone performs a role. Like the actors in the spotlight, the judges and legal representatives of the parties to the case play the largest roles, speaking often and shaping the legal content in prescribed fashion, abiding by rules of speech, deference, form and delivery. The audience, on the other extreme, is expected to be silent. In stark contrast to the theatre experience expected in early German theatre, where there was much more interaction between the audience and the main actors (Fischer-Lichte 2008: 38),[17] in the courts, as in

17 The description of the type of interaction in eighteenth-century German theatre warrants extensive depiction, as it brings to life the types of co-construction possible in the sculpting of a theatre experience, and by imaginative extension, the co-construction of a performing a legal ritual. Fischer-Lichte notes: 'Max Herrmann demonstrated that the specific mediality of performance consists of the bodily co-presence of actors and spectators. Performance, then, requires two groups of people, one acting and the other observing, to gather at the same time and place for a given period of shared lifetime. Their encounter – interactive and confrontational – produces the event of the performance. To use traditional terminology: performance must satisfy specific conditions of "production" and "reception." The actors act, that is, they move through space, gesture, change their expression, manipulate objects, speak, or sing. The spectators perceive their actions and respond to them. Although some of these reactions might be limited to internal processes, their perceptible responses are equally significant: the spectators laugh,

contemporary theatre, that interaction is much more tightly regulated. However, this does not mean that there is no interaction. Fischer-Lichte describes the changing of the 'subject-object relationship' in theatre as begging the question whether the interaction between the audience and the performers 'establishes a community of co-subjects or merely recreates the old relationship in a new guise' (Fischer-Lichte 2008: 40). In making a comparison to the theatre, it is useful to think of this idea of a 'community of co-subjects' in relation to court trials as well. Interactions among all people involved, not simply the actors, as 'bodies-in-the-world' shape the experience of the ritual and the content of the legal application and legitimacy rendered during the court trial.

The script: stating the 'facts'

Any trained lawyer or astute law student knows that the statement of facts stipulated at the outset of any case is a powerful determinant of not only the legal outcome of the case, but also the parameters of legitimate legal inquiry. That which is not included in the legal statement of facts is regarded as too trivial to be included in analysis of the legal issue at hand – in this case, an assessment of culpability. Here, the official charge was a negligent failure to prevent Oury's death, and this was based on the presumption that Oury had committed suicide by lighting himself ablaze. So, in Oury's case, the pieces left out of the facts are seemingly the most important pieces of the puzzle for those looking to find the totality of the circumstances of his death: they beg the question of who started the fire. Litigating the charge of negligence leaves no room in the legal case to ask the questions that activists want to ask. For example, who were the two men who were alleged to enter the cell shortly before Oury was set ablaze? How

cheer, sign, groan, sob, cry, scuff their feet, or hold their breath; they yawn, fall asleep, and begin to snore; they cough and sneeze, eat and drink, crumple wrapping paper, whisper, or shout comments, call "bravo" and "encore," applaud, jeer and boo, get up, leave the theatre, and bang the door on their way out.

Both the other spectators as well as the actors perceive and, in term, respond to these reactions. The action on stage thus gains or loses intensity; the actors' voices get louder and unpleasant or, alternatively, more seductive; they feel animated to invent gags, to improvise, or get distracted and miss a cue; they step closer to the lights to address the audience directly or ask them to calm down, or even to leave the theatre. The other spectators might react to their fellow spectators' responses by increasing or decreasing the extent of their participation, interest, or suspense. Their laughter grows louder, even convulsive, or is suppressed suddenly. They begin to address, argue, or insult each other. In short, whatever the actors do elicits a response from the spectators, which impacts on the entire performance. In this sense, performances are generated and determined by a self-referential and ever-changing feedback loop. Hence, performance remains unpredictable and spontaneous to a certain degree'.

would anyone manage to light a fireproof mattress while highly intoxicated and handcuffed to the wall?[18]

This type of story is sadly not unprecedented, considering that every year asylum applicants lose their lives in police custody all across Europe.[19] However, the extreme circumstances of Jalloh's death have fuelled an already keen sense of awareness among Black people in Germany that they are targeted and brutalised by the police. One reason that the case has acquired so much attention is the trial that followed, alleging that the police acted negligently when they failed to prevent Jalloh's death. Another reason, and probably the more important one particularly for Black Germans, is the looming suspicion that the on-duty guards had *actual* knowledge of the fire when it happened or, worse yet, started the fire themselves. To see how law and justice are read into the way that Jalloh's story has been narrated by activists and intellectuals, one must examine the symbols and communication techniques recognised and employed by Black Germans in the context of mobilising around the legal issues.

Reading between the lines: silence, omission and erasure

In a trial, an omission of evidence or a silence in testimony on an issue can be as damning or exonerating as hard evidence. Legally, this is because one is innocent until proven guilty of a crime, at least in Germany and the rest of Europe, and without appropriate evidence one cannot be held liable under the standard of negligence. Considering this, it is easy to understand how the activists pushing the Oury Jalloh trial forward could come to experience certain evidentiary omissions and testimonial silences as a great weight suppressing closer engagement with the events of Oury's death.

I describe these omissions and silences as a type of violence. This violence has a legal character, enabling and co-constituting societal violence.[20] Among various episodes, I will discuss three silences and omissions during the course of this trial illustrate the repetition of scenes of violence that reinjure, remind and reinvigorate those involved in pushing forward the trial who understand and experience this violence.

The first is the lack of discussion around the medical examiner's racial remarks about Jalloh at the police station. The second is the differences in physical condition noted between the police autopsy and the independent autopsy of Jalloh's body. The third is the blank section of the crime scene

18 See 'Pressemitteilung: Wir Fordern Die Mordanklage! – Aufruf Der Initiative in Gedenken an Oury Jalloh' 2012.

19 See United for Intercultural Action 2012.

20 See Spade 2011. Spade discusses a concept that he terms 'administrative violence', which he discusses in terms 'administrative systems', such as identity production (31–32) and sex segregation by birth sex (7–11).

investigation footage.[21] These issues, while not necessarily central to the legal questions presented at the civil negligence trial, supported the presumption of foul play and potential murder in the minds of many Black people and other civil rights activists. These elements all point to all-too predictable components of pattern racism, which repeat the experienced reality of racial violence for Black people each time they occur. These issues, taken together, also highlight what it means to be Black in Germany in terms of an epistemology of racism.

The first issue, discussed during the first trial in 2007 in Dessau and carried forth into the second trial in Magdeburg, concerns a remark made by the medical examiner who took a blood sample from Jalloh the night he was detained. When Officer Schubert[22] called the examiner to examine Jalloh, the examiner replied that he is never able to find veins in dark-skinned people.[23] To this remark, Schubert laughed and suggested that he should bring a special instrument to draw blood.[24] This exchange evidencing the general fact that Jalloh's skin colour and heritage became a topic of conversation among the medical examiner and the arresting officer during the examination prompted the Black community and others to look for the meaning of this exchange. The racial undertones were familiar, recognisable. What was this 'special instrument', and why was the matter funny? The impression among Black people and activists involved in the trial was that this comment sounded sinister at its worst, latently racist at its most benign. This did not sound like a statement of overt racial disdain or xenophobia, but it was, for many, informed by fears and fantasies of the white majority. A psychoanalytic reading of the statement might suggest that the doctor's description revealed his preoccupation with racial difference – this guiding sense that Black people are so different that they evade his capacity to medically treat them – that their humanity, like veins, was difficult to identify, obscured under dark skin. Racism operates through these types of images and metaphors (Kilomba 2008: 86–91).[25] Though the doctor may not have meant this consciously, the statement publicly revealed by way of testimony to a community already in a defensive posture, exposed the horrors of what he could potentially have meant. This reinforces mistrust and the assumption of racial foul play – after all, Jalloh did die hours later, and what happened in between this exchange and his death is contested and obscured.

21 'Stellungnahme Zum Laufenden Revisionsverfahren Um Den Tod Von Oury Jalloh Vor Dem Magdeburger Landgericht' Initiative in Gedenkan an Oury Jalloh e.V.' 2012.

22 See Urteil v. 28.2.2012 – 5 K 1026/11.KO (Verwaltungsgericht Koblenz 2012).

23 Ibid.

24 Urteil v. 16.12.2008 – 6 Ks 4/05 (Landgericht Dessau-Rosslau 2008) 7–8.

25 Here, in her chapter entitled 'Skin Politics', Kilomba discusses the role of fantasy and associations in her description of racialised thinking.

The second issue is an omission that echoed an act of physical violence was the failure of the police autopsy to find that Oury had sustained a broken nose and a perforated eardrum.[26] From members of the Initiative in Gedenken an Oury Jalloh, e.V. (Initiative in Remembrance of Oury Jalloh) (IOJ), one gathers that after the initial police autopsy, Oury's body was scheduled to be repatriated by the state to Sierra Leone.[27] Activists of what is now the Initiative, then concerned friends and members of the community in Dessau, collected funds and paid for an independent autopsy because they were sceptical of the credibility of the state-sponsored autopsy. If Oury's death was indeed the result of police abuse or neglect, the Black community and many other concerned Germans suspected that there may be cooperation between the police and those administering the autopsy, as it would not be in the interests of the state to discover unfavourable information during the examination. When the independent autopsy confirmed the fears predicted by members of the IOJ, many thought it most likely that the police were attempting to obscure their roles in having brutalised Oury. The lack of evidence would have alienated the community from being able to articulate this potential case of abuse in a legally recognised way had it not insisted upon and paid for an independent autopsy.[28]

Third, the gap in the crime scene investigation footage caused a great deal of alarm for those sceptical of a thorough prosecutorial investigation, and the discussion of this gap set a particularly moving scene in the courtroom. The blank section of the footage is debilitating for future prosecution because, as it potentially revealed forensic clues not recorded elsewhere, the lack of footage may be a convenient way to support the defence's assertion that Oury's death was a suicide. The clear question that remains on the minds of many activists is: was the footage erased?

Taken together these singular elements outline the frame of a greater crime, commonly known as conspiracy. While the Black community has not used this term to characterise these evidentiary issues, likely because the term has a social connotation of being a reactionary accusation without sound factual basis, such issues are quietly understood and discussed as a type of institutional coordination to suppress the due process concerns of Black people and asylum seekers. So, while conspiracy was never formally alleged, activists have spoken of a closing of ranks, an enforced silence around the circumstances of Oury's death.

26 The autopsy independent from state forensics engagement and supported by the IOJ reported broken nose or eardrum and subsequent medical examinations did find these conditions. This has been verified in later burn incident reports, all of which are on file with author. See *Leichenöffnung Oury Jalloh* (*Autopsy of Oury Jalloh*), (31.03.2005), on file with author.

27 I discussed this with Mouctar Bah, interview, Magdeburg, 1 April 2011.

28 *Leichenöffnung Oury Jalloh* (*Autopsy of Oury Jalloh*) (31.03.2005), on file with author.

The trial transfixed: a moment out of character

In the court, everyone has a role to play. There was one instance, however, in which the rigid barriers of the roles softened to allow for an almost tender moment to occur in the courtroom. It was a tense but quiet moment of introspection. It was the day that the police forensics examiner testified in relation to the video of Oury's body that he filmed shortly after the fire was extinguished. The video was allegedly cut short before it could capture images[29] of what lay beneath or directly to the sides of Oury's body, including the remnants of the lighter that was controversially supposed to have been in the vicinity when he was burned.

The witness described how it was that the video footage was cut short in the middle of filming. He said that he was in the cell with Oury's body, he filmed the body and then he placed the camera on a tripod and plugged it in, and when he plugged it in, the camera must have shorted out the electricity in the building because everything went out, including the lights. He claims to have continued to film, but that the camera was not on. The audience then watched the film in question.

The legal relevance of what the court would witness when watching the film was clear – it would either support or indict the witness' account of how the film came to be cut short. What was more interesting was the effect that watching the video itself had on the courtroom. The film was displayed on a large screen toward the back of the courtroom. The courtroom was completely silent and over the speakers of the large monitor, one could hear the clicks of the camera equipment, the footsteps of the forensics examiner as he descended the steps into the basement of the police department, and his voice as he mentioned into the camera that he was going to see about the person who set himself on fire.[30] Once he arrived at the room and walked into the cell, Oury's body was fully visible. Much of his skin was blackened like charcoal, some still brown or red and intact. His body had swollen slightly, to the point where various segments of his skin had ripped open. His body was jerked away from the wall, it was visibly apparent that he had been trying to move about.

The silence in the court was deafening, and from the upper-level of the court, I was able to see the faces of all of the participants in the trial, including the judges, the lay judges, the defence attorneys, the defendant, the state prosecutor and the attorneys for the family. This was the first time that the video was shown during this remanded trial. It was as if an apparition had entered the court, the person about whose life this trial was about had

29 A second unanswered question is whether the images were ever captured to begin with, or whether the footage was interrupted and not resumed.

30 This was a point of controversy after this trial day, given that the forensics examiner had not yet seen the body and had already made a decision about who had set the fire.

come in a physical form to weigh in on the trial with a gravity that would surely haunt the participants in the court in one way or another.

The footage showed the body, and then, as the camera was positioned hovering over the body, swaying noticeably with the person holding the camera, it abruptly went black. The camera had clearly not been placed on a tripod. I felt goose bumps, and wondered if others did as well. The goose bumps were partially because I felt like I had just seen a real-life nightmare on film, seeing Oury's body, lifeless in the real-time of moving video footage. Mostly, however, it was because the detailed story that I had just heard from the forensics examiner had not been corroborated by the film.

Outside the theatre

The discussion of the tension between the narratives of material reality as shaped within formal discourses produced in the theatre of the court changes here to one of the slightly less formal setting beyond the courtroom doors, where rules of decorum that strictly limit behaviour are replaced with less stringent legal and social expectations. The communication between the same or similar actors outside of the courtroom, while they take on a very different tone, have everything to do with what is going on in the courtroom.

Physical barriers to the possibility of dissent

The scene began uneventfully. Upon entering the foyer of the Magdeburg Regional Court building, one would encounter three police officers, who would ask guests to place their mobile phones into a brown paper envelope, which would be stored in a cardboard box in the corner of the foyer, just behind the officers. In return for a phone, one would receive a green index card with a number on it for later collection. Pockets were to be emptied and contents shown. Guests walked through a metal detector and, occasionally, it beeped and officers scanned their bodies with a metal-detecting wand. The interaction was similar to security checks at most airports.

Dirk,[31] a member of IOJ, who had attended nearly all of the eight court dates for the appellate trial to this point, had entered the building in the morning and left the building at lunchtime with a few others to either smoke a cigarette or take in fresh air. While he was having a cigarette, a local Magdeburg resident known for being disruptive in formal settings such as the courtroom, entered the building and, once recognised by police, was checked more thoroughly than most. The insides of his pockets were examined and his small wallet was searched.

31 This is a pseudonym.

When Dirk re-entered the building, the police officer in the foyer asked him to present his wallet. He took his wallet from his pocket and held it in his palm. The officer asked him to open it so that he could examine its contents. Dirk asked him why he should need to open his wallet for close inspection when this was not common practice. The police insisted on searching Dirk's wallet, looking underneath the cards and fingering the small flaps of the billfold. Dirk asked again why his wallet was being examined, and the visitors and officers who had been standing in the foyer turned to see what was going on. The officer told Dirk to refrain from being aggressive. Dirk replied that it was the officer who was being aggressive by scrutinising his wallet unduly to create the suspicion of criminality. A woman from the IOJ said from the small crowd now forming at the door, '*Sie müssen uns nicht kriminalisieren*' ('you should not criminalise us'). Dirk repeated loudly, '*Sie kriminaliseren uns, sie sollen das nicht tun*' ('You are criminalising us, you should not do that'), and the officer looking a bit confused, placed his hand on Dirk's chest as if to indicate that he should not get any closer. '*Fassen Sie mich nicht an!*' ('do not touch me!') was Dirk's response. He was clearly outraged by the officer's behaviour. '*Seien Sie nicht so aggressiv*' ('do not be so aggressive') was the officer's response, '*oder Sie gehen garnicht darein*' ('or you won't go in there at all'). Dirk responded that the officer was not authorised to forbid him entry, as this was a public trial. Someone in the crowd said quietly in the din of commotion, '*er versucht uns zu kriminaliseren*' ('he is trying to criminalise us').

As I stood there in the foyer and watched the situation escalate, scribbling mental notes furiously onto an invisible pad, I could not help but think of the concept in Germany of the left-wing extremist, the activist portrayed to go one step too far in challenging the state on any number of issues. I thought of the security precautions and the available justifications that police would have to take extreme precaution. As a security precaution, it seemed exaggerated to leaf so carefully through this man's billfold, but then security checks serve not only to find unwanted items, but to create the perception of control and intelligence gathering. In this sense, the check was to establish a relation of control with those coming into the courtroom. Given the nature of the trial, this clearly did not sit well with the activists working to find out whether the police had killed Jalloh, particularly because of the nagging suspicion that his Blackness had something to do with it and that Dirk, a Black man, was the only person of those who regularly attended whose wallet was intricately inspected.

Such episodes in the interactions of members of the IOJ, particularly the Black members of the Initiative, colour their perspectives on the treatment of Black people by the German police. The episodes demonstrate the continuities of prejudice and power that are experienced by Black people in Germany on a regular basis. For Dirk and those Black and non-Black onlookers of this scene of physical examination, resembling a checkpoint or immigration border control, the wallet search was not a random inspection. It was also not a justified search because of increased security. For them, it was a way to control Dirk, to put him in his place by subjecting him to more invasive scrutiny. Was the assumption that he was hiding a razor blade under his bank card? For them, it was about the spectacle of creating a scene where Dirk was the criminal entering a space where he would need to be inspected, observed and physically controlled. This space was not for his protection, but rather a space in which he was to be viewed as a threat to protect against.

Bad reviews: intimidation of courtroom critics

'Coming back from the court, two cops stopped us at the Magdeburg Central Train Station. They made us show our passports and told us that their colleagues would be acquitted'.[32]

Mouctar Bah, a close friend of Oury Jalloh, has been a prominent figure in orchestrating the effort to, first, bring legal charges against the officers of the Dessau police station and, second, clarify the totality of circumstances surrounding Oury's death. Mouctar, a man in his thirties and of Gambian decent,[33] became a public presence in Dessau after speaking out at numerous vigils and demonstrations regarding the impending trial between 2005 and 2007, when the proceedings actually began. In this time, Mouctar attests to having been the victim of bullying by an institutionally concerted effort between the police and the local court.

Mouctar's harassment by the police became a central issue that activists took up during the course of the trial. Mouctar lived and worked in Dessau at the time of his friend's death and mentioned to me on numerous occasions that, due ostensibly to the fact that he had been keeping the issue in the public eye, police raided the internet café that Mouctar ran. The café had also been the place where the IOJ regularly met. Eventually, in 2006,[34] the police issued Mouctar an official notice restricting his right to manage the café, whereupon he became an employee. This type of harassment by police has been a regular part of Mouctar's life since 2005. I called Mouctar in late December, the day that the German Federal Court was originally scheduled to announce whether it would grant an appeal against the acquittal of the officers in Oury's case, and he explained to me that the police had once again raided the cafe in Dessau the previous evening. It was clear to Mouctar that they wanted to divert positive media attention of a potential reversal and remand of the trial court decision with negative

32 Mouctar Bah, interview, Magdeburg, 1 April 2011.
33 Paraphrased from interview with Dirk and Marta, IOJ.
34 'Polizeiaktion Gegen Telecafe Und Mouctar Bah Vor Gerichtstermin Im Fall Oury Jalloh' 2009.

presumptions of criminality that inevitably accompany a police raid on the internet and telephone cafe.[35]

In the time following Oury's death, Mouctar felt harassed by the police in another way as well. A police officer accused Mouctar of calling him a '*Negerkiller*' in Dessau. Mouctar appeared before a judge in Dessau to defend himself and to insist that he had neither used that term nor verbally badgered a police officer. Due to a lack of consistency of corroborating testimony given by other officers, Mouctar was ultimately not charged and the incident was dismissed. Mouctar experienced this encounter as a form of harassment and a tactic meant to intimidate him, to make him pay for his activism by making his life in Dessau difficult.[36]

These insights regarding retribution by the police and others are important ones to note for a more holistic understanding of Black scepticism around law and enforcement. There is a presumption that demanding rights will lead to the punishment of Black and immigrant communities. This punishment is violent both physically and epistemologically. Such insights have become the subject of a play called *The Most Unsatisfied Town*, written by American playwright Amy Evans, who has spent a great deal of time living and working in Germany. Using the themes of retaliation and community punishment, the play narrates the story of Oury Jalloh and those still fighting for justice around his case.[37]

Activists and human rights organisers have recognised that the police have singled Mouctar out as a troublemaker for speaking out against what he perceives as injustice. Among the demonstrations against this bullying was one held on 19 December 2009 in Berlin, and it was termed by the organisers and participants, including leadership of the International League of Human Rights, as a demonstration against the police repression of Mouctar Bah in Dessau. Mouctar has also been commended for his pursuit of justice by a Berlin-based human rights organisation. The scapegoating of Mouctar has produced a related strand of activism to fight off what amounts to a further oppression and silencing among Blacks in Germany, reminding them that mentioning the traumas they face will lead to more injustices being perpetrated against them. This ultimately describes the pain that Kilomba speaks of when she describes the process of decolonising knowledge in the context of post-colonial relations (Kilomba 2008: 31–34).

During the course of the new trial, as remanded from the Bundesgerichtshof (German Supreme Court) (BGH) back to the regional

35 This incident was also reported in an online article posted on the website of Die Karawane. See ibid.

36 Mouctar Bah, interview, Magdeburg, 1 April 2011.

37 I attended and spoke about the Jalloh trial at a reading of this play at the Institute for Cultural Inquiry in Berlin, 27 April 2010.

court level, this time in Magdeburg, Mouctar and others faced additional harassment by police officers. After one of the trial days in the beginning of the trial in early 2011, Mouctar, Dirk and others were being driven to the main train station, which is only a few kilometres away from the Magdeburg Regional Court. According to Mouctar, he and Dirk were seated in the back seat of a car, and two white German colleagues were in the front. Police pulled the car over, shined lights on Mouctar and Dirk, and had them produce passport identification. They asked the group where they were travelling to and they followed the group to the train station. It was at the train station that, when the group asked the police why they had followed them to the station, the police remarked that their colleague would be acquitted in the trial. It was presumed that everyone knew what trial they meant, they showed that they knew who group was and what the group was doing in Magdeburg. Mouctar and Dirk have both described this incident as a tactic of intimidation.[38]

To both commemorate the seventh anniversary of the death of Oury Jalloh and raise awareness around and galvanise support for the ongoing trial against the police, the IOJ held a demonstration in Dessau. A few days before the demonstration took place, local officers in Dessau arrived at Mouctar Bah's telecafe and told him that the Initiative was legally prohibited from using the slogan '*Das War Mord!*' ('That was murder') in the future, and if posters displayed this slogan at the demonstration, they would be confiscated. They were implying that such a slogan would violate slander laws.[39] However, this very issue of the use of the slogan was decided publicly by a judge in the early days of protests around Jalloh's death, in 2006.[40] The slander law would not apply to a situation in which the message is not proven to be false, and to impose such a speech restriction would impair the freedom of opinion (*Meinungsfreiheit*).[41]

The members of the IOJ knew that a previous judgement had deemed the slogan legally permissible.[42] This had been the slogan of the Initiative since its inception, and it cut to the heart of their social message – that this was presumed to be murder, particularly given the circumstances that included missing and contradictory evidence, paired with initial charges that presupposed suicide without testing alternative possibilities. The sudden enforcement of an injunction against use of this seven-year-old slogan in the middle of the retrial seemed more than arbitrary, it seemed strategic.

38 Mouctar Bah, interview, Magdeburg, 1 April 2011.

39 There was coverage of the issue in mainstream news sources. See for example, 'Strafbar Oder Nicht?' 2012 See Beschl. v. 31.03.2006, Az. 2 M 156/06 (Oberverwaltungsgericht Magdeburg 2006).

40 'Strafbar Oder Nicht?' 2012.

41 Ibid.

42 Interview of Dirk and Marta, IOJ.

On the day of the demonstration, members of the Initiative did display posters with the slogan on them, as per usual. The police forcibly confiscated some of the posters, and not others. At some points, the police physically beat some of the protesters. One of the police officers head-butted Mouctar and knocked him unconscious. They also physically injured Dirk and a number of other prominent members of the Initiative. Mouctar was hospitalised for four days.

This type of harassment by law enforcement agents does not merely illicit the response of a general mistrust in police of their abuses of power in stifling protest, but it also begs specific questions as to the propensity for legal codes of conduct to be set aside for political and ideological motivations in making arrests. This reinvigorates the question: why was Oury Jalloh really arrested and detained in the first place?[43] The return to the beginnings of this legal encounter bring us to the ideological component of recognition and treatment by state bodies based on having a certain subject position. This process of recognition and treatment based on an interpolation of a particular type of other, while difficult to translate into terms of quantifiable or explicit prejudice, is a well-observed process among people of colour in Germany.

Conclusion

The examination of the basic elements of this trial, including the social discourse surrounding the trial, sets the stage for the rest of the book. It provides a central illustrative example of the synthesis of racially informed ideologies and state power in the rendering and enforcement of legal rules. It also sets some of the basic terms for the discussion of racism and structural violence in Germany more generally.

The trial serves as a starting point for a wider critique that attempts to remap, to a certain degree, the parameters of the discussion of racism in Germany. It provides traction for identifying the important social interactions that may not be conventionally regarded as important modes of knowledge production. For instance, examining the experiences of the activists outside of the courtroom suggests a more holistic engagement with institutional resistance and truth-seeking in a somewhat hostile environment, which is perhaps not taken very seriously by state authorities or mainstream media and, thus, broad swaths of the German population.

This chapter has introduced the basic 'facts' of the Oury Jalloh case in the conventional sense, outlined the legal parameters of the case, and explored a perspective for understanding the trial in the context of recog-

43 The IOJ refers to 'racially-based arrest' ('*die rassistisch begründete Verhaftung*'). See 'Pressemitteilung Zum Ende Des Gerichtsprozesses Im Fall Oury Jalloh' 2008.

nising institutional racism and structural violence against certain targeted groups. The importance of doing this is multiple. First, it enables us to put the legal story, comprising the 'official narrative of events', into perspective. The activists who call for truth around the death of Oury Jalloh speak of the trial in a way that configures the legal process as a show trial, a mask of sorts. This way of speaking about the trial presents a set of assumptions that contests the functional purposes of certain apparatuses of the state. The mode of analysis describes the function of this particular trial, as a way to placate the public with the impression of due process without the substance of such process. This poses a critique of the limits of law and the justice narrative of the legal process in general. Additionally, where the show trial concept indicates a level of façade that is ostensibly meant to obscure some hidden relation, the activists have publically identified this extra level in an effort to expose the structures and processes that maintain it.

The next chapter takes up some of the themes discussed in the case of Oury Jalloh, delving further into the activist responses to and descriptions of institutional racism, particularly with regard to police violence.

Chapter 4

The politics of remembrance

Narrating state violence

The ways in which one experiences and interprets encounters with certain institutions can reveal a great deal about one's relationship with those institutions. Mechanisms of governance and law can have profound effects on the ways people negotiate and articulate aspects of their identity, and paying close attention to how people deal with this process can help to distil aspects of life in Germany. The subject positions of Black people living in Germany can serve as a lens for viewing law. The aim for using this view is to identify how state institutional logics interrelate with the ways Blackness is experienced in Germany. Certain confrontations that Black people have with German law expose a critical dialogical tension on difference and state violence that crystallises in ideological dissonance as to the law's purposes and objectives.

Black people's responses to the types of legal violence[1] in Germany discussed in this chapter are characterised by three recurring interventions, each of which gives some insight as to what is at stake and how one might conceive of the violence itself. The first is a deliberate process of naming institutional racist violence and its technologies. This includes describing ways in which judges, advocates and law enforcement officers marginalise, vilify and silence this process of naming. This characteristic of resistance illustrates the necessity for anti-racism activists to confront the paradigm of de-historicised individualism that frames mainstream understandings of racial violence by, instead, describing the episodes as interrelated, systematic and ideologically informed. The second is acknowledging the pattern of repeated instances of institutional racism as a structure. This includes recording and referencing similar instances of violence and legal aftermath and building a sort of collective memory around them. The third is a dual-pronged approach that on the one hand

1 By 'legal violence' I am referring to the violence that is inherent in the coercive enforcement of any judicial order. There is a significant literature on the violence inherent in processes and principles of law, particularly law's enforcement. See Sarat and Kearns 1992: 193–194.

criticises institutions for their racism, and on the other hand engages with a rights-based approach to achieving a just outcome for previous and potential victims of violence. This two-pronged approach is, thus, an appeal both to governmental structures as well as to non-governmental actors and the public at large to understand the dynamic of this contemporary resistance against racial violence in order to achieve both ideological and structural change.

This chapter describes and analyses the three aforementioned described interventions that Black activists in Germany have made in public discourse on police brutality in order to highlight connections between state violence, national identity and racial exclusion. Alongside the analysis of the interventions, the chapter aims to describe a historical narrative of highly visible acts of racialised violence in the last two decades in Germany. It also aims to illustrate some key differences between mainstream media reporting on these acts and activist and Black community responses to them, articulated via online and print media sources. The latter part of the chapter assesses the current ideological tensions between official legal posturing, mainstream media narratives and anti-racism activist narratives, with particular emphasis on the prospects for critical examination of how these tensions impact ideas about racism and national belonging.

Police brutality and racism: a European discussion

A rich example of the recognition of structural racism, one that has gained popular recognition not only in Germany, but also in the rest of Europe, is police brutality. Its presence in discussions of racism and xenophobia across Europe has forced European states to look not only at what distinguishes them from one another, but also at what makes them similar, what stories are shared among those who reside in various parts of Europe. The recognition of structural racism and certain shared experiences of Black people with regard to law enforcement are commonplace in Black European discourses on race and the law. These ideas run counter to the conventional notions in much of Europe that racism can be accurately measured by observing right-wing extremist violence alone – a logic that has caused some writers, such as Loïc Wacquant, to claim that Europe is not invested in the type of obsession with race that the United States of America is invested in (Wacquant 1999: 46–49).[2] Black thinkers in Europe, including community organisers and activists, have recognised that racism can and should be observed as existing structurally in such public and

2 This essay is a critique of uncritically importing identity constructs from the United States of America to Europe. However, in characterising race as a construct that is largely not relevant to Europe, it fails to acknowledge the shared experiences of and communication within marginalised communities transnationally, particularly diasporic communities.

private sector institutions as those relating to education, law enforcement, media and commerce.

While conventional narratives on racism in Europe vary from state to state, certain conventional European logics suggest that racism is not much more than the sum total of right-wing violence that occurs in the state. While a hegemonic narrative of racism might, for public policy purposes, attempt to measure racism by the amount of violence that occurs on the basis of race or ethnicity, Black narratives may describe racism using the vernacular and following the logics of those who experience it, which encompasses more than just physical violence. Contemporary academic writing and cultural and artistic expression reflects that Black Europeans experience racism as part of everyday structural processes including institutional exclusions, violence by the state, media portrayals and discrimination.

Intellectual and cultural work on racism from within Black European communities creates new spaces in European discourses on identity and difference by creating institutional memory around racism in Europe (for example, Beriss 2004, Essed and Trienekens 2008, El-Tayeb 2011). It creates a new vernacular that illuminates the possibility of talking about racism in Europe. Creating this new vernacular forces Black Europe in general, and Black Germany more specifically, to grapple with heterogeneous goals and views of its different communities, which includes carefully considering intersections with gender, sexuality, class, nationality, ethnicity and regional difference (El-Tayeb 2011: 60–79).[3]

In Germany, particularly over the last decade, public discussion on institutional racism in relation to Black people has identified police violence as a central concern. If the 1980s could roughly be characterised as a period focused on the gaining of cultural space and the 1990s could be characterised as one in which Black activists were fighting various types of neo-Nazi violence, the 2000s seem to have shifted gaze to one that confronts state violence, particularly in the area of law enforcement, alongside more widespread informal, social over-policing of Black people in certain areas of public life.

Naming violence

It is through the language of violence that one can best articulate the pain and disappointment experienced by Germany's Black community in the wake of Oury Jalloh's death. The anguish and frustration caused by legal and social handling of the physical violence against Jalloh constitutes a

3 El-Tayeb discusses the 'central role of transnational black feminist positions within the Afro-German community'. She also discusses a shift to 'queer of color' activism that represented changes in organising as well as articulation of community as a political project.

re-instantiation of that violence in very real ways. Calling this 'violence' offers a lens for interpreting the invocation of collective memory and a basis for exploring the focus on contemporary events in light of such processes of remembrance. The experience of racial violence helps to unify a diverse community of actors among Germany's Black citizens and residents, and the common language of this pain provides a basis for the epistemological reckoning that takes place between Germany's Black community and the ideology of the state.

Subsequent to the initial demonstrations in Dessau around the Oury Jalloh case, a small number of activists compiled footage of the demonstrations in order to publicise future protests. One of these compilations was posted on the Internet with the title *We are all Oury Jalloh,* a slogan that addresses various audiences, depending on who the 'we' references. The 'we' could mean all German residents, Black Germans or asylum seekers, but it sends a prompt for the reader or listener to question whether or not he or she feels included in or identified with the 'we'. It calls on uniting concerned people around a due process issue that is potentially more far reaching than it may at first appear. A great deal of ideological work is packed into the slogans – '*Oury Jalloh, Das war Mord!*',[4] 'We are all Oury Jalloh!' and discussion of the death as part of a larger genocide of Black people.[5] These declarations interpret history into the present and position Black people within that violence with direct, unabashed language. This language helps to identify the experience as ongoing violence, rather than to obscure it in the contingencies of fact that may well exist.

On this idea of unity prompted by a sense of affect to law, English professor and cultural critic, Lauren Berlant, notes the unifying effects of such scepticism:

> In the conjecture 'utopian/traumatized' I mean to convey a logic of fantasy reparation involved in the therapeutic conversion of the scene of pain and its eradication to the scene of the political itself. Questions of social inequity and social value are now adjudicated in the register not of power but of sincere surplus feeling: worry about whether public figures seem 'caring' subordinates analyses of their visions of injustice; subalternized groups attempt to forge alliances on behalf of radical social transformation through testimonial rhetorics of true pain; people believe that they know what they feel when they feel it, can locate its origin, measure its effects.
>
> (Berlant 1999: 57)[6]

4 Translation: 'Oury Jalloh, that was Murder!'.
5 Translation: 'Genocide'. See for example, 'Press Release: The Persecution of a Word and a Call for Action' 2007.
6 See also, Johnson-Reagon 2000.

Berlant references Freud in her conception of mourning and what she views as the 'theory of infantile citizenship', considering it the nation's duty to eradicate the pain of its citizenry (1999: 57). Transposed, this scene echoes the allegory of the police as protectors and the doubly painful trauma that ensues when they are perpetrators of pain. I do not wish to dwell here on the concept of trauma, but rather on the aspect of pain that inhabits experience in this context. For those involved with the Initiative Oury Jalloh, to counter the violence evidenced by the pain and frustration of the case, it was important to make sure the larger issue of due process regarding deaths in police custody was balanced with the more community-specific issues of racism and the treatment of asylum seekers in Germany. There was a sense, as Berlant phrased, of converting the scene of pain and its eradication onto the 'political scene', and in this scene, the pain was shared and publicly staged and exposed. The retelling of Oury Jalloh's story, and the subsequent stories of the community harassed for speaking out, produced a spiral-like repetition of sharing and exposition, etching a new vernacular into the institutional and collective memory of the Black community in Dessau and Berlin.

The type of pain to which Berlant refers also prompts affected communities to build coalitions with one another. For instance, in the present case, the Black community and the refugee community built close alliances with groups of predominantly white activists from, for example, socialist organisations and migrant assistance organisations. These alliances embody what Berlant deems as a concerted call on the state to protect. However, in practice, the Black interest community organisations, including the IOJ, were careful to control the strategy, language and narrative produced by their group. Within the Initiative, which is made of a diverse group of citizens and residents, the Black majority of the organisation closely protected the position of producing experience-based knowledge about racism and assured that this knowledge permeated the group's position on Jalloh's death. Protection of the space within which to produce this specialised knowledge was one of the reasons activists developed an independent group, rather than join a pre-existing mainstream group.

Berlant's use of pain as a rhetorical scheme helps reorient one's interpretation of the concerns of Black people towards the racism and xenophobia potentially lurking beneath the legal stumbling blocks and ultimately behind the cause of Jalloh's death. To further elaborate this idea, indeed a politically relevant extension of the psychoanalytic term of trauma, I prefer the racism-specific interpretation of the 'pain' of being 'trapped within a colonial order' offered by Kilomba:

> We could actually say that in the white conceptual world, it is as if the collective unconscious of Black people is pre-programmed for alienation, disappointment and psychic trauma, since the images of

> Blackness we are confronted with are neither realistic nor positive. What an alienation! To be forced to identify with heroes who are white and reject enemies who appear as Black. What a disappointment! To be forced to look at ourselves as if we were in their place. What a pain! To be trapped in this colonial order.
>
> (Kilomba 2008: 19)

Through the writing and critique of psychoanalysts and cultural critics in the Black German community, most notably Kilomba, as well as the relative centrality of Frantz Fanon (1963, 1967) in some contemporary Black German intellectual thought, the language of colonial power relations central within the emergent decolonial turn in psychoanalysis is becoming accessible to more people of colour in Germany. Here, Kilomba is analysing the circumstance that psychoanalyst Frantz Fanon found himself in, explored thoroughly in his groundbreaking *Black Skin, White Masks* (1967), wherein he problematises the depictions of Black people in the cinema of the 1950s in France and French territories. He suggests in a footnote that Black people from the Antilles sitting in French cinemas would be 'petrified' for, unlike in the Antilles, in France, among mostly white French people, they would be confronted with recognising themselves not in the protagonist Tarzan, but in the Bushmen in the film (Fanon 1967: 152–153).[7] Kilomba notes that the witnessing and internalising by Black people of the position of being trapped within the fantasies of white people. This disappointment and pain is part of what Kilomba points to as the wound or pain of the colonial order.[8]

The pain of this type of violence reproduced in the trial and wider public discussion on Oury Jalloh's death goes beyond the issue of protection, which Berlant highlights, and touches upon notions of differential subjectivity and alienation from the ability to set the terms of one's own subjugation in society. Taken together, Berlant and Kilomba offer a complex notion of pain relevant to Black legal existence in post-colonial Europe – that the state, envisioned as a protector and characteristically white, is staged within a colonial scene that is susceptible to reproducing the sequence of violence, alienation and disappointment described by Kilomba in *Plantation Memories* (2008) and by in Fanon with his experience in the cinema.

Racism and xenophobia are predominant themes in the Black community's narration of Jalloh's death. I contend that this is not the result of a knee-jerk assumption that police officers were motivated by race to let Jalloh die, or indeed to bring about his death, in their custody. However,

7 See Fanon's footnote 15.
8 See Kilomba 2008: 99.

particularly considering the missing pieces of key evidence, the hostile reaction by law enforcement to Mouctar Bah and others in the IOJ, and the ineffectiveness of the court to ask the right questions, the circumstances reinforced and exacerbated the feeling that Jalloh's death and its investigation were suspicious and coloured by racial bias. The feeling was that the judicial process was not adequately investigating the circumstances of Jalloh's death and that this lack of regard was reproducing the same racism that may have contributed to his death in the first place.

Motive was never really a main aspect of the trial itself. The police were prosecuted for negligent failure to act quickly enough to prevent Jalloh from dying, so the bulk of the liability determination revolved around how long the police took to rescue Jalloh after admittedly ignoring multiple smoke alarms.[9] However, even within the context of the negligence claim, the *reasons* that they may have purposefully let Jalloh perish were never focused on in court. Nonetheless, the issue of motive was an undercurrent within activist circles. More specifically, activists assumed that the police regarded Jalloh's life as having little value, and that they 'othered' Jalloh to justify treating him with less care than a citizen or a white person, and certainly less than a white citizen, would normally receive. An informal consensus among many Black people and some non-Black activists is that German authorities systematically discriminate against Black people and refugees, among other groups. This presumption is also linked into modern intellectual and political thinking among Black Germans concerning whiteness and global racism (Nghi Ha 2004, Eggers 2005).

Experiences of racial space

The first day of the remanded trial in Magdeburg was set to begin at 9:30 a.m. It was an important day, during which activists and journalists from all over the country would convene. Some local residents and campaigners would be present. There was a press conference the night before for interested members of the press, and some of us involved in the trial slept in Magdeburg to be fresh for the trial's opening session. Our housing was generously arranged by a local migration organisation, along with a meeting space for after the trial session. Magdeburg was a challenging place. The kindness and warmth of the residents who housed us and, for example, the friendliness of the woman who runs the bakery across from the courthouse were one side of Magdeburg. The other side of spending time in Magdeburg was, at times, witnessing the visible neo-Nazi presence.

There had been some talk a few days before arriving in Magdeburg that the first day of the trial would coincide with a large neo-Nazi meeting

9 Regina Götz, Application for Appeal in the case against ./. Schubert (in der Strafsache ./. Schubert) – 6 Ks 4/05. On file with author.

happening somewhere in the city. Indeed when I disembarked the train from Berlin on the day of the press conference, I crossed paths with a number of young people in the station, mainly men, some with shaved heads wearing insignia that indicated their affiliation with neo-Nazi groups. It was eerie and I could not help but feel that I had entered a hostile environment, not only because I was visibly not white but because I was there partly to observe a case that was implicated in racism. A number of us typically travelled together, this time included, as we understood that there was safety in numbers. The weight of the trial was quite heavy already, and the extra energy it took to be vigilant of my surroundings, cognizant of the danger of indiscriminate physical violence and verbal abuse made the first few days in Magdeburg quite draining. Apart from a few stares at the train station, nothing happened to me personally. However over the course of the trial, campaigners were spat upon by passers by and racially profiled and harassed by local police.

While racism should not be seen only in terms of right-wing extremism by any means, alone the visible presence of neo-Nazis is taxing for people of colour to experience. When I walked amongst the neo-Nazi 20-somethings in the train station, I could not help but think of Ermyas Mulugeta, who was beaten into a coma by a young man in 2006 in Potsdam, close to where I had completed a legal internship. I thought of my friend, a doctor originally from Cameroon, who was confronted one night on an S-Bahn in Kottbus by three neo-Nazi males. They told him they were going to throw him under the train; no one in the carriage came to his defense. Luckily, the three men ultimately left him alone, though shaken. These experiences have shaped the way that I think about my safety when I know that the environment that I am in at a given moment is cohabited by right-wing extremists and when there is a silent acceptance of the like. In the Magdeburg train station, I asked myself: how many ordinary citizens' silent acceptance of the neo-Nazis' presence was also a tacit objection to my own? I imagine, of course, that many people who may have objected to the presence of the neo-Nazis would have been perhaps unwilling to cause a serious disturbance in the station, risking personal injury. But the silence was distressing – it was a denial of sorts. That being said, we who were there for the trial also did not protest. We walked straight ahead and went to the vans outside that brought us to our housing. We would have to be strategic about our protests in our everyday lives; each of us had learned that somewhere along the way.

On the danger of silence

Silence around the real physical danger associated with high levels of neo-Nazi activity became a visible national issue during the world cup in 2006. But before I discuss that, I will reflect on an earlier episode in my own experience in Germany as a student that caused me to distrust the way in which right-wing violence had been regarded by mainstream society.

It was 2002 and my fellowship was coming to an end. I had decided to stay in Germany to continue postgraduate studies and now, in order to save money, I contemplated moving from my apartment in Prenzlauer Berg into student accommodation (*Studentenwohnheim*).[10] I arrived early to the office hours at Studentenwerk Berlin, an office that handles student housing, and was greeted by a very friendly white German woman. I explained that I was a student at Humboldt University, looking for a room in a *Studentenwohnheim*. She said that many of the buildings were full, such as the one in Friedrichshain (which is the only one I had any knowledge of and was hoping had available rooms). She mentioned, however, that there were rooms available in the building in Mahzahn, and that I could move in at the beginning of the upcoming Autumn term. Mahzahn. The name set off alarms in my head. It was the place just east of central Berlin on the S-Bahn, only 30 minutes away, but a world away in terms of the safety that it ostensibly did not afford people like me. Close German friends from the university, white and non-white had, unprompted, offered advice not to travel to Mahzahn or Lichtenberg (a borough between central Berlin and Mahzahn) at night or alone, and they mentioned this with such consistency and spontaneity that it had become a part of my mental map of the city. I did not trust that I would be safe there. 'Is it safe?', I asked the friendly housing advisor. She assured me that it was, she even looked puzzled that I would ask that. To make it clearer, I told her about my mental map, that I had heard that Mahzahn and Lichtenberg were risky areas for people with my skin colour. '*Ach, quatsch*' ('Oh, nonsense') was her response, and she brushed off the suggestion with a briefly wrinkled brow, and a moment of silence, before she asked me whether I would want a single room or a shared room. I ultimately decided to look for a second job instead, so I could afford to remain living in the city centre once my fellowship ended.

What puzzled me about this exchange at the time also puzzles me now. Was it that this friendly Berliner was not aware of the potential danger that I would face living in Mahzahn as a person of colour? And if so, was it disbelief that allowed her to brush off my worries as nonsense? Or did she have some knowledge about the risks, and still decide to shirk off my concerns to avoid an embarrassing confrontation with the ever-paralysing topic of racism in Germany? I thought of this discussion years later, when contemplating the public debates on mapping out no-go areas for non-white visitors to the World Cup, hosted in Berlin in 2006.

It is important to note, as was noted during the discussion of no-go areas in 2006 in Berlin-Brandenburg, there is a danger in depicting racial

10 Translation: student residence halls.

violence as an East German problem. However, there was the danger of viewing racism as only an issue of right-wing physical violence, rather than attitudes and institutional exclusion that shape the lives of those even in metropolitan centres. Racism and racial violence are more widespread, and while there seems to be a concentration in the East, failure to understand racism and racial violence as structural issue risks mischaracterising institutional racism and trivialising the violence that takes place outside of the eastern parts of the country.

Considering the real threat of physical violence that exists for Black people and other people of colour in Germany, the slogan 'Break the Silence', which was adopted as a central slogan of the IOJ, takes on a certain urgency. In this sense, silence around this violence provides the conditions in which such violence can exist, and exposing it gives German society a chance to identify and diminish it. Discursive work thusly takes on an important role as resistance to physical violence.

Repetition of violence in law

In 2010, there was a performance protest held at the Magdeburg Regional Court to commemorate and raise the profile of Oury Jalloh's death in the midst of the trail against the police. Three men from the IOJ, dressed in red pallbearers' robes, carried a coffin slowly to the courthouse steps as a symbol for not only the death of Oury Jalloh, but for those who have died under what can be characterised as similar circumstances, within a pattern of institutional violence. This is a public declaration of the recognition of institutional violence. The gesture of symbolically bringing Jalloh physically back into the space where his story was to be revised and debated, some five years after his death, placing his coffin at the steps of the court, was meant to underline the injustice of his death and the importance of the issue. This was one of many artistic or theatrical protests staged to urge onlookers to pause and reflect on institutional racism and police violence. It was also meant to communicate that those who cared about this issue and the systematic violence that it represented were engaged in a constant mourning and constant witnessing of death – so were those who did not care as much, whether they knew it or not.

Coming down the stairs of the courthouse after the 2012 appeal verdict was announced was a sad and disappointing descent for many of us. As a trial observer, I expected the verdict that was rendered, since there was no indication that the charge would be changed leading into the final stages of the trial. The activists also expected the verdict that was rendered. Despite their push to change the discussion to one about murder rather than negligence, social pressure had not translated into decisive action on the part of the state prosecutor or the presiding judges. After the announcement of the verdict against the accused police officer of negligently causing death (UK and US: involuntary manslaughter),[11] activists placed crosses on the steps of the courthouse to symbolise others who have died in police custody under suspicious or unclear circumstances.[12] The crosses were not there at the beginning of the day, but at the end of the day, when people left the courthouse, they were waiting on the steps as a reminder that this day was an important part of a larger pattern and that there were people who noticed. The court was a space of death, where death would be witnessed and memorialised over and over again.

Reporting Black deaths as narratives

Since German reunification in 1989, racial and ethnic violence has been a prevalent feature of many people of colour in Germany, particularly (but by no means exclusively) for those living in certain areas of former East Germany (Hügel et al. 1999: 206–233). Scholars have attributed this to a variety of factors, such as new pressures for economic integration of the East by the West and newfound freedom to dissent and distinguish among various segments of the working class in post-communist East Germany.[13] These explanations are coupled with some writing on racial and ethnic violence in the Cold War period and the increased visibility of immigrant groups and people with so-called *Migrationshintergrund*[14] during this period.[15] Law enforcement played a role in the period right after reunification in socially marginalising non-white Germans. These included identity checks on the basis of appearance and harsher treatment during encounters with police. A major example of police inaction was documented in the now infamous 1991 riots in Rostock-Lichtenhagen, in which hundreds of right-wing militants threw stones and petrol bombs at an asylum residence.

11 The legal term in German is *fahrlässige Tötung.*

12 This image can be seen on the cover of this book.

13 For a multi-variable analysis of youth cultures after reunification, critically examining a single-factor explanation for violence, see Frindte et al. 1996. See also Linke 1999: 206–207 (discussing violent ideologies in everyday language, and that unification relied on a reinvesting in a collective identity based on rhetorics and motifs of negation and opposition).

14 Translation: 'migration background'. The term *Migrationshintergrund* is commonly used to describe people who have themselves migrated to Germany or whose parents or ancestors migrated to Germany from elsewhere. Some argue that this conceptualises the 'native German' as a static group, able to be easily defined, which reinforces the myth of the ethnic German. For a thoroughgoing critique of the term *Migrationshintergrund,* see Utlu 2011: 445.

15 See Göktürk 2011. Göktürk discusses tensions among Turkish and Black people on one hand and the majority society on the other after reunification, focusing on the articulation of the changing relationships in German cinema.

The Black community in Germany has not been the only community to take note of tragic deaths of people of colour either in custody of or at the hands of the law enforcement agents. Other groups, including anti-fascist organisations, refugee organisations, media watchdog organisations and anti-police brutality activists[16] have demonstrated and written against police abuse. In depicting these deaths as systematic, a politics of exclusion is iterated that transcends a simplistic view of racism, articulating instead a multi-valenced set of power relations that incorporates racism, sexism, xenophobia and the relationship of citizens to the state.

At least ten deaths since 2000 stand out as anchoring points in discussions about systematic police violence against Black people in Germany. These deaths either transpired while the deceased person was in police custody[17] or were attributed at least in part to police action or inaction. Each of these examples garnered at least some mainstream media coverage, and this coverage generally diverged from the ways in which Black anti-racism activists have depicted the events. Importantly, instances of physical violence are compounded, from the perspective of anti-racism activists, by severe legal mishandling of the cases, which many times becomes an equally or perhaps more important extension of the physical violence. The legal mishandling of these cases is thought by many to be informed by racial prejudice not wholly unrelated to the type of prejudice that instigated the original physical violence.[18]

These narratives to which Black activists direct our attention are important as they change the nature of the discussion from a value system based on vicissitude of fact finding[19] and faith in positive legal outcome to one based on exposing unspoken racial prejudice.

Though some mainstream media sources did cover the Jalloh's death critically, there was a lack of continuous coverage over the span of time since Jalloh's death in January 2005. Refugee organisations the Voice and die Karawane, alongside the IOJ, have provided fora for those concerned to produce an alternative narrative to the official one that was being produced by police reports and courts, being mediated and filtered by the

16 'Pressemitteilung: Vorgang Oury Jalloh Aus Polizeijournal Gelöscht. Vom Gericht Auf Die Straßen Berlins Geht Die Initiative in Gedenken an Oury Jalloh e.V. Am 16.7.2011' 2011.

17 I define custody here as being under the control of the police, whether in public, private or in a police station.

18 By this, I am referring to the interconnectedness of interpersonal instances of racism with institutional and structural racism. See Essed 1991: 185–188.

19 It is important to note that the concept of 'fact finding' in legal settings has been critiqued from an anthropological perspective. See Engelke 2009: 45 (critically discussing the notion of objective truth in the context of expert testimony). See also Bruce-Jones 2009: 337–338 (discussing the concept of co-construction of reality rather than 'finding' of fact).

mainstream news reporting. During and after the initial civil trial against the Dessau police officers, the commonality among these alternative narratives is the portrayal of pretence underlying the legal treatment of investigations into Jalloh's death.

The stories

> We have the feeling that our freedom of movement is limited, that we can not even move the way we want to. The African has tried for years to convince the government and agencies in Berlin and Brandenburg that there is a specific form of racism against Black people, they should prepare a catalogue of precautionary measures so that everyone who comes to Berlin and Germany knows that there are places where it's just dangerous. And we called that No-Go-Areas, actually that does not mean that one can not go there, one still can, but we say, you can, but now there's danger.
>
> (Mouctar Kamara in *Angstträume*)[20]

I would like to return to examine the ways that Black people in Germany have discussed overt racial violence in relation to certain spaces, particularly the eastern parts of the country. If you are Black and living in Germany, chances are you are familiar with the type of narrative that Mouctar Kamara describes. You may hear stories about the way people look at you in a certain small town. You may have had tense encounters with neo-Nazis in your own neighbourhood at the edge of a big city, heard racial epithets on the U-Bahn (metro), been verbally threatened in broad daylight, or maybe you have been the victim of direct physical attack. You may have been told that you do not belong, that you are out of place, leaving you to wonder whether it is because of the way you look. In any event, there is recognition among Black people and others that, in terms of at least physical danger, certain areas in Germany are best entered with extreme caution and preferably not alone. Green Party parliamentarian Cem Özdemir has publicly acknowledged that the danger for Black people in certain areas is real and should not be trivialised.[21]

20 Mouctar Kamara, in an interview a video called *Angstträume. Alltag schwarzer Menschen in Berlin und Brandenburg.* Christoph Hartmann and Lennart Laberenz, Air Miami, 2006. Original: "*Wir haben das Gefühl, dass unsere Bewegungsfreiheit begrenzt [ist], dass wir nicht mehr uns bewegen können, wie wir möchten. Der Afrikaner hat versucht seit Jahren, die Regierung und die Behörden in Berlin und Brandenburg zu überzeugen, dass es ein bestimmter Form von Rassismus gegen schwarze Menschen gibt, die werden eine Katalog von Vorsichtsmaßnamen erstellen, damit alle die, die nach Berlin und Deutschland kommen, wissen, es gibt Orte, wo es einfach gefährlich ist. Und wir haben das No-Go-Areas gennant, eigentlich, das heisst nicht, dass man kann da nicht hinfahren, kann man immer noch, aber wir sagen, das kannst Du, aber jetzt gibt's die Gefahr*".

21 'Özdemir: No-Go-Areas Für Schwarze in Deutschland Realität' 2006.

There has been a significant number of highly publicised deaths of people of African descent in police custody or related to police action or inaction. The stories of those who have lost their lives exemplify situations that have the potential to arise in the everyday lives of Black Germans in their encounters with law enforcement in certain circumstances. While this is not to suggest that these stories are necessarily descriptive of the 'norm' in terms of police behaviour, they do provide real scenarios that Black anti-racist thought has located as important for discussing the landscape of police violence. Due to the fact that these deaths resemble one another to varying degrees, it is helpful to describe them chronologically to first lay out a particular historical trajectory. Additionally, though the first story mentioned does not concern a custodial death, it is nonetheless very important to the conversation on institutional racism in Germany over the last decade.

The first story to consider is the death of Alberto Adriano, originally from Mozambique. Alberto Adriano had been in Germany for 20 years and was beaten to death by three young men (two were 16 and one was 24 years old) in a public park in Dessau in 2000.[22] The three young men were neo-Nazis from nearby cities. They kicked him with steel-toe boots and stripped him naked. The beatings left Adriano brain dead and he passed away some days thereafter.[23] It was reported that the police arrived in the park a half-hour after the beating took place, although the three young men were identified and taken into police custody the same night. The three were prosecuted and charged with murder.[24]

Adriano's death prompted a very public and visible national discussion about neo-Nazi violence. In response to his brutal murder, Afro-German recording artists called Brother's Keepers released a song in his honour as both a tribute to Adriano and as a social intervention describing and condemning systematic racism, including racially disproportionate identity checks and social silence around racial violence. The song, titled *Adriano (Letzte Warnung)* (translation: *Last Warning*) was a commercial success, and the accompanying awareness campaign about racism reached out to youth through school visits. The then chancellor, Gerhard Schröder, visited the site of Adriano's death to lay a wreath and pay his respects.[25]

The second story is that of Mareame Sarr. In 2001, a Sudanese woman named Mareame Sarr was shot in her home by police officers in Aschaffenberg. Sarr, who was in a dispute with her husband at the time, was said to have threatened police with a breadknife, an assertion that has not been corroborated. This incident was particularly controversial because

22 Broomby 2000.
23 Ibid.
24 'Kein Vergeben, Kein Vergessen – Alberto Adriano' 2010.
25 Broomby 2000.

Sarr was not only in her own home, but she was in the company of three males (her husband and two police officers) who could have attempted to subdue her had she threatened with a knife instead of fatally shooting her through the chest in front of her young child. The death of Sarr was followed by a series of demonstrations by members of Germany's Black community and other communities.[26]

The third story is that of Achidi J. In 2001, Michael Paul Nwabuisi (known as John Achidi), originally from Nigeria died at 19 in Hamburg when forcibly administered an emetic and 800 ml of water through a tube put through his nostril and into his stomach. According to media reports, Nwabuisi collapsed after the emetic was administered and too long a time elapsed before police tried to revive him. Nwabuisi fell into a coma and died after three days.[27] An anti-racist organisation, No-Racism, posted on its website an article that included a few details not widely reported in newspapers, which was that Nwabuisi was panic stricken and thought that the liquid was going to kill him. Because he panicked, four police officers held him in his chair while a doctor inserted the feeding tube that he resisted[28] The legal press release in the complaint filed against the police following his death also describes a violent scene, focusing on the nearly immediate fatal reaction the treatment caused to Nwabuisi's body[29] rather than to

26 New York-based playwright Amy Evans, who lived in Germany from 1997 until 2004 and visits Berlin regularly, wrote a play that recounts the deaths of Sarr and John Achidi, who was killed when an emetic procedure was performed on him by police officers. Her approach to using playwriting to analysis social issues was used in courses she taught at Humboldt-Universität zu Berlin in 2003 and 2004 called Scripting Rage, in which she used scriptwriting techniques to examine how one might rethink and reframe perspectives taken by the media and witnesses in recounting such events as Sarr's death. She attempted to bring a human element into the depictions of the events, including the banal activities of each relevant player in the event, in an attempt to help participants to identify with being enmeshed in that particular set of power relations, beyond the legal framing of events.

27 Denso 2006. See also Bausch 2005: 1–2.

28 'Michael Paul Nwabuisi – Tod Nach Brechmitteleinsatz in Hamburg' No Racism website 2001.

29 See 'Presseerklärung: Klageerzwingungsverfahren Beantragt' 2003). '*Im Institut für Rechtsmedizin wird er zu dem "Behandlungsraum" gebracht. Schon da torkelt er gegen die Wand und bricht zusammen. Von zwei Polizisten zur „Behandlung" geschleppt, reagiert er mit Panik, ruft, er werde sterben. Die Polizei ruft Verstärkung. Fünf Polizeibeamte schließlich fixieren den immer noch Gefesselten mit Gewalt am Boden. Die Jacke zerreißt, der Hosenknopf springt ab, die Jeans rutscht in die Kniekehlen. Die Gerichtsmedizinerin Prof. Dr. L. ist unbeeindruckt. Das Kinn wird auf die Brust gepresst, eine Sonde nach mehrmaligem erfolglosen Versuch durch die Nase eingeführt, Brechmittel und fast ein Liter Wasser in Achidi John hinein gekippt. Er röchelt, sein Körper verkrampft sich, er nässt ein, bleibt dann reglos liegen. Wahrscheinlich ist dies der Zeitpunkt des Herzstillstands. Die Ärztin wertet es als "Einsicht" und entfernt sich. Später wird sie behaupten, sie habe Achidi John die folgenden Minuten liegen lassen, um ihn nicht zu stören. Nach einigen Minuten findet man, er sehe schlecht aus. Da ist der Puls ist bereits weg. Die von der Ärztin vorgenommenen Rettungsmaßnahmen sind dilettantisch*'. Translation: 'At the Institute for Forensic

describe the situation in less graphic terms as the 'administration of an emetic'.

The fourth story is that of Oury Jalloh. Jalloh burned to death in a holding cell in Dessau while chained by his hands and feet to the tiled wall of the cell and to the floor alongside a fireproof mattress. Police turned off the smoke alarms that indicated a fire in the building and claim not to have known that he was burning until it was too late to save him. Substantial amounts of physical evidence are missing, and many police witnesses testifying in the trial claim not to remember information that would describe the cause of his death. On appeal, the case was returned with a verdict of negligence for the officer on trial.[30]

The fifth story is that of Laye-Alma Condé, who also died in police custody in 2005. Condé was drowned in Bremen when the police officers who had detained him on the suspicion of drug possession forcibly administered an emetic and several litres of water through a hose forced into his nose. This was to force vomiting to try and recover evidence for a drug conviction. In 2012, the Federal Supreme Court (*Bundesgerichtshof*) struck down the second acquittal of officers from the charge of negligent killing, and the case was retried a third time in Bremen in 2013.[31] The third trail ended with a third and final acquittal.[32]

The sixth story is that of Dominique Koumadio. Koumadio was shot and killed by police officers in Dortmund in 2006.[33] Officers reported that Koumadio had a knife and threatened them with it.[34] Koumadio has been

Medicine, he is brought into a "treatment room." There, he was already staggering against the wall and collapsing. Dragged to "treatment" by two police officers, he reacts with panic and calls out that he will die. The police call for reinforcements. Five police officers ultimately pin the already hand-cuffed man violently to the ground. His jacket rips, the button on his trousers pops off, and his jeans slide down to his knees. The forensic medical doctor, Prof. Dr. L., Is impressed by this. His chin is pressed against his chest, a probe is led through the nose after several unsuccessful attempts, and an emetic and almost a litre of water are poured into Achidi John. He wheezes, his body cramps, he wets himself and then lies motionless. This is probably the time of his cardiac arrest. The doctor considers this as "observed" and leaves. Later she claims that she left Achidi John to lie there for those minutes that followed so as not to disturb him. After several minutes, one sees that he looks bad. By then, his pulse is already gone. The resuscitation measures executed by the doctor are amateurish'.

30 This case is discussed in detail in Chapter 3.

31 Pollähne 2012.

32 'Bremer Brechmittel-Prozess: Am Ende kein Urteil' 2013.

33 See 'Aufruf: Tribunal in Gedenken an Dominique Koumadio, Oury Jalloh Und Alle Anderen Opfer Rassistischer Staatsgewalt', the Caravan website 2008. In this press release, the Caravan points to the fact that Koumadio's sister posed questions to the state prosecutor about why the police had not tried to overpower Dominique before shooting him twice, fatally injuring him.

34 See 'Dominique – Von Polizei Erschossen' No Racism website 2006.

regularly memorialised since 2006 as part of a line of people killed unjustly and without clear legal consequence.[35]

The seventh story is that of Ermyas Mulugeta. Mulugeta was beaten into a coma on a street in Potsdam by two men who shouted racial epithets at him before the beating.[36] Mulugeta managed to survive the beating, and there was a prosecution against these men. However, the prosecution refused to acknowledge that racial animus may have played a part in the beating.[37]

The eighth story is that of Marwa El-Sherbini and her husband Elwi Ali Okaz. El-Sherbini, 32 years old, sat on the stand in a Dresden court in July 2009, having sued a German man of Russian descent for insulting her, calling her a terrorist in a public park. As she, her husband and her three-year-old son attempted to leave the courtroom, the defendant stabbed El-Sherbini more than 15 times and as the husband tried to help her, he was also stabbed. In the course of this, a police officer shot Okaz, rather than the assailant. El-Sherbini died and the assailant was tried and sentenced for murder. Meanwhile, a separate investigation was made into why the officer shot Okaz and why there was not sufficient protection in the courtroom to have prevented El-Sherbini's death and Okaz's near-fatal injuries. There was a discussion about potential racism in the shooting of Okaz El-Sherbini, but those discussions were prevented from taking place in certain contexts, such as the summary penalty order against a professor for making statements about the possible racial implications of the police shooting.[38]

The ninth story is that of Christy Schwundeck, who died on 19 May, 2011. Schwundeck, a Nigerian-German woman, was shot and killed in a job centre in Frankfurt am Main after an altercation with the police, during which she injured an officer's arm with a steak knife. After an initial investigation, the state prosecutor in Frankfurt decided not to bring charges against the officer who shot Schwundeck, arguing that the officers' claim of self-defence was adequate to repel charges of wrongful death. An African news source mentions, in its account of the story, Schwundeck's history of mental illness, raising the question of whether the police should have been aware of the potential for someone with certain psychological issues (such as addiction problems) when it received the call from the job centre, since this particular job centre was designated for people with addiction problems in the local area.[39]

35 See 'Kundgebung in Gedenken an Dominique Koumadio' Flüchtlingsinitiative Berlin-Brandenburg website 2009.

36 See Diehl 2007. The aggressor called Mulugeta '*Scheißneger*' (roughly: 'fucking nigger'). See also Friedrichsen 2007.

37 See Schauka 2007.

38 Fekete 'Freedom of Speech on Racism under Threat' Institute for Race Relations website 2010.

39 See Izoya 2011. See also 'Reaction from Kassel Branch: 'The German Police at It Again' No Racism website 2011.

The tenth story concerns a man named Ousman Sey, who died in police custody on 7 July 2012. According to witnesses and reports, Sey experienced chest pain and called the paramedics twice, and they told him that his symptoms were not severe enough to warrant a trip to the hospital. He began to cramp up and became aggressive, so he smashed a window in his apartment and a neighbour called the police. When the police arrived, he continued to complain of chest pains. A neighbour, who was a nurse, advised the police to bring him to a hospital, but the police instead put him in handcuffs and took him into custody, where he died.[40]

The eleventh story is that of Emrah Kara, who was killed on 20 December 2013. Kara, who lived with his sister and mother in Holzminden, Germany, was in the midst of a mental health episode, during which he became volatile. His family called a doctor and the police. The police deployed a special command unit (*Sondereinsatzkommando*, or SEK), which arrived with what has been reported as over a dozen officers. The officers sent a policing dog into Kara's room to subdue him, and Kara killed the dog. The SEK unit then opened fire on him, shooting the 29-year-old fatally in the chest (Bruce-Jones 2014).

Stories as a basis for articulating patterns

Highlighting the structural nature of police violence has been a process of excavation. In the case of those working on the Oury Jalloh case, this has required committing painful stories of the last decade to institutional memory. The Voice, die Karawane and the IOJ, alongside regular press releases and articles on their respective websites, co-published a small yellow booklet called *Break the Silence*, the fifth edition of which, under the subheading 'institutional racism and due process in Germany' highlighted cases of other Black and Asian asylum seekers killed by the police or in police custody between 1999 and 2007.[41] It recounts the death of Sudanese born N'deye Mareame Sarr, for example, who was shot by police in her home in Aschaffenburg in 2001. It also recalls the death of Laye Condé, who drowned in Bremen in 2004 when water was forced into his lungs during the administration of a procedure meant to make suspects of drug possession vomit. Recounting these and the other deaths in the pamphlet, in addition to archiving the systematic use of fatally excessive force by the police, reopens the wounds of the past decade to expose the body politic to a reckoning that is both deeply painful and potentially profoundly healing. It, once again, brings the past into the present, and describes the present as a place characterised by violence.

40 See 'Warum Starb Ousman Sey? Mahnwache Am Dienstag!' Initiative Christy Schwundeck press release 2011.

41 The pamphlet is on file with author.

The stories of the individuals in the yellow booklet, alongside the stories of other Black people and people of colour killed in Germany in the last two decades (notably the Turkish and Greek men and women killed by the NSU between 2000 and 2007) form the discursive landscape for making sense of the ongoing pattern of deaths, including their circumstances, legal issues and media reports. They are relevant not only as an explanation as to what is happening (institutional and structural racism), but also as an explanation for the relentless activism in bringing these deaths to light. Criticism of these violent episodes has been pitted against institutions and structures rather than individual independent acts of abuse perpetrated by 'bad apples'.

The stories have similarities that make subsequent stories sound hauntingly familiar, and this familiarity perpetually renews the feeling of a need for action. For example, the death of Christy Schwundeck in 2011 echoed back to the death of N'deye Mareame Sarr ten years earlier on the basis that police officers fatally shot a Black woman in possession of a knife, and no prosecution was launched.[42] It also echoed the deaths of Dominique Komadio and Emrah Kara, each fatally shot in possession of a knife. These deaths indicate a pattern of disproportionate violence, if one considers that there are ways to disarm people without killing them. Knowing of these patterns shapes the expectation of people of colour vis-à-vis the police in Germany and indeed across Europe. The stories give names and details to the pattern of violence, offering a technical awareness of the idea of the disproportionate response.

The story of Ermyas Mulugeta resonates with the story of the Lübeck fire – while both instances of violence were prosecuted, racism was not immediately acknowledged by the courts to have played a role in the violence, despite quite convincing evidence to the contrary. In turn, the Lübeck fire, the arson attack on an asylum residence, evokes memories of the burning of a particular asylum residence in Rostock-Lichtenhagen by right wing groups and local residents, which turned into a mob scene that the police was, by some accounts, unwilling to properly control (Fekete 2000).

The Oury Jalloh case is very particular in its facts; however, in the process of discussing both the episode of violence that led to his death as well as the legal responses that ensued, activists regularly mention cases that are similar on distinct points. Some of this has to do with the temporal proximity of the other cases to the Jalloh issue. For example, the same year in which Jalloh died in police custody in Dessau, Laye-Alma Condé was killed in police custody, which means that Condé is mentioned at some of the rallies and demonstrations held to honour the life or support the trial of Oury Jalloh.

42 See Wirner 2001.The article also mentions that police used ammunition on Sarr that would catch in the body, doing it more harm, rather than to exit the body and potentially hurt others. The type of ammunition used may have contributed to Sarr's death.

Also, the 2011 trial on the death of Jalloh was punctuated by two other custodial deaths – Schwundeck in 2011 and Ousman Sey in 2012. The temporal proximity of these two deaths and separate but connected outcries for rallying around them bolstered the analysis of disparate racial violence in Germany, particularly police violence, as a pattern.

A main feature that has been echoed in most of the cases has been the reliance on racialised stereotypes to criminalise the victim of violence in order to make him or her into a perpetrator and thereby justify some violence, making the situation appear somewhat symmetrical and the police response arguably appropriate. This has happened in most of the cases described above. Condé and Nwabuisi were seen to have committed criminal drug offences, legally warranting the use of an emetic under German law (Bausch 2005). Sarr, Koumadio, Schwundeck and Kara were depicted as belligerent, knife-wielding attackers, and so shooting them was depicted in mass media as primarily self-protection (Bruce-Jones 2014, 2015).[43] Jalloh and Sey are depicted as out of control and violent, and they are put in restraints, which is instrumental in their deaths. Okaz, rushing to the aid of his wife, is shot by police, mistaken as a perpetrator in the 'chaos of the situation', and reporting of the issue as potentially informed by racial stereotypes (Okaz being Egyptian) is silenced.

Defining structural racism: institutional memory praxis

It is with these intertextual stories in mind that one must view the strategic engagement of anti-racist activists with the current state of police violence in Germany. This engagement includes exposition of and education about institutional racism in Germany as well as the assertion of rights-based remedies for instances of violence against people of colour. However, these two prongs do not always use the same vernacular, nor do they always have the same immediate goals, even if they are, to some extent, coordinated efforts. They are part of a concerted discussion on racism and police accountability more broadly.

What makes a struggle 'Black'?

> Against this background, I would deny the existence of a 'black point of view' or a 'black voice' in any essentialist (or racialist) sense. Yet that doesn't answer the particular questions that are relevant to the political and cultural arguments for large-scale affirmative action. The first of these is whether minority communities would get, from a much larger minority legal intelligentsia, a scholarly output that would better

43 Shooting these individuals in non-fatal regions, or with rubber bullets, or attempting another mode of restraint is not discussed.

> serve their diverse political, social and economic interests than does what they get from an overwhelmingly white legal intelligentsia. The second is whether the legal academic community as a whole would get a more valuable total corpus of scholarship.
>
> (Kennedy 1995: 168)

To ask what makes any struggle specific to a certain group already makes a statement about the struggle – namely that it is of specific interest. It also makes a statement about the group to which the struggle belongs – that there is something, whether political or ideological, that the group shares. Neither of these statements is completely true on its own, but they approximate a type of relative importance that certain issues may carry across particular segments of society, not to the exclusion of other segments. But the issue may enjoy heightened visibility or immediacy for those who may see the struggle as 'their own'.

The selection above is from a collection of critical essays entitled *Critical Race Theory*, and in it, legal scholar Duncan Kennedy offers an intervention into the US affirmative action debate as regards diversity hiring policies in higher education. He contends that there is no uniform view that Black people in the United States hold, which seems a straightforward proposition if one is to acknowledge the political, ethnic and historical diversity of American Black people. However, he does estimate that larger representation of Black voices in legal scholarship might better address certain structural challenges facing Black people and, perhaps, the academic community as a whole. Kennedy continues on in his article to argue for increasing diversity of minority professors in legal scholarship, and within academic institutions (Kennedy 1995: 161–162). This suggests an interesting point about power and scholarship. Kennedy challenges conventional tenets of scholarly meritocracy by acknowledging that the integration of minority professors can be an asset rather than a liability in representing minority interests as stakeholders in academic projects. This suggests that Black scholarship in legal academia has a unique ability to contribute to overall legal scholarship by reflecting on the very aspects of privilege and power that are currently ignored.

The United States example is relevant for the European idea of Black political and social engagement for a few reasons. First, Black people in Europe are quite diverse and occupy a broad range of positions across the political spectrum. Second, and most importantly, exploring the US example as a contemporary point of comparison shows that, in certain circumstances, using 'race' and 'Blackness' as analytical categories enables us to look at how certain groups organise politically around identifying as and being categorised as Black. This community organisation occurs around the racialised term 'Black', despite the contested nature of the translatability of the category 'race'. Black people in Europe, like Black people in many parts of the Americas, live in social conditions in which they are simultaneously hyper-visible and invisible (Reddy 2010). The particular positions that Black subjects occupy in the contemporary Western world make it useful to explore transnational continuities that bind Blackness and Black people.

With regard to the discussion of legal subjectivity, hegemonic narratives of what constitutes European-ness are relevant not only to the question of authenticity and identity, but also to access to rights. Conventional notions of the role that law plays in structuring social behaviour and issues of entitlement are critiqued in this project from a Black perspective to effectively describe the epistemological struggle of Black Europeans and their families.

A central issue that uncovers competing narratives about subjectivity is the concept of *jus sanguinis*, or blood ancestry as a main criterion for citizenship. European member states have, to varying degrees, systems of citizenship recognition that privilege those who can prove blood descendance from a citizen over those who can not do so but were themselves born on the country's soil.[44] This type of policy contributes to the understanding of citizenship as an ethnically informed notion of entitlement.

A second issue that invokes law, though on a broader conceptual level, is the idea that formal citizenship is and should be the mechanism through which rights are conferred. This is the normative legal proposition that nation states are the conveyors of rights and protections and, without citizenship, humans would be stripped down to bare life.[45] This can be problematic inasmuch as it may imply a paternalistic relationship between states and citizens and it may foreclose other alternative ways of conceiving of justice or redistribution that fall outside of a rights framework.

A third big issue is discrimination. The debates surrounding discrimination range in focus, including discussing statues, court decisions, actions by local municipalities and enforcement against individual private actors. Here, the tension is one that speaks to the notion of state responsibility towards marginalised Black citizens and residents of European countries in a context where, at least in the cases of Germany and France, discriminatory treatment of Black people is not rigorously tracked because little or no data collected by the state about service provision or access to employment, housing or education is disaggregated by race (Bruce-Jones 2008).

44 For an example of a blood ancestry-based citizenship law, see Citizenship law (Staatsangehörigkeitsgesetz) of July 22 1913, amended by law on August 21 2005 Germany. Sections 4–5 (stating that individuals born in Germany before July 1, 1993 of a German father and a foreign mother must first apply for German citizenship, which requires a paternity test or confirmation of fatherhood, regular residence in Germany for the three years preceding the application, and the submission of the application before the end of the year in which the applicant turns 23). See also Bruce-Jones 2008: 457–458.

45 For a discussion of bare life within critical legal scholarship, see Agamben 1998. For a discussion of the relationship between race and bare life, see Weheliye 2014.

Black German political groups are especially active in the capitol city of Berlin. There is a large number of people with African heritage living in the capitol, which enables a higher degree of social organisation and political coordination than in other cities. Paulette Reed-Anderson (2000) traces the presence of Africans in Berlin back to the 1600s, painting Berlin as an historic city for Black people in the German context.[46] Due to a relatively high concentration of Black people, Berlin serves as a good central meeting point for events, exhibitions and demonstrations, though by no means does this limit organizing and event-hosting in other areas of the country.

Despite the centrality that the metropolitan centre occupies in terms of the potential for networking, organising and visibility, the Internet and electronic media are have an ever-growing ability to influence and even host the discussions that are happening face-to-face on the streets of Berlin, in exhibition galleries and in classrooms. This changes the way that members of the Black community communicate and network with one another. It also enables groups to publicly respond to issues as they arise and to form strategic alliances on specific issues. Meanwhile, it helps organisers to rapidly communicate and mobilise their constituencies. All of this, because it is done electronically, is easily saved in digital form or converted into print media, which allows it to be institutionally recorded, an important step for strengthening the overall momentum of the social justice aspects of Black German political formations.

The Oury Jalloh trial: early days

The year is 2008, three years have passed since Oury Jalloh was found burned to death in a police cell, and there are still demonstrations in Dessau. In this small city of around 90,000, there is a small but visible Black population, and a substantial number of the Black men and women in Dessau live just outside the city in residences for asylum applicants. The scene is striking. A crowd of predominantly African men and women is gathered on the steps of the Dessau police precinct, where Jalloh died. Their fists are raised in the air in the iconic manner of the American Black Panthers of the 1960s Civil Rights Era, and they are singing *N'kosi Sikelel' iAfrica,* the post-Apartheid South African National Anthem, in Xhosa. How has the demonstration of a man's death been framed as a fight against racial apartheid, echoing the clenched fists and liberation songs of distant countries in the small city of Dessau, Germany?

The discursively intertextual references between the German and other political contexts is a hallmark of diasporic political thinking – publically

46 For further detail, see Chapter 5.

showing a unified Black response to local subjugation that draws on the lessons learned from similar past subjugation elsewhere in the world. This does not exclude dissent or imply a monolithic perspective, but emphasises the focus on similarities and recognition of patterns of oppression in historical perspective among those who take part. The Black community that has rallied in this way around the Oury Jalloh case takes an ideological position in this encounter with violence and sets out to identify and describe patterns of injustice, rather than individual justice.

Dual-pronged approach: anti-racist political praxis

At the same time as the activists of the IOJ were funding and pushing for the trial to go forward, with its problematic assumptions and insufficient legal articulations of the issue, they were using the platform of the trial as a 'show trial' to get across more pressing social messages and keep public scrutiny and the opportunity for dialogue open on what actually transpired in the cell. This illustrates the basic dual-approach that the Initiative has taken to the issue: balancing the defence of legal rights with a larger criticism of the social unawareness of structural and institutional forms of racism and marginalisation, particularly with regard to state violence, police brutality and the complicity of law in meting out such violence.

I was able to gain some insight on this negotiation of rights and broad-based social thinking-through of structural racism with my involvement in the planning stages of the independent commission to investigate Jalloh's death. The purpose of the commission that we were in the process of forming was to bring to light those crucial circumstances surrounding Oury Jalloh's death which were not investigated during the legal proceedings, thereby rectifying a potential miscarriage of justice and highlighting the need for legal and policy reform around deaths in custody. The commission's fact-finding component would seek to be as non-biased as possible in light of available evidence, identify gaps in protection of those in police custody and develop a narrative of Oury Jalloh's death that lay closer to 'the truth' than the one that the legal proceedings had proposed. The findings would be written up in a report and issued as a policy reform brief to relevant stakeholders and government bodies.

However, this reformist political goal was birthed from an activist orientation that was much narrower in its original aim, which was to expose the circumstances of Jalloh's death, including the possibility that the police killed him with intent. The IOJ, a social activist organisation dedicated to securing a sense of justice for Jalloh and his family, adopted the slogan '*Oury Jalloh, das war Mord!*' ('Oury Jalloh, that was murder!').[47] The slogan

47 'Justice for Mouctar Bah – Fax Campaign against the City of Dessau-Rosslau' The Voice Refugee Forum press release 2008.

aims not only to prompt Germans to recognise the violence that occurred, but also to suggest that a further injustice was committed when murder charges were not brought by the state prosecutor. During the development of the commission, the IOJ remained focused on winning the legal trial and subsequent appeal.

The first task for the commission was to assert that a potential injustice had occurred without suggesting that it was looking to prove the guilt of the on-duty officers, all the while preserving the objective tenor of legal reasoning. This mission sounds straightforward, but separating the commission's aims from those of the IOJ was a question not only of organisational integrity, but of community cohesion. The strategy of separating out the litigation focus of the IOJ from the fact-finding approach of the commission seems like good idea because two different and independent perspectives promise better odds of producing reform than one. However, the fact-finding commission could not suggest that the police indeed had knowledge of Jalloh's impending death before gathering facts and highly probative evidence if it wanted to maintain credibility with other organisations and actors as an independent and impartial investigative body. This bifurcation of approaches is insulting to some people who believe that, even without further fact finding, it is ultimately clear that he could not possibly have died without being set ablaze, and that the police must have known or done it themselves. Accordingly, some thought that, considering that the legal trial was a farce, the Black community should focus on bringing publicity to the issue in the unmitigated terms of murder.

The IOJ press release campaign

The IOJ regards exposing a broad range of police brutality issues as vitally important for society.[48] According to one IOJ member, there are multiple dimensions to the IOJ's work around the particular case of Oury Jalloh. One goal is to create a precedent in German law to address racially motivated crime that will engage with the past and present deaths-in-custody. Another goal is to address the repression by police against those who bring cases like the litigation around Jalloh's death.[49]

The IOJ has had an ongoing campaign of press releases and blog entries over the past years since Jalloh's death in 2005. During the most recent trial, in Magdeburg, the campaign has demonstrated a number of characteristics that balance legal rights-based remedies with broad educational messages about racism, power and the law. The elements that the press releases demonstrate consistently are: (1) reflection on the temporal context of the events, which serves to both signal the immediacy of the

48 Interview with Dirk and Marta, IOJ. Berlin, 6 March 2012.
49 Ibid.

release and to mark the passage of time as an indicator of progress in an ongoing discussion on larger social issues, (2) iteration and repetition of questions left uninvestigated or unasked during the legal proceedings, (3) indication of perceived interests and motives of legal actors or law enforcement agents as a commentary on institutional posturing strategies, (4) calls for recognition, solidarity and action on the part of civil society. These aspects and their relevance to both legal processes and widespread social thought will be discussed here in turn in the analysis of five recent press releases.

The first characteristic of relatively recent press releases of the campaign is reflection of the temporal circumstances, including the trajectory of the case, the highlighting of other events relevant to the case, and an emphasis on the passage of time (and a corollary lack of progress). In a press release from 7 January 2013, the IOJ recalls previous deaths that occurred in the Dessau-Roßlau police station where Jalloh died and, in the process, describes a pattern not only of deaths, but also of inconclusive investigations regarding the causes of the deaths in 1997, 2002 and 2005.[50] This pattern does not rely on racism. In another published statement, the IOJ asks 'how many of us will they kill?', which acknowledges a pattern of behaviour that orients the reader to the past in describing the urgency of its call to action.[51] This is a pedagogical technique as well as a persuasive rhetorical element, as it resists viewing the present incident as an isolated event and insists on interpreting the incident through the catalogue of experiences over the previous decade and a half. This response to the trial goes beyond the scope of the case, which began formally in 2005, and positions it within a trajectory so that Jalloh's story becomes one that is a community's story, which began much earlier than 2005, when Jalloh died.

The second characteristic is presenting questions unanswered from the legal trial, mostly related to the failure to investigate forensically or to enter into a certain line of judicial inquiry. For instance, in a press release from 14 November 2012, the IOJ points to the court's rejection of requests by Jalloh's family lawyers, Phillip Knapp and Gabriele Heinecke, to investigate whether there may have been fire accelerant used in the burning of Jalloh.[52] The release supports Heinecke's assertion that, because pure alcohol is easily accessible at any apothecary, it should be considered a practical possibility in this case.[53] The same press release also discusses the lack of DNA traces from Jalloh, or fibres from the mattress[54] or Jalloh's clothing[55]

50 'Pressemitteilung: Mörderische Verhältnisse im Polizeirevier Dessau – Roßlau!' 2013.

51 'Stellungnahme Nach Dem Urteil Des Magdeburger Landgerichts – Wie Viele Von Uns Werden Sie Noch Töten?' 2012.

52 'Pressemittilung: Kommen Sie Mit, Wir Kaufen Reinen Alkohol' 2012.

53 Ibid.

54 Ibid.

55 See 'Stellungnahme Der Initiative Vom November' 2012.

on the lighter that was said to have been found in Jalloh's cell. These questions are both distilled into easily accessible, non-lawyer language and they are questions that go to the heart of the evidence in the case – evidence, or a lack of evidence, upon which the thesis of Jalloh's self-immolation rests. In a statement addressed to the Magdeburg Regional Court and published on the IOJ website, the IOJ laid out some of the main questions that remained un-investigated in the court's assessment of the events that killed Jalloh.[56] These questions serve two functions – to inform those interested about the central evidentiary gaps in the narrative of what happened to Jalloh and to persuade the general public that the court is choosing not to follow up on leads that could potentially change the parameters of the trial and reveal more about how Jalloh died.

The third characteristic element of the campaign is the revealing, with clear language, of perceived motives of various arms of the state, including the courts and law enforcement, to obscure the issues in the trial and to thwart dissent by the IOJ and others. There is a sceptical an accusatory tone taken with the courts, law enforcement and government agencies that serves to identify them as active players in obscuring the circumstances of Jalloh's death. In a press release from 14 November 2012, the IOJ states that there is an administrative 'silence' around what happened in the police station on 7 January 2005 that the responsible offices are in a position to break. The same press release also suggests that the presiding judge and the state prosecutor 'simply turn away from all the contradictions in the witness testimony' and ignore questions that would lead to a line of reasoning that diverges from the suicide thesis.[57] It continues 'Meanwhile,

56 See for example, 'Pressemittilung: Kommen Sie Mit, Wir Kaufen Reinen Alkohol' 2012 (which asks what the clear liquid was that was reported by some to be on the ground near Jalloh's bed). See also 'Pressemitteilung Zum Ende Des Gerichtsprozesses Im Fall Oury Jalloh' 2008 (which asks how Jalloh could have set the mattress on fire with bound hands, how the lighter wound up in the cell even after it had been inspected and how Jalloh's nose was broken). For a thorough discussion of the questions left unanswered from the trial at first instance, see Narr and Vogelskamp 2010.

57 'Pressemittilung: Kommen Sie mit, wir kaufen reinen Alkohol' 2012. Original: '*Der Prozess plätchert underdessen weiter unter der Parole ‚Es Kann nicht sein, was nicht sein darf'. Polizist_innen lügen, die Justizbehörden decken und in diesem Sumpf können Mörder_innen ungeschoren davon kommen*'. See also 'Stellungnahme nach dem Urteil des Magdeburger Landgerichts – Wie viele von uns werden sie noch töten?' 2012: '*Das Gericht wollte sich, angesichts der neuen Indizienlage, die immer eindeutiger in Richtung Mord weist, so schnell wie möglich aus der Affäre ziehen. Ein schnelles Urteil mußte her, obwohl die Widersprüche zum Himmel schreien. Es kam sowohl in Dessau als auch in Magdeburg nicht darauf an „Recht" zu sprechen, sondern nur darauf, dass überhaupt verhandelt wurde*'. Translation: 'The court, when faced with the new set of leads pointing more and more towards murder, wanted to pull out of the affair as quickly as possible. A quick judgment had to be produced, although the contradictions cry to the heavens. In Dessau, like in Magdeburg, it did not come down to "law" but rather down to the fact that there was a trial at all'.

the trial continues to lap up against the slogan "What must not be, cannot be." Police lie, the justice authorities cover, and murderers can get out of this swamp unscathed'.[58] This sceptical outlook regarding the motives of the justice system was echoed by lawyers for Jalloh's family in March 2012, when, after multiple refusals to investigate evidence regarding the cause of Jalloh's death, they petitioned for the removal of the judges for bias.[59]

The fourth characteristic element is a call for action and solidarity. This takes the form of empowering language and identification with the reader through positioning the speaker of the press release as a citizen or resident with expectations of due process before the law. In a number of press releases by the IOJ and cooperating groups, the pronoun 'we' is used very liberally,[60] and while it can be understood to describe the groups themselves, it can also be taken to prompt the reader to identify with the 'we'. Many of the press releases, which contain vital information about the ongoing process, end with a call to action, building on the sense of outrage which the reader is expected to develop while reading the press release. This call to action is in the form of demonstrations, attendance of the court sessions in Magdeburg and general solidarity with the IOJ.[61]

One member of the IOJ states, 'the press releases are our weapon'.[62] Another member states that among the most important aspects of the formulation of the press releases are that the writer was actually there, unlike some mainstream media reporters. The press releases are written collectively, and accuracy and linguistic rigour are seen as very important to getting the IOJ's messages across clearly and persuasively. They create a discursive defence to the legalistic and official narratives of Jalloh's death. Their drafting and publication constitute a discursive practice: a naming and critiquing of legal practices, discursive and administrative, that shape the nature of the court sessions. The public discursive confrontation with the edicts and genuflections of the trial allow the lay person to tap into the discussion. Although it seems an obvious risk to use such language that challenges the state in an explicit way, attracting the characterisation as *Linksradikale* ('left wing radical'), the IOJ, through this campaign, keeps true to one of its main mantras: 'Break the Silence!'.

58 'Pressemittilung: 'Kommen Sie mit, wir kaufen reinen Alkohol' 2012.
59 See 'Stellungnahme Nach Dem Urteil Des Magdeburger Landgerichts – Wie Viele Von Uns Werden Sie Noch Töten?' 2012.
60 See for example, 'Pressemitteilung: Wir Fordern Die Mordanklage! – Aufruf Der Initiative in Gedenken an Oury Jalloh' 2012.
61 Ibid.
62 Original: '*die Pressemitteilungen sind unsere Waffe*'.

Conclusion: the political act of remembering

Demonstrating and protesting frequently outside of the courtroom in which the Jalloh and other similar cases are tried, at memorial sites for the deceased and on main public roads may seem at first glance to the public, and to the police, to be political acts. Indeed they are political acts. However, they are certainly also personal acts, important for the positioning of certain groups in German society (e.g., Black groups, asylum seekers, anti-racist groups) and for the ethos of a nation of people trying to understand itself in relation to German identity, German history and the German state. As the most recent instantiation of the Jalloh trial closed on 13 December 2012, one of the activists was overcome with grief and wailed in frustration: 'Where is Oury Jalloh? Where is Oury Jalloh? Oury Jalloh was killed! This is a disgrace for Germany! How many of us have to die?'.[63] His frustration was shared by many observers in the courtroom, some met outside the building, weeping beside the crosses laid at the steps of the courthouse as visual reminders of the pattern of violence that has become familiar to those paying attention.

It is important to recognise that the activists, in responding to the physical violence done to Black Germans, also make statements about the reproduction of that violence in the legal arena and about the way that that violence is mirrored back onto the social conditions that produced it. They are engaged in an ongoing process of exposing violence and raising public interest and awareness through press releases and demonstrations. In this way, they are giving public visibility to an issue that that they view as fundamental to life in Germany at this juncture.[64]

The next chapter takes a closer look at the historical narratives that shape some of the racial ideologies underlying the treatment already discussed in the previous chapters. It does this through examining a growing body of Black German writing that has challenged normative ideas about German history, policy and national discourses of exclusion.

63 Original: '*Wo ist Oury Jalloh? Wo ist Oury Jalloh? Ermordet! Das ist eine Schande für Deutschland. Wie viele von uns müssen sterben?*'.

64 In imagining what is at stake for bringing visibility to issues of racialised state violence, I am informed by the concept of social death, articulated by Orlando Patterson. See Patterson 1982.

Chapter 5

Gender, colonial history and contemporary social movements

Germany's Black community has reflected on legal themes in writing over the past quarter century in various ways – despite that, there has not been a great deal of what has come to be known in legal academia as 'critical legal scholarship' on race in Germany. In other words, critical writing about race and law has not tended to come from within the legal discipline in Germany. There have been important writings and political engagement before the 1980s by Black people in Germany. The 1980s saw a proliferation of work by Black writers. Using the 1980s as a turning point helps locate the significance of the process of this writing as a matter of historical record; it is a sort of process of archiving and reflection – looking back, and positing and positioning contemporary Black thinkers within the German historical landscape. The way in which material has been studied, recovered and recast invokes the adage that the 'personal is political'[1] in countering racism – that it has become part of the life's work of a number of people and, seen through the lens of a necessary and vital circumstance, countering racism can be regarded as embedded within the fabric of the experience and work of writers, organisers and artists. Such perspective on a multi-dimensional confrontation of racism can illuminate strands of thinking that cut across that which constitutes *the particular* among institutional barriers and touch upon broader-reaching rationales and ideologies. This chapter traces writings by Black people in Germany that engage with legal issues as they create historically reflective narratives. These writings offer observations about the ways in which the legal technologies of the state shaped and continue to shape the lives of Black people in Germany and identify modes of continued engagement on legal issues that build on historical examination.

1 This adage, popularised by bell hooks and Audre Lorde, among others, has been an important concept for Black feminist writers.

A community of archivists

In the summer of 2012, I attended a day-long public symposium of Black artists in Berlin, and I took the opportunity to ask the panel a question about recording and formally archiving the experiences that they had had as artists in bringing their material to the public or challenging exclusionary norms that tend to marginalise the visibility of their work. I gave the example of rukus!, a British community organisation of LGBT Black artists that began to archive its work in the London Metroplitan Archives. Noah Sow, an activist, writer and musician, responded, 'everything we do is an archive'. The boldness and directness of her response affirmed my own sensibility about the importance of 'the product' of art, music, study and journalistic commentary in mapping out the institutional memory of a place. A constant drafting and redrafting of history as well as the present. It is important to pay attention to texts when doing research on resistance. Text is crucially important, not only as a product of intellectual exercise but also as a process of remapping, reimagining and reconstituting an archive of knowledge.

Black German writing forms a foundational anchor for much social and political engagement in anti-racist activism among Black people in Germany. In this sense, what I mean by 'activism' is social engagement for the purpose of social change. First, as Sow suggests, the excavation, documentation and engagement that the Black German community regularly engages in is a form of archiving – recording, testifying, critiquing and integrating all of this back into social praxis and social discourse. Second, I contend that much of the activism among Black Germans has happened on the page – while there have been largely important political acts that are also discursive acts, text is a large part of the project for establishing a space to be both Black and German, culturally, historically and otherwise. This chapter attempts to draw out these two key points by mapping some of the texts that have formed a politics of situating Black German-ness, focusing to some extent on strands of legal discourse that are woven into the textual accounts.

Another issue that looking at activism through the lens of text brings to bear is the conception of community. One of the links that I see between community in its multiple sense and the idea of political formation can be found in the phrase 'the personal as political', (Lorde 1984)[2] which has been further elaborated by Lorde and built upon by bell hooks (1984) in

2 See Lorde's essay 'The Master's Tools Will Never Dismantle the Master's House' in her 1984 book. This term was re-signified by Black feminists, originally used by white feminists as a slogan to politicise women to become a part of first-wave feminism and the women's movement in the US. Ika Hügel-Marshall also refers to this slogan as informing her views during the early years of her politicisation. See Hügel-Marshall 1998: 81.

the contexts of writing and activism.[3] Both the personal and political aspects of people's stories were important in forming a political community. Black identity politics in Germany is quite political to begin with because of the proclamation it makes about German-ness. If German-ness coincides with Blackness, then we can predict the tension that arises between the assertion of Black community or political formation on one hand and structural and institutional logics of anti-Black racism and exclusion on the other. How are the interests of the community or political formation constrained by the state and its laws? How does this tension relate to deeper questions of ideology, belonging, authenticity and humanity? How does this tension affect the individual and, by extension, the group, its dynamics and the way it communicates its messages?

The term 'community' can be broadly imagined to describe a network of people who share a certain experience, affinity or background. A rigid, conventional idea of community as a geographically isolated or socially insular group may reinforce already entrenched thinking about how to measure one's belonging within a given space that cuts against the radical potential of the concept of diaspora. For instance, conventional ways of identifying a community would have been to focus on indicators of demographics, language, cultural affinity, common politics, common nationality and external recognition as a group. Black European positions require a more creative lens for viewing. Creativity is not to be seen as contriving the possibility of community, but locating 'Blackness' in the European project mandates a much longer discussion than this section can indulge. However, to challenge the notion that Blackness is akin to mere voluntary political affiliation devoid of the 'real' basis for community ostensibly provided by common culture, ethnicity or nationality, the ethnographer or social theorist must actively decide to deploy Blackness as an analytical category and to reflect on the experiences offered by interlocutors – that Blackness is an important basis for shared experiences (Eggers 2012: 228–233).

Excavation

The reformulation, narration and recovery of certain historical anchoring points for discussing German racism and the relationship between Black Germans and German majority society has been an important aspect of academic and socio-cultural inquiry for Black people in Germany. It has been a foundational aspect of Black German writing and continues to undergird a great deal of academic, artistic and political life. This historicising of Blackness in Germany takes on various issues, but here, my intention is to highlight those aspects that articulate legal tropes (state

3 See especially the essay 'Feminism: A Movement to End Sexist Oppression'.

regulatory, administrative and constitutional aspects) in this process of excavation. One reason for this is to insist that some work on these topics is available and has been done – there has not been an absence of legal historiography on this issue within the renaissance of contemporary Black German writing.

First, one must consider the writing that recounts historically significant ways in which the German state has regulated the social lives of Black people in Germany since the colonial period. Reflection on this type of regulation helps to draw out the role of legal institutions in formulating ideas about racial and cultural difference in this specific context, but also comments on German-ness as a state ideology. The texts highlighted in this section are important to Black people in Germany for the way they imagine the German context as having a particular legacy of anti-Black thought. They paint a broad picture but are important for contextualising some of the stances taken by certain Black anti-racism activists in Germany, whether combating violence or fighting for social inclusion more broadly. This section is important inasmuch as contemporary activism around policy reform and legal justice regard today's issues as rooted in the social and historical legacy of state complicity in stereotyping, racism and institutional exclusion.

The centrality of colonial frames

> Today's unveiling of the memorial plaque here at May Ayim Bank is a small step on a long way, that is why I would like to begin my comments with a saying from my Ghanaian ancestors: the Adinkra Proverb *San-ko-fa* bids: 'go back and take it'. This refers to the necessity to look backwards into the past and to grapple with history in order to be able to understand the present and shape the future.
>
> (Joshua Kwesi Aikins 2010)[4]

In 2010, Gröbenufer, a street that had been named after Otto Friedrich von Gröben for his service to Brandenburg-Prussia in helping Germany to set up a colonial fort and slave trade terminal in Ghana,[5] was renamed

4 Joshua Kwesi Aikins, speech at unveiling of the May-Ayim Ufer memorial plaque, 2010, Original: '*[D]ie heutige Einweihung der Gedenktafel hier am May Ayim Ufer ist ein kleiner Schritt auf einem langen Weg, deswegen möchte ich meine Anmerkungen mit einem Sprichwort meiner ghanaischen Vorfahren einleiten: Das Adinkra Proverb San-ko-fa lädt ein: "Geh zurück und hole es Dir". Gemeint is die Notwendigkeit, in die Vergangenheit zu blicken, sich mit Geschichte auseinanderzusetzen, um die Gegenwart zu verstehen und die Zukunft gestalten zu können*'.

5 See 'A Shift in Perspective: The May Ayim Ufer' Amadeu Adriano Stiftung website 2010. According to the Stiftung, 'Otto Friedrich von der Gröben, in duty to Brandenburg-Prussia, co-founded the Groß-Friedrichsburg colony in modern-day Ghana. The fort was a defense base for the German colonies, as well as a slave-trade terminal'.

May-Ayim-Ufer. The permanent inscription above the street sign reads 'May Ayim. Afro-German scientist,[6] author, pedagogue and activist of the Black movement in Germany'.[7] Ayim's name has been inscribed onto the landscape of Berlin with a footnote that explains her importance.This fact represents a social process described above by Aikins in his recalling of the meaning of *San-ko-fa*: go *back* and take it (emphasis added). The process of identifying a painful history, positioning oneself with respect to the legacy of that history and making a decision to honour a figure of hope in that history is indeed a political act. It is not an historical erasure, as argued by some. Rather, it is an ongoing, iterative process that showcases historical points and people for particular reasons. This particular shift recognises the importance of Ayim's work and the appropriateness of bringing her

Figure 5.1 May-Ayim-Ufer, Berlin Friedrichshain-Kreuzberg

Source: Photograph by author

6 In German, the term 'scientist', *Wissenschaftler/in*, includes social scientists, and May Ayim was a historian.

7 See Figure 5.1.

presence into the present, into the everyday-ness of the lived environment, and honouring the legacy of writing she has left Afro-Germans and indeed all Germans.

May Ayim passed away in Berlin in 1996. She ended her own life after suffering a series of mental breakdowns. Her essays, historical texts and poems continue to inspire Black people to carve out a space and a vocabulary for critically examining German life vis-à-vis the experiences of being Black – which is certainly intellectually challenging and generally inspiring to those who are not Black. The light that she shed on the connections between different Black experiences, the details of living with everyday racism, and the structures of racial power and exclusion continue to help formulate the tense relationship with Germany that people of colour have. Her thematic references reflect the almost unspeakable omnipresence of colonialism and help people to gauge what has and has not changed since the 1980s and early 1990s when she wrote the majority of her material. It is the insistence upon a feminist and artistic Black German voice that provides the community with leadership and a firm foundation. Her timely reflections coincided with some of the most important times in the last quarter century, including the transition from divided Germany to the unified *Bundesrepublik*.

Though she has passed away, her observations are not closed cases. In fact, quite the contrary; a central feature of her poetic work is that it creates a type of temporal openness that demands that seemingly contemporary local problems be addressed with a commitment to historical and global power relations. Her analysis on the structure of racism in Germany draws the past of colonialism into the present neo-colonial[8] arena and sets the stage for imagining a future for Black people in Germany. In her iconic poem 'blues in black and white', Ayim makes the connections between the legacy of colonialism, contemporary global geopolitics and life within a newly reunited Germany.

The German colonial era

The German colonial era, and its presentation in reflective historiography, memoir, poetry and art by Black people in Germany, functions as one of a few anchors in discussions of contemporary racism and representations of Blackness in Germany. Over the past three decades, a great deal of work has been done to recover and describe the German colonial period in

8 I refer to post-colonial in the way that Aikins and Hoppe describe it, not as an era after colonialism, which suggest a critical rupture from colonial logics, but rather a continuity of colonial logics even after the formal constitution of colonial regimes in Africa have ceased to exist. See Aikins and Hoppe 2011: 521, footnote 1.

Africa and its relevance. German colonial administration in Africa was particularly focused on East Africa after the 1884/85 Berlin Conference, and it endured roughly 30 years (Ayim et al. 1992). Although not formally from within the discipline of law, Black people in Germany have written historical, biographical and cultural-critical work that reflects on colonial relations and the effects that they have had on race in contemporary Germany, particularly with respect to Blackness in the German social imaginary. Given the highly state-regulated interpersonal relationships between Germans and Africans during the colonial period, much writing on the period involves some explicit discussion of legal regimes.

Fatima El-Tayeb, in her book *Schwarze Deutsche* (2001), discusses German racial discourse and German national identity, with particular focus on discourses around Blackness during the period from 1890–1933. In the introduction to the book, El-Tayeb notes that both public and academic discussions of German racism are shaped by the discursive techniques that marginalise Black thought and experience in German society. This fundamental assertion is important in the context of researching and discussing colonialism because it also suggests that the relevance of colonial relations vis-à-vis Black German subjects are relegated to the periphery of historical significance. The recovery of historical significance is of central importance in El-Tayeb's project, and not only do aspects of German colonial relations find prominence in her historical renderings of German racial thought, but connecting colonial miscegenation laws in German South West Africa to the so-called '*Mischlings-Debatte*'[9] in Germany stands out as a direct recovery of a particular legal discursive trajectory, the social reverberations of which are recognisable in various forms in German life (El-Tayeb 2001). Importantly, El-Tayeb points out that the discussion of German colonialism and ideologies of race are not seen to 'anchor' German society as they are seen to anchor discussions in the USA, France and England, which El-Tayeb challenges (2001: 14).

In 2000, Paulette Reed-Anderson, an African-American researcher who has lived for many years in Germany, authored the aptly titled volume *Rewriting the Footnotes*, an archival study on Berlin's Black history. In it, she describes the institutional relationships between Africans and German institutions in East Africa: the German Foreign Office, German legal institutions and society at large, which shaped their lives (Reed-Anderson 2000). She traces these relationships from before the colonial period until the end of the NS regime. This work builds on some of the work that Black Germans had been producing in the prior two decades related to German colonialism.

9 Translation: 'cross-breed debate'.

Colonial symbolism in contemporary activist discourse

> That Justice is a blind goddess
> is a thing to which we Blacks are wise:
> Her bandage hides two festering sores
> that once perhaps were eyes
>
> (Aimé Césaire)[10]

Reference to colonial history and colonial logics, but also corresponding modes of struggle against colonial logics are commonplace in the vernacular of contemporary social organising around the issues of racism and state violence. A poignant example of this is can be seen in a statement made by the refugee and migrant rights and empowerment organisation, The Caravan (Die Karawane), which prefaced the announcement of demonstrations against the wrongful death of Oury Jalloh with quotes from French Négritude movement leader and one of Frantz Fanon's political role models, Aimé Césaire. Calling upon collective memory of past injustice,[11] Césaire describes the paradox of a blind goddess upon whom some violent act has been committed so that she can no longer fulfil her duty of administering justice. He notes that Black people, in particular, understand this and in this remark is the suggestion that there is a reason for this 'wisdom', one related to colonial power relations and racialised experience. He suggests that there is knowledge not only about justice, but beyond justice, and that such knowledge can be accessed through an embodied view of the world, echoed by notable contemporaries such as Frantz Fanon (1967)[12] and W.E.B. Du Bois (1969).

The mention of Césaire in this context identifies him, and at the very least his ideas, in relation to his experience grappling with the machinery of colonialism, as an intellectual or, at least, political guide, one who has waged similar battles and gained knowledge about both physical and epistemological struggle in the process. After all, colonial governance was articulated through the vernacular of law and administration, and this vernacular relied on the language of a racialised social hierarchy and discourses of civilisation and nation for its meaning. For this reason, colonial references undergird certain aspects of Black political organising, from the aesthetics of argument to the symbols chosen and the metaphors crafted to illustrate the substance of contemporary intersections of race, power and nation.

10 'Press Release: Die Verfolgung Eines Wortes Und Ein Anruf Zur Aktion' 2007. This quote from French Black activist Aimé Césaire appeared on the website of Die Karawane to promote a demonstration in remembrance of Oury Jalloh and Dominique Koumadio. Césaire is most widely known for his development of the Black empowerment movement Négritude.

11 Ibid.

12 Fanon relies on Césaire to describe the psychology of colonialism and structural racism.

A number of examples illustrate the use of colonial references in current political activism, revealing continuities between historical colonial violence and contemporary forms of violence. A short article on the death of Dominique Koumadio[13] written for The Caravan website contained a quote from a speech by Patrice Lamumba on Congolese independence. The excerpt from Lamumba's speech reads:

> We have experienced, how our land,
> in the name of supposedly just laws,
> has been carved up, which only goes to show
> that rights are with those more powerful.
> We will not forget the massacre,
> In which so many have died,
> Nor the cells into which
> They were thrown who did not
> Subordinate themselves under a regime
> Of oppression and exploitation.[14]

The use of this selection in opening a discussion on the alleged disproportionate response by the police in fatally shooting Koumadio, said to be armed with a knife, is relevant in at least two ways. First, it highlights the continuity of exploitation of people of African descent, which is a core facet of understanding neo-colonial relations with respect to racial subordination. Second, it is important that the speech is in the context of the Congolese people, because Koumadio was, himself, a Congolese national. The historical relevance of the Congolese genocide under the Belgian rule of Leopold II is crucial here because Leopold was issued the Congo at the partition of Africa at the 1884–1885 Berlin Conference. One he acquired the Congo, with the charge of eliminating the slave trade, Leopold introduced laws to effectively privatise certain rubber harvesting enterprises and enforced brutal measures against Africans who did not produce certain quotas of rubber, including torture, chopping off limbs, and murdering children and whole families (Delathuy 1989). This historical context makes a more general link between Koumadio's situation and Congolese history – the role of power in mediating law's violence. Lumumba speaks of 'supposedly just laws' and 'rights of the powerful', which suggests that facial

13 See Chapter 4 for details of his death.

14 'Pressemitteilung: Für Eine Gesellschaft Frei Von Mord Und Todschlag' 2009. This quote appeared in German on the website, which reads: '*Wir haben erlebt, wie unser Land im/ Namen von angeblich rechtmäßigen Gesetzen/ aufgeteilt wurde, die tatsächlich nur besagen, / dass das Recht mit dem Stärkeren ist./ Wir werden die Massaker nicht vergessen,/ in denen so viele umgekommen sind,/ und ebenso wenig die Zellen, in die/ jene geworfen wurden, die sich einem Regime/ der Unterdrückung und Ausbeutung/ nicht unterwerfen wollten*'.

neutrality of laws does not necessarily indicate what violence may face people in their everyday lives. He also points to the suppression of resistance to the 'oppressive and exploitative' regime of subordination, which is echoed in the feelings of criminalisation and silencing of dissenters in Koumadio's and other cases of police brutality in Germany.

Why are these colonial references so important? What type of communication do the references engender? One aspect of referencing the colonial past is a reorganisation of such past as present – the colonial relations in contemporary times. This brings to bear reflection on structural racism and geopolitical power relations that shape social policy on migration, equality and the interpretation of various rights-based claims.

Discussion with Katharina

I met with Katharina Oguntoye to ask her about her book on German colonialism. Katharina is a prominent member of Germany's Black community, having co-edited the benchmark work *Farbe bekennen* in 1986 and having since worked as a historian and the director of a cultural centre in Berlin. I wanted to ask her about the process of writing her subsequent book, *Eine Afro-Deutsche Geschichte: Zur Lebenssituation von Afrikanern und Afro-Deutschen in Deutschland von 1884 bis 1950* (Oguntoye 1997), and particularly, why she felt at the time of writing the book, in the late 1990s, that this historical work was important in contemporary Germany.

When I arrived at Joliba, the cultural centre that Katharina directs near Görlitzer Park in Berlin-Kreuzberg, Katharina was hard at work, busily planning a newsletter for Joliba and organising stacks of papers. We hugged, and it occurred to me that I had not seen Katharina since I left Berlin some years earlier. We chatted in English and German, slipping in and out of both languages. This is a familiar aspect of our communication with one another, as some English phrases carry a nuance that better articulates a given idea or is more contextually appropriate than the German, and vice versa. For neither of us is communicating in the other's first language a 'distant grammar'.[15]

Katharina showed me how Joliba had changed since I had last visited it, four years earlier. The main room now had large table in the middle of it and the small back room now housed artwork prepared some weeks before by children in Berlin, who had completed a workshop with a local Afro-German artist on identity and self-reflection. After viewing the artwork and preparing some tea, we sat down and had a chat about the book.

15 This term is borrowed from Clifford Geertz in discussing Kroeber and anti-relativist positions within anthropology. In some ways it is distant, in other ways it is profoundly shared. See Geertz 1984.

Katharina first briefly reflected on her reasons for writing the book and what drew her to the project of writing *Farbe bekennen*. She told me, 'in *Farbe bekennen*, we wanted to distance ourselves from this blood stuff. In the NS era it [blood] was used as an exclusionary mechanism. But we don't want to use that to define Afro-Germans. It's not about blood'. Katharina was referring to the idea of blood ancestry, a commonly understood idea of ethnic German identity associated with a certain notion of German authenticity still related to certain social and legal privileges.[16] Katharina then took me through a few of the issues discussed in her book regarding the mechanisms of legal exclusion experienced by Black people living in Germany during the German colonial period, from the 1880s until before 1920. She mentioned that she knew the topic was a broad one, and that her professor at the time (the book was originally a master's thesis) would have rather she chosen a narrower one,[17] but it was important to her to do this work in the way that she did – interviewing people and doing archival research to put together an historical narrative that had previously been missing. Of her engagement with those she interviewed, Katharina says, 'my work was to find these people. They were invisible. Some of them did not want to speak very much. But they were, for us, the opening into history'.

Mapping race and gender regulation through narrative strands

The German state has, through regulatory and administrative action, formulated formal rules around race but also stressed already strained social relations. It may be helpful to focus on three areas of regulation and administration that have been, in some form, persistent in the lives of Black people. The first is state violence in its direct and explicit, even physical, form. The second is the regulation of sex and family life. The third is the regulation of citizenship. These categories all describe processes of exclusion and subjugation to some degree, and they overlap. However, these broad areas serve as examples for discussing a trajectory of the relationship between Black people and the German state and identify present-day continuities that remain important for contemporary social critique. It is useful to highlight aspects of these areas as discussed by Black writers in the last few decades in order to understand how writers have linked past and present forms of race-based regulation of social life.

16 See Bundesvertriebenengesetz [BVFG]. BGBl. III/FNA 240-1. Germany. Art 4. Spätaussiedler. 1993.

17 Katharina mentions 'I could have chosen a narrower topic, I took on a big one. But I didn't care. My teacher did not understand the meaning of the work I did. Or maybe it bothered her'.

In describing some of the policies that shaped the lives of Black people in Germany since the colonial period, this section examines four texts that use descriptive narratives, autobiographical memoir and, in some cases, reflective interviews: *Farbe bekennen* (Oguntoye et al. 1986), *Eine Afro-Deutsche Geschichte* (Oguntoye 1997), *Daheim Unterwegs* (Hügel-Marshall 1998) and '*Neger, Neger, Schornsteinfeger!*' (Massaquoi 1999). In examining the narratives presented in these works, it is useful to consider four time periods they cover: the colonial period (1884–1914), the interwar period from (1915–1933), the Third Reich (1933–1945) and divided Germany (1945–1989).[18] While discussion of these periods highlights specific aspects of state regulation and is not meant to offer an all-encompassing account of racial laws, these aspects together describe a set of trajectories of narrativising the role of law and state policy in shaping the lives of Black people. Laws and state policies do not present a holistic impression of the lived experiences of racial violence or marginalisation, particularly considering various important non-legal ideological forces that have shaped racial thinking; however, it is important to demonstrate that the study of law and policy has not been omitted in various historical and biographical narratives rendered by Black Germans in the past few decades.

Colonial period 1884–1914

During the mid-to-late nineteenth century, amidst industrialisation and after German unification in 1871, acquiring spheres of influence overseas went from being a project of merchants and missionaries to one of national interest (Friedrichsmeyer et al. 1998: 9). This led to a state effort to acquire parts of Africa in the 'scramble for Africa' in the late 1800s (Friedrichsmeyer et al. 1998). Germany's colonial period is described by some authors as a period of experimentation (Zimmerman 2010: 111–123)[19] that had significant consequences on the continent of Africa. After Africa was divided into colonial regions at the Berlin Conference of 1884–1885, Germany acquired Namibia, Togo and Cameroon (Friedrichsmeyer et al. 1998: 10–12). It also acquired present day Rwanda, Burundi and Tanzania, which were to be known collectively as German East Africa (Friedrichsmeyer et al. 1998: 12). Colonial rule was, at times, met with broad resistance, which was suppressed with devastating violence. This is most apparent in the 1907 Maji Maji rebellion, and with the killing of tens

18 The period from 1990 onwards is taken up in the next section, on contemporary criticism.

19 For example, Zimmerman discusses the cooperation of German colonial forces and US-American institutions, including the Tuskegee Institute, in introducing agricultural reforms in the colony of Togo.

of thousands of Herero in 1904 in Namibia in what has been described as the first genocide of the twenty-first century (Friedrichsmeyer et al. 1998).[20]

During the colonial period, anti-miscegenation laws existed in the colonies to prevent German settlers and African people from having sex, relationships or children.[21] Historian Frank Becker describes the development of anti-miscegenation laws as part of a broad social policy regarding racial mixing that was applied to all of the German colonies, including the Samoan Islands, and became more restrictive in the early 1900s. Becker writes:

> The number of marriages between white men and indigenous women never exceeded the number of 150 at any time in all of the German colonies. From 1904, during the great revolts in the African dependencies, marital unions as well as the general 'mixing of the races' were subjected to criticism. These forms of integration were now regarded as a threat to power politics and as an overstepping of the boundaries. Also, 'mixed people' were perceived as dissatisfied: while they considered themselves above the Africans, they were not accepted as equals by white people; as a consequence, they were expected to strive for freedom from white rule in order to rise to the top of the social hierarchy on their own. Besides, interracial marriages and 'miscegenated' children challenged the colonisers' desire for control: their very bodies bore testimony to the possibility of bridging the gap between the races. The debate also included aspects of gender insofar as the interethnic unions were regarded as proof of the physical and moral degeneration of German men, imperilling German predominance as well as German prestige.
>
> (2008: 242)

Becker continues on to discuss the prohibition of interracial marriages in German South West Africa in 1905 and German East Africa in 1906, which he credits partially to the threat that 'mixed' children posed to the German

20 See also Oguntoye et al. 1986: 35–36, quoting Carl Peters, founding member of the Society for German Colonisation, who reports that violence is the only way to control the Massai people was by shooting them. He states: '*Ich habe versucht, den Massai durch Waldbrände, durch Leuchtraketen, ja durch eine zufällig am 23.12. eintretende Sonnenfinsternis zu imponieren, aber ich habe gefunden, daß diesen wilden Söhnen der Steppe schließlich doch nur die Kugeln der Repetiergewehre und der Doppelbüchsen, und zwar in nachdrücklicher Anwendung gegen ihren eigenen Körper, imponiert haben*'. (Translation: 'I have tried to impress the Massai with forest fires, with flares, and with an eclipse that happened coincidentally on 23.12., but I have found that these wild sons of the step are, in the end, only impressed with bullets from a repeater rifle and a double-barrel rifle used insistently against their own bodies').

21 For discussion of racial ideology underlying racial mixing before and during the German colonial period, see El-Tayeb 2001: 53–54.

tradition (*Volkstum*) (Becker 2008: 243). Mixed children were given special education and treated as indigenous African children, as a matter of social policy (Becker 2008). This regulation of sexual, marital and familial relations functioned as a racial/national ideology, and the deliberate separation of the 'races' would extend not only beyond the colonised geographies of Africa and the Samoan Islands into Germany, but it would intensify there after the colonial period.

During the early 1900s, alongside Germans settling in Africa, Africans were brought to Germany as workers. Reed-Anderson, in her archival research, documents that African men and women were brought to Germany as contract workers to perform at the First German Colonial Exhibition in 1896 in Berlin (Reed-Anderson 2000: 29). There was a group from present-day Cameroon, one from Togo and a group each of the Suaheli, Massai, Khoikhoin and Herero people. Reed-Anderson describes the participation in the *Völkerschauen* as exploitative and degrading for the African people involved, and that the shows helped influence 'initial and future circumstances for the people in the developing African Disapora in Berlin' (Reed-Anderson 2000: 22–24).

During my discussion with Katharina Oguntoye, Katharina honed in on an aspect of citizenship during and after the German colonial period in which administrative reasoning was used to block African people from attaining German citizenship (Oguntoye 1997: 106–107). This, accompanied by the outbreak of World War I, led to a decline in the number of African people living in Germany, as evidenced by the rapid decline of the number of Africans in Berlin from 1915 to 1916 (Reed-Anderson 2000: 26).[22]

The colonial period was a very brutal period, not least of all because of the mass killings and generally exploitative relationship between Germany and African groups under its colonial rule. Marriage between the colonised and the colonisers was regulated quite strictly during this time. Though some Black people were given German citizenship, this was not a straightforward ordeal. The dynamics of citizenship recognition changed rapidly, but only after the formal colonial period had ended.

World War I until the rise of National Socialism: 1915–1933

The beginning of World War I marked the formal end of most of German rule in Africa (Oguntoye et al. 1986: 45). In 1918, American, Belgian, French and British forces occupied the German Rheinland region (El-Tayeb 2001: 142–143). This occupation quickly and persistently took on a highly racialised character in the German imaginary, and this led to the Germans

22 Anderson notes that the number of Africans registered in hotels, hostels and pensions in Berlin dropped from 1800 to 18 from 1915 to 1916, according to statistical registers.

forming a campaign against Black soldiers stationed by the French forces in the region (Oguntoye et al. 1986: 45–50). This campaign was a deeply gendered political and social response to the presence of armed men of African descent and their sexual relationships, real and imagined, with white German women. The authors of *Farbe bekennen* highlight that Adolf Hitler wrote about the Rheinland campaign in 1928 in *Mein Kampf*, wherein he asserted that Jewish people had sent Africans to the Rheinland to effectively damage German racial stock in order to subsequently become superior to and rule over the Germans (Oguntoye et al. 1986: 53).[23] This campaign, a curious intermingling of anti-Semitism and anti-Black racism, is known historically as the *Schwarze Schmach* (Black Scandal) or the *Schwarze Schande* (Black Shame) (Oguntoye et al. 1986: 49–51).

It is important to note that the Black men who were deployed were not imagined to be in control of the situation. They were thought to be deployed as agents of the French military or other armed forces (Oguntoye et al. 1986: 45–46), or imagined to be sent by the Jewish people, and imputed to have possessed ravenous sexual appetite. They were imagined to have been set off like animals to rape white German women (Oguntoye et al. 1986: 50).[24] They were seen, then, as dangerous pawns, wild tools of political rivals.

Emphasis on this campaign is important in the context of excavation of Afro-German history, particularly with regard to law and state violence, for two reasons. First, the campaign positions Black people within central social and political discourses that shaped German nationalist thought in the crucial period leading from World War I into the NS era. The *Schwarze Schmach* campaign had already begun to influence policies aimed at addressing 'racial dishonour'. Such policies would become much more pronounced during the late 1930s. Second, the campaign took on a global tone, both in being linked to occupation by other European powers and the fear of racial subjugation (of Germans), but also as a comment in a transnational discussion about the social and legal position of Black people. Policy makers analysed sexual relations between Black men and white women by drawing from other sexual/racial paradigms from other colonial settings in order to make a case for the protection of white women. In this context, the authors of *Farbe bekennen* cite the speech of an assemblyman of the Bayern

23 See Hitler 1933: 357: '*Juden waren es und sind es, die den Neger an den Rhein bringen, immer mit dem gleichen Hintergedanken und klaren Ziele, durch die dadurch zwangsläufig eintretende Basterdierung die ihnen verhaßte weiße Rasse zu zerstören, von ihrer kulturellen und politischen Höhe zu stürzen und selber zu ihren Herren aufzusteigen*'. Translation: 'It was the Jewish that brought the Negro to the Rhine, always with the same ulterior motive and clear goals, through forced bastardisation, to destroy the white race they despised, to bring them down from their cultural height and to become their masters'. See also Pommerin 1979.

24 For contemporary analysis on the instrumentalisation of sexual stereotypes of Black people in constructing national and citizenship identity, see Partridge 2012.

People's Party in 1919, beginning with reference to the United States of America:

> where a Nigger is lynched if he has hit on a white woman, and England, which requested before the war that no woman should work in front of coloured people in India or Ceylon in the future, in order not to degrade the white woman.
>
> (Oguntoye et al. 1986: 50)[25]

The comments by the assemblyman are revealing, not only for the specific arguments for protecting the sense of worth of white women, but the connections between race and colonial rule. A parallel is drawn with the United States and the lynchings during the late 1800s and up until that point, which had claimed the lives of many Black women and men, where a common reason for the lynching was sexual transgression of some type (Allen 2000). The other parallel made is with reference to white English women who are living in the colonial territories of India and Ceylon who were not to work in the presence of *Farbigen* (lit. coloured people). This racialised gender relationship, while it did not take the exact same form in these different colonial contexts, was iterated with the similar characteristic that racial, and effectively, civilisational status was a pre-scripted performance of racial gender relations that functioned not only to oppress people of colour using extreme violence and degrading treatment, but also to maintain the superior position of colonial settlers by advancing notions of social difference and emphasising the need to enforce sexual and, thus, biological separation. This dynamic, as evidenced in the descriptions of the *Schwarze Schmach* campaign, was not only a stratifying practice of colonial outposts, but also practiced in the German Rheinland during the interwar period (Oguntoye et al. 1986: 48–54).

Third Reich 1933–1945

The period of the Third Reich was a tumultuous era for Black people in Germany. The system of 'rassification' put in place by the National Socialists had been built upon some of the ideological positions on biological difference taken during the Weimar Republic with respect to Black people, Jewish people and Roma people, among others.[26]

25 Original: *'wo ein Neger gelyncht werde, wenn er sich an einer weißen Frau vergangen habe, und England, welches vor dem Krieg verlangt habe, daß keine Frau in Indien oder Ceylon in Gegenwart von Farbigen arbeite, um die weiße Frau nicht herabzusetzen'.*

26 This is evidenced by the German participation in the burgeoning Eugenics movement of the late 1800s and early 1900s, and the establishment of the Society of Racial Hygiene in 1905 and initial laws regarding sterilisations on the basis of 'eugenic indicators' from 1919 and into the 1920s in Germany. See Oguntoye et al. 1986: 52, 70–71.

The NS party rose to power in 1933, and in 1937, a policy was put into place in the Rheinland to sterilise children born of Black fathers and white German mothers (Oguntoye et al. 1986: 54–58). Historians note significantly that, while this was an explicit state policy, it did not have a legal basis, even under the NS laws (Oguntoye et al. 1986: 54).[27] Frieda mentions sterilisations that she was aware of as a young woman. She remembers in an interview in *Farbe bekennen*: 'Many coloureds were sterilised, Gerda, Hanna ... Christel was hidden by her mother in a convent near Cologne. They took her out of there and sterilised her too. Our nephew also. He was sent home immediately after the sterilisation, he was not even able to rest' (Oguntoye et al. 1986: 75).[28] She also remembers being spit upon and called 'bastard' or '*Mischling*' on the streets of Berlin (Oguntoye et al. 1986: 69). In school in the early 1930s, she was made to take a course called '*Rassenkunde*', where part of the pedagogy was to communicate that racial mixing was worse than the mere fact of racial difference.[29] From family relations to educational curriculum, social forms of exclusion and marginalisation were, to a large extent, supported by racial ideologies perpetuated and maintained by the state.

Katharina Oguntoye interviews the same daughters when describing the experiences of the Diek Family in the Free State of Danzig, before and during NS rule. In interviews with the two daughters of Mandenga Diek, she describes the economic marginalisation of the family. Customers who had previously used the family's wholesale supply services were afraid to place orders under NS rule (Oguntoye 1997: 155). Economic difficulties meant that the family needed to move into a smaller flat somewhere less central within Danzig, but this was difficult when the flat owners found out that Diek was African. She notes that children were treated harshly during this period, mentioning the steady rejection of one of the daughters as a young woman (referred to by a pseudonym in *Farbe bekennen* but whose real name, Doris, was disclosed in Oguntoye's later work) by her best friend,

27 Ibid.: 54. This is despite the 1933 law based on eugenic principles that required sterilisation of certain German women for reasons of race hygiene (*aus rassenhygenischen Gründen*). See Gesetze zur Verhütung erbkranken Nachwuchses, GVeN, 14.7.1933. See generally Pommerin 1979.

28 This quote was given by Anna G. when interviewed in *Farbe bekennen*. Original: '*Viele Farbige wurden sterilisiert, Gerda, Hanna ... Christel war von ihrer Mutter in einem Kloster bei Köln versteckt worden. Dort haben sie sie rausgeholt und auch sterilisiert. Unseren Neffen auch. Nach dem Sterilisieren wurde er sofort nach Hause geschickt, er durfte sich noch nicht mal ausruhen*'.

29 Oguntoye et al. 1986: 70. Frieda remembers: '*Ich hatte an dem Fach »Rassenkunde« teilzunehmen und mußte mir Slogans anhören wie: »Alle Weißen und Schwarzen hat Gott gemacht, die Mischlinge stammen vom Teufel«, oder: »Die Mischlinge können nur die schlechten Eigenschaften von beiden Rassen erben«*'. Translation: 'I had to take the subject "Raciology" and was made to hear slogans like: "All whites and blacks were made by God, the crossbreeds come from the devil"or: "the crossbreeds can only inherit the bad characteristics from both races"'.

who suddenly began to ignore her, and members of her bible reading group and typing course, who wrote her letters asking her not to attend (Oguntoye 1997). Oguntoye, reflecting on this social shunning, remarks that like Doris, who tried to find her place in society despite constant rejection, many Afro-Germans were in a difficult situation that forced them to experience both extreme rejection and to find a way to survive. She remarks, using Doris as an example:

> One notices that, despite the rejections, she kept on trying to find a niche for herself. This reflects her courage and will to live, but also the desperate attempt to continue to participate in social life. Life in the conflict zone of opposites, on one side the 'lack of dignity' in being excluded and ostracised and on the other side to have the possibility to continue to live one's own life, is the most typical characteristic for the situation of Africans and Afro-Germans in Germany in the NS era.
> (1997: 156)[30]

Here, Oguntoye touches on a central dilemma to the Black condition during the Third Reich, which is the negotiation of the circumstances with persistence. This characterisation challenges the notion that Black people were simply victims during this repressive period, but rather shows their deployment of agency in a way that is complex, as it describes an attempt to participate in a social world that attempts to exclude the Black subject but also needs the subjugated Black subject to enable the ideology of racial supremacy.

In 1939, after the Free State of Danzig is taken over by the NS regime, Frieda comments on the changes to their citizenship that have taken place. Frieda remarks that her and her father's passports of the Free State of Danzig had been taken away and, after not having any passports for a year and a half, they were issued *Fremdenpässe*, or foreigners' passports (Oguntoye et al. 1986: 72). Anna had married a man from Cameroon, and since it was a French colony, he applied for and was granted French citizenship at the French consulate, and his citizenship was subsequently conferred to Anna (Oguntoye et al. 1986).

An important characteristic of a number of the narratives of Black experiences in the Third Reich is the tension between, on the one hand, a categorically oppressive and violent set of legal rules and practices, and on

30 Original: '*Es fällt auf, dass sie trotz der Ablehnungen immer wieder versuchte, für sich eine Nische zu finden. Das speigelt ihren Mut und Lebenswillen, aber auch den verzweifelten Versuch, weiterhin am sozialen Leben teilzunehmen. Das Leben im Spannungsfeld der Gegensätze einerseits als "lebensunwert" ausgegrenzt und geächtet zu werden und andererseits die Möglichkeit zu haben, das eigene Leben weiter zu leben, ist das typischste Merkmal für die Situation der Afrikaner und Afro-Deutschen in Deutschland in der NS-Zeit*'.

the other hand, a negotiation of those rules and practices that was made possible by the ambiguities of the position of Black people in Germany. Hans-Jürgen Massaquoi recalls, as a young boy, that he wanted to participate in the *Hitler Jugend* (Hitler Youth or HJ) because all of the other boys in the class were participating in it, and though he did not understand the ideologies behind the movement at the time, he was drawn to the power and sense of identification that was sure to accompany being accepted as part of the group (Massaquoi 1999: 128–134). He recalls asking his teacher whether he could be a part of the HJ. His teacher replied:

> 'I thought you knew that you can't join the *Jungvolk* because you are a non-Aryan,' he began. 'You know that your father is African and that Africans and other non-European people count as non-Aryans. Non-Aryans are forbidden from joining the Hitler Youth'. 'But I am so German,' I sobbed beneath tears. 'My mother says that I am German, just like all the others.'
>
> 'You are a German boy' Mr Schürmann admitted sympathetically, 'but unfortunately not like all the others. I'm sorry, my boy, I wish I could help you, but it won't work. The laws are just that way'.
>
> (Massaquoi 1999: 130)[31]

Massaquoi remembers the explanation from his teacher, painful to hear at the time, and the rejection from the HJ leader some days later when he and his mother went to the HJ offices to make an appeal to have him admitted, which was denied on the same grounds. The rules were such that Massaquoi's identity was the reason for his exclusion because it was to be constructed in terms of Aryan-ness, not German-ness, though it is doubtful that his German-ness was seen in as credible a light, considering that being Aryan was what entitled Germans to German passports and non-Aryans to *Fremdenpässe*. However, Massaquoi, and his mother, had tried to have young Hans-Jürgen admitted to the HJ as a mechanism of protection, so that he might avoid standing out as the separation between Aryans and non-Aryans was codified and put into various other forms of practice. The idea was to negotiate the danger of a venomous state-imposed social structure by partially blending into it, as problematic and dangerous as this may have been.

31 Original: '*"Ich dachte, du wüsstest, dass du nicht ins Jungvolk darfst, weil du Nicht-Arier bist", fing er an. "Du weißt doch, das dein Vater Afrikaner ist und dass Afrikaner und andere nichteuropäische Menschen als Nicht-Arier gelten. Nicht-Ariern ist es untersagt, der Hitlerjugend beizutreten". "Aber ich bin doch Deutcsher", schluchzte ich unter Tränen. "Meine Mutter sagt, dass ich Deutscher bin, so wie alle anderen".*

"Du bist ein deutscher Junge" räumte Herr Schürmann mitfühlend ein, "äber leider nicht wie alle anderen. Es tut mir Leid, mein Junge, ich wünchte, ich könnte dir helfen, aber das geht leider nicht. Die Gesetze sind nun mal so" '

Professor of Women's Studies Tina Campt's oral history ethnography, *Other Germans* (2004), highlights aspects of early-twentieth century German state policy that greatly affected the lives of Germany's Black residents, including the *Schwarze Schmack* campaign and the NS sterilisation policies (Campt 2004). Campt's interviews with survivors of the Third Reich reveal some of the ways in which legal and administrative laws have been addressed in the historical narratives of Black Germans, and they open up ways to think about state policies on race over the last century. In her interview with an Afro-German man named Hauck, the son of an Algerian father and a white German mother, born in 1920, Hauck reveals that he was one of the children sterilised by the German state (Campt 2004: 25). Hauck reveals that he participated in the HJ organisation to protect himself from certain exclusion and violence, insisting that he could not imagine what his life would have been like during the Third Reich had he not joined the group (Campt 2004: 197–201). This suggests a mode of negotiating inclusion and exclusion that was precarious and complicit, utilised to minimise visible difference that would otherwise trigger the ideological sticking point for the majority society and the real physical violence and social exclusion.

Other examples of avoiding perils associated with the NS era that are specific to the circumstances faced by Black people in Germany can be thought of as serendipitous coincidences that complicate the stratification of identity during the NS era and beyond. This includes another attempt by Massaquoi to identify with those Germans in power by joining the Nazi war effort. This was thwarted, in a similar way to his attempt to join the HJ, because he was considered racially 'impure' (Massaquoi 1999: 132–134). Frieda also mentions that, in Danzig, because she was issued a foreign passport instead of a German passport when Danzig was annexed by the NS, she was spared persecution when Russian forces took control of the region (Oguntoye et al. 1986: 72). These instances demonstrate how certain forms of social exclusion, here from military and civic participation, had consequences that affected the experiences of Black Germans in ways that were not completely predictable, owing to their in-between status during the Third Reich.

Alongside heightened regulation of sexual relations between Black people and white Germans, Black people in Germany were subject during the NS regime to being interned in work camps and concentration camps (Oguntoye et al. 1986: 74–77). However, Black people were instrumentalised by the NS regime in other ways. To gather momentum for building a colonial empire, some of the Black prisoners interned in camps, along with Black prisoners of war from the United States, were gathered and made to act in colonial films about Africa (Oguntoye et al. 1986: 78). Others stood as models for photographic advertisements for such films or for circus attractions (Oguntoye et al. 1986). This demonstrates the role that Black people were forced to play in commercial and imperial state-building endeavours of the Third Reich.

Divided Germany 1945–1989

The period of divided Germany is described as a period of intense social stigma for Black people, which was coupled with state regulation of family life, particularly of children born of foreign soldiers who had been stationed in Germany after World War II. Ika Hügel-Marshall (1998) reflects on her experience growing up in divided Germany. Among her most poignant reflections on this particular era are the discursive turns that identify her as a symbol of national political turmoil and, as such, someone who was not afforded full acceptance in German society. She reflects on the familial regulation by the state, a coordinated effort between the state and civil society, when she notes the era's widespread policy of placing children born of the war into children's homes.

As a young girl, Hügel-Marshall, the daughter of a white German mother and an African-American father stationed in Germany after World War II, was called a *Besatzungskind* (child of the occupation) (Hügel-Marshall 1998: 41) and a *Heimkind* (home/institution child) (Hügel-Marshall 1998: 31) during her childhood. She, like many children born to soldiers occupying the Rheinland after World War II, was sent to live for most of the year in a boarding house (Hügel-Marshall 1998). The significance of this social expectation is an important aspect of thinking through the lives of many of those, including non-Black children, who were seen as children of occupation and not fully integrated into the social and moral fabric of the nation. Hügel-Marshall's description of her experience of this aspect of her upbringing makes it clear that being not just any child of occupation, but a Black child of occupation, made her time particularly difficult both at home and in the boarding house, as the only Black child in both settings (Hügel-Marshall 1998: 31, 41–45). In her childhood and early adulthood, Hügel-Marshall describes how she has faced one challenge after the next, from home, to finding solidarity in family (Hügel-Marshall 1998: 59–60)[32] and friends, and partner (Hügel-Marshall 1998: 75–77),[33] and in the memoir, she reflects on these aspects as part of a broad social discrimination that is contoured by aspects of the national.

32 Hügel-Marshall describes her despair and feeling of betrayal when her sister claims that she is just a friend when asked about her relationship with Hügel-Marshall in a social setting. Hügel-Marshall, however, describes her simultaneous commitment to understanding her sister's point of view as a mechanism for surviving in a world where she also found it difficult to survive.

33 Hügel-Marshall describes being harassed on the street for holding hands with her white partner, and she reflects on the toll that social stigma of her interracial relationship may have taken on the relationship itself.

She describes her time in school as unchallenging and frustrating, because, aside from facing constant racial insult (Hügel-Marshall 1998: 46–47), her intellect was generally unrecognised or she was accused of cheating to produce superior work (Hügel-Marshall 1998: 47–48). Instead of being encouraged when she told an overseer in her boarding house that she wanted to become a teacher, she was told that she would only ever be fit to do social work, such as childcare (Hügel-Marshall 1998: 54, 74). She describes her emotional plea to the head of school to repeat her *Realschulabschluss*,[34] identifying systematic marginalisation and hindrance by her teacher and classmates (Hügel-Marshall 1998: 62–63). In her description of the reactions that she would hear from people on the street when she went hand-in-hand through the city with her partner, she reflects upon thoughts about not only race, but nation and national identity (Hügel-Marshall 1998: 75). People said things like: '"Look at that, she must think that that she's better with a white man by her side." "Well, that won't go well for long between them." "Can she not look for someone like her? Must it be a German?"'[35] (Hügel-Marshall 1998: 75).

These comments echo some of the racialised nationalist thinking that was continuous with previous eras in which race and reproduction were discussed as contentious, attacks on the nation. The first remark in the selection above circumscribes a place for Black people, as both spatially separate and subordinate. When the white male is by her side, she is said to *think* that she is better than she is, but, the remark follows, she is no different, she is merely configured differently vis-à-vis power. Gender is also very prominent in this example, as the white male is not lambasted in this critique, but seen as a source of power to which someone else opportunistically attaches.[36] The second remark indicates that such a pairing is destined to fail. The third remark builds the aspect of nation into the language of race, and conflates whiteness (or, at least, this particular man's outward appearance) with German-ness. Furthermore, it positions this German-ness as passive in this constellation, reinforcing the idea that the Black woman has chosen him, a national commodity to which she had questionable rights, rather than treating the white man as a thinking agent who also chooses.

Hügel-Marshall, in reflecting upon her experiences growing up and coming to terms with German racism, organises her thoughts into a

34 Translation: 'real' school diploma, a type of elementary school diploma.

35 Original: '*Sieh dir die an, die glaubt jetzt wohl was Besseres zu sein mit 'nem weißen Mann an ihrer Siete.« – »Na, lange wird das nicht gutgehen mit den beiden.« – »Kann die sich nicht einen ihresgleichen suchen? Muß das ausgerechtnet, n Deutscher sein?*'.

36 In comparison, Hügel-Marshall's mother was referred to disparagingly for having betrayed white patriarchal relations for sexual or love relations with a Black male, and Hügel-Marshall remembers that she was called a *Negerhure* (nigger's or negro's whore) by many, and told that she should be ashamed of herself. See Hügel-Marshall 1998: 41.

catalogue of experiences and observations that helps to guide her as she moves into adulthood. This catalogue acts as a sort of knowledge archive, in which she stores important aspects of her life experience, processes them and draws on them when necessary. *Daheim unterwegs* reads, in some respects, almost as a pedagogical memoir, where the narration is reflective on issues that help the reader and author mutually acknowledge societal and structural forms of racism, as well as methods for dealing with racism's effects.

Contemporary legal interventions in writing

With the steady growth of an Afro-German literary and artistic body of work during the 1980s and 1990s and into the present, there has been constant reflection on past eras in order to make sense of the present and to change the circumstances of Black people and other marginalised groups in Germany. It puts historical facts and experiences together to form narratives and create institutional memory, which serves as a crucial educational platform for moving Germany forward as a society.

Reckoning with the past in contemporary social critique

Various contemporary social critical writings by Black Germans reference the past, including the colonial era, and note the longstanding presence of Black people in Germany and the presence of Blackness in the German imaginary. Some of these writings discuss law and state policy, which reveals that, while these narratives are not necessarily ensconced within the genre of legal academic writing, they are engaged with ideas that are important in the discussion of legal and state regulation of race and racism.

Black people in Germany have written on what has been termed 'everyday racism', or racism that is experienced persistently in daily interactions (Essed 1991: 284–286),[37] and have connected everyday racism to legal and policy structures that can be important for understanding the totality of legal issues surrounding race. One such writer is Noah Sow, with her 2008 book *Deutschland Schwarz Weiss: Der Alltägliche Rassismus* (*Germany Black White: Everyday Racism*). Sow describes contemporary forms of racial violence with explicit reference to a trajectory of violent state policies from the colonial period and through the Weimar era and the Third Reich (Sow 2008: 84–95). She highlights the political might of German colonial rule over parts of Africa, the mass killings of tens of thousands of Herero in 1904–1906 and hundreds of thousands of Maji-Maji in 1905–1908, and the execution of hundreds of resistance fighters in Cameroon in 1914 (Sow

37 Here, Essed discusses the importance of valuing experience-based knowledge about racism.

2008: 84–86). She also highlights the seizure of German passports once held by African residents of Germany from former German colonies and the negative impact that this compromised rights status had on their life circumstances (Sow 2008: 93). She highlights the *Schwarze Schmach* campaign of the 1920s, the sterilisation of hundreds of Black children in the Rheinland and the internment of Black people in work camps. What is important about this part of Sow's work is not that it is newly discovered information, but that she connects historical excavation of these policies explicitly to types of racism that Black people in Germany may encounter presently. She describes power dynamics involved in discussing past racism as, themselves, racially informed. She gives examples of how the history that she highlights is not examined critically or adequately reflected upon by white Germans when they are engaging in public discussions (Sow 2008: 96–97).[38] Sow discusses the word '*Neger*' at length, focusing on its etymology in historical context before applying her historical reading to contemporary social debates, including an exchange that she had with editors of Langenscheidts Dictionaries, wherein the editor justified the French translation of '*Neger*' as '*le Noir/al Noire*' or simply Black (Sow 2008: 122).[39]

Sow, in her book, examines, partly through the lens of her work as founder of the media watchdog group, Der Braune Mob, primarily discursive forms of exclusion and perpetuation of racist stereotypes with an eye toward public policy. She examines various types of media, including casting and advertising for theatre and television (Sow 2008: 158–170), general newspaper reporting (Sow 2008: 147–157), public campaigns for financial donation to Africa and children's books, and she links the messages she

38 For example, she analyses the frustration one Black visitor on a tour of *Konzentrationslager* (concentration camp or KZ) *Neuengamme* experienced when the tour guide described a Black woman's relegation to kitchen and waiting service, rather than some other type of work, as privileged. She describes her own further shock at the supposition made by the tour guide that the overseer of the camp rather liked Black people, suggesting that this is why the work that the Black person had to do in the KZ was 'not as bad' (96). Sow also mentions her frustration at the reaction to the 2005 situation of an African crafts fair being solicited by the zoo in Augsburg as a venue, and the discussion that ensued between the zoo's director and critics of the move (96–97).

39 While the definition did accompany a cautionary note that the word could have a negative connotation, Sow argues that this was translated incorrectly and that the extremely insulting use is the primary use of the word.

A court case concerning the use of the term '*Neger*' is mentioned by Aretha Schwarzbach-Apithy in her essay 'Interkulturalität und Anti-Rassistische Weis(s)heiten' ('Interculturality and Anti-racist Whiteness/Wisdoms'). In the case, in which the ISD raised a claim against the Volksbühne in Berlin for using the term '*Neger*' in the title and advertisement for a play, Schwarzbach-Apithy notes that the judge at the Regional Court in Berlin argued that '*Neger*' is a term only found objectionable by academics, suggesting that the common usage is more benign. Schwarzbach-Apithy disagrees, and argues that it is an inherently violent term that people of African descent are confronted with constantly as everyday racism. See Eggers 2005: 250–251, 260.

distils from the texts and images to larger social discussions that demonstrate the pervasiveness of racial stereotypes and the negation or minimalisation of German colonial history. Interspersed with her examination of print media, she makes connections with racial stereotypes and racial violence, describing such stereotypes as pervasive parts of German public discourse and such violence as institutional rather than interpersonal (Sow 2008: 133, 171–181).

A second area of writing in which Black Germans, along with other people of colour and white German thinkers, have made significant contributions to historically-minded contemporary critique is in writing on post-colonial relations and historically-focused critiques of race politics in Germany. For example, a 2011 edited volume called *Wie Rassismus aus Wörtern spricht: (K)Erben des Kolonialismus im Wissensarchiv deutsche Sprache* (Arndt et al. 2011) relates colonial events and colonial thinking to types of racialised thinking that resonates with people in present-day Germany. The volume is arranged as a glossary and the majority of its entries are written by Afro-Germans and people of colour living in Germany. The entries are broken into four parts which cover racism and colonialism, concepts relating to knowledge production in hegemonic white society, conceptual terms ('interventions') by people of colour and terms that are deployed as racist remarks in everyday speech (Arndt et al. 2011). This volume contributes to making connections between German history, including colonial history and twentieth-century history and contemporary racism in language and ideology. Other volumes have contributed similarly (for example, Arndt et al. 2004). Still other volumes discuss Germany as a post-colonial society, centring colonial thinking as an object of study and an lens for viewing contemporary thinking on race, gender and sexuality in Germany (for example, Nghi Ha 2004, 2007, 2010, AG gegen Rassismus in den Lebenswissenschaften 2009).

Legal interventions

> The origins of my question lie in observations made whilst working as a legal researcher in Berlin. I was often struck by the fact that I was the only Black woman in law seminars or at law conferences. Where I did meet another legal scholar of colour, she or he was also only temporarily in Germany. My lack of interaction with any other Black legal professionals may have simply been due to missed opportunities or bad timing, but I often wondered why there was an absence of colour in law faculties and at legal conferences both in Berlin and elsewhere.
>
> (Solanke 2004: 179)

Law professor Iyiola Solanke reflects on the relatively small number of Black people, and people of colour more generally, who participate in the legal profession or legal academia in Germany. She analyses in her piece 'Where are the Black Lawyers in Germany?' some aspects of general education, legal professional education and entry to the bar which may be hindrances to certain groups to formal participation. However, there is a discussion around race and law that is not limited to legal professionals, but still thematises law and legal provisions in central ways. While Black people have been shaping this discussion in various ways, the discussion is not led in all cases by Black people.

There have been a number of writers who have made specific interventions in the area of CRT, either from within the Black German community or building upon knowledge about race and racism in Germany that has proved important in critiquing current legal approaches. These writers have a foundational idea in common – that racism is a component part of the German legal order, and must be considered in a profound structural sense in order to adequately deal with racial disjuncture in German society.

CRT is based on the idea that legal structures are informed by ideologies of power, including but not limited to racial ideologies, in such a way as to render the judgments of courts and norms of legislative decision-making, for example, as inextricably connected to normative power relations. Such a theory suggests that the study of racism, sexism and heteronormativity, for example, are essential to understanding the effects of law. This has been taken up by legal academics such as Crenshaw (1995) and others in the US context, and it has been applied in the German context by Solanke (2009), Möschel (2007),[40] Barskanmaz (2011)[41] and Bruce-Jones (2009: 2015).[42]

However, it is not only legal academics that have scrutinised the law as a central mode for unpacking contemporary racism. Playwright Amy Evans, a Black American playwright who lived for many years in Germany, penned two plays that deal with accusations of institutional police brutality and racism. The first of these is called *Achidi J's Final Hours,* and it deals with the death of John Achidi (see Chapter 4). The second of these is *The Most Unsatisfied Town,* which was written about Oury Jalloh's community in Dessau and the context of the legal trial. This play was written during first trial and workshopped in Berlin with academics, activists working on the trial and members of the general public before the retrial occurred.

40 Möschel makes a case for the relevance of racial analysis to the legal systems of various European countries.

41 Barskanmaz criticises the move to erase the term *Rasse* from the German Basic Law without a critical discussion of the construct, the lived experience of racism and the symbolic gesture of erasure.

42 In 'Race, Space and the Nation State', I compare German and French approaches to recognising the category of race in each country's anti-discrimination law and constitutional equal treatment provisions. In 'German Policing at the Intersection' I use an intersectional lens to analyse institutional biases in policing.

Both the technical interventions by legal academics and the contextual interventions by playwrights and authors who focus on racism in legal structures as an aspect of social racism put historical violence and structural violence into a framework for thinking about contemporary race and racism. They scrutinise the legislature and judiciary as failing to account for racially biased effects in its judgments, its promulgation of statutory law and its self-regulation and openness to critique and reform.

The culmination of historical and legal reflection provides fertile ground for the reimagining of German law and society. The social and legal aspects of racism in Germany have been linked to varying degrees by both those who experience racism in Germany and by those who are examining legal structures in Germany. This fascinating contemporary era provides a rich context for bringing issues that have been central to the experiences of Black people in Germany to a space of visibility and a starting-point for reflection on German national identity and German legal institutions.

The reparations case

A culmination of colonial historical reflection, post-colonial geopolitical relations and thinking through legal remedies was brought into sharp relief with the 2001–2004 legal proceedings for compensation for what has been termed 'the Herero Massacre' during German colonial administration of what is now Namibia.[43] The proceedings were launched a few years before the hundredth anniversary of the Herero Massacre, which occurred in 1904. The Herero People's Reparation Corporation (HPRC), an entity established to examine the possibility of compensation for mass killings of Herero during the colonial period, filed a complaint in a superior court in Washington DC against the German government and several German companies for US$2 billion.[44] The complaint was removed by defendants to the federal district court in DC,[45] where it was dismissed in 2003 for failure to state a cause of action,[46] relying on the lack of personal jurisdiction sufficient to engage DC's long-arm statute to allow it to adjudicate the case.[47]

43 For a detailed account, see Olusoga and Erichsen 2010.

44 'Herero Massacre: General's Descendants Apologize for 'Germany's First Genocide' 2007.

45 The Herero People's Reparations Corporation, Et. Al. V. Deutsche Bank A.G. and Woermann Line, D/B/a Deutsche Afrika-Linien Gmblt & Company, U.S.App.D.C. Reports. Decided 11 June 2004.

46 Spiegelberger 2003.

47 The Herero People's Reparations Corporation, Et. Al. V. Deutsche Bank A.G. and Woermann Line, D/B/a Deutsche Afrika-Linien Gmblt & Company, U.S.App.D.C. Reports. Decided 11 June 2004, 5–6. The defendant company was deemed by the court not to have had adequate contacts with the District of Columbia in the United States to give the court jurisdiction over the company.

The HPRC appealed their claim's dismissal in 2004, but the appeal failed, based on there being no statutory basis authorising the DC court to be able to adjudicate the issue, absent any personal jurisdiction over the defendant company.[48]

Law professor Rachel Anderson advances several arguments supporting the Herero litigants in their cause of action, relying mainly on the assertion that the German government acted unlawfully at the time of the massacre according to customary international law principles, as well as conventions that were in existence at the time (Anderson 2005: 1172–1180). She does not engage thoroughly with the DC district court's argument that there was no personal jurisdiction in this case, but rather focuses on establishing the violation of international law by the German government.

Alongside the formal litigation, there was a social discussion occurring in Germany about the practical solutions and public-relations-facing response that the government would offer, in light of the growing discussion and media coverage around the hundredth anniversary of the killings. Parliament discussed whether to give Namibians some form of compensation. The German government argued consistently that it had already been giving general financial aid to the government of Namibia, but this reasoning did not engage explicitly with the context of colonial violence, a foremost concern of the Namibians who were pushing for a German response on facing up to the massacre.

A further dynamic was added to the issue when it was announced that skulls of those Herero killed in 1904, found safeguarded in the Medical History Museum of the Charité Hospital in Berlin and at Freiburg University, would be returned to Namibians.[49] The status of recognition of the massacre remains a contentious subject today. Mainstream news source, *Deutsche Welle*, published an article in 2012 on the failure of the German government to acknowledge the mass killing as a genocide.[50] A formal apology has been one of the core requests of Namibian people, and despite the 2007 apology given by descendants of 1904 Genderal Lothar von Trotha, who waged the attack on the Herero, and the 2004 apology by the German Development Minister Heidemarie Wieczorek-Zeul,[51] there has been no formal apology issued by the German government. In Namibia in 2005, Herero people protested Germany's petition to gain a permanent seat at the United Nations, citing their refusal to recognise past injustices committed against them.[52] After the skulls were returned in 2011, an organisation

48 The Herero People's Reparations Corporation, Et. Al. V. Deutsche Bank A.G. and Woermann Line, D/B/a Deutsche Afrika-Linien Gmblt & Company, U.S.App.D.C. Reports. Decided 11 June 2004.

49 BBC News, 30 Sept 2011.

50 Schmeller 2012.

51 'Germany Asks for Namibians' "Forgiveness"' 2004.

52 Bause 2005.

called the Ovaherero Council for Dialogue on the 1904 Genocide issued a press release, disapproving of the tabling of the motion in the German parliament that would have recognised the massacre as genocide.[53] A film has also been made by activists, and was screened in 2013 in Berlin, on the calls for reparations since the mid-2000s.[54]

The ongoing discussion on the responsibility of Germans not only to issue some material compensation for the violence of colonialism, but also to recognise the effects of its colonial legacy is a very current one. It is one that has purchase not only among historians, more recently, politicians and international lawyers, but of activists working on German domestic racism (Sow, 2011: 126–128).[55] On 22 March 2012, Black Germans, people of African descent, along with people of other backgrounds, protested in front of the German Bundestag, reading statements by Namibian organisers, carrying placards that read '*Völkermord verjährt nicht*'[56] and demanding an apology for genocide. This was a diasporic organising campaign, important to people in Germany not only because of a feeling of connection with descendants of Herero, but also owing to the importance of positioning oneself with respect to historical power relations for epistemological survival in the German nation. As Widenroth-Coulibaly (2007: 403) states, 'memory work is also a [form of] resisting'. Here, those protesting in front of the Bundestag were resisting the silence around its colonial legacy and calling upon the nation to calculate its past into its present.

Conclusion

This chapter locates some of the ways in which Black people in Germany have uncovered and interpreted historical social events and described the circumstances in which Black people in Germany find themselves. Through this they have been able to reconcile with history and interpret the present. This chapter presents select narratives of social life since colonial times that Afro-Germans have written since 1985, all of which deal, to some extent, with state regulation of their everyday lives, informed by notions of racial difference and, in particular, Blackness as a historically contextual identity. It is important to recognise in this process of excavation not only that Black researchers have been active in locating historically

53 'Press Release: The Position of the OCD 1904 on the Genocide Motion in the German Bundestag' 2012.

54 Nikolai Alber & Hilke Rusch, Directors. *Deutsch-Südwas?! – Erinnerung an einen deutschen Völkermord* (Film), German with English subtitles. 2012.

55 Here, it is argued that the failure to grapple with Germany's colonial past, including the massacre of the Herero, constitutes a type of 'forgetting', which I argue speaks to a larger issue of the epistemology of identity regarding the German self-conception.

56 Translation: '[the claim of] Genocide does not expire'.

significant aspects of Black experiences in Germany, but also that this excavation has helped to situate Germany's Black community politically and socially by creating a shared set of resources and experiences to draw from and honour in constructing a way of being at home in the ideologically challenging terrain of the nation-state.

Part III

Unruly work on race and the law

Chapter 6

Towards a European anti-racism

> Those who commit the murders write the reports, and hence these blots upon the honor of a nation cause but a faint ripple on the outside world. They arouse no great indignation and call forth no adequate demand for justice. The victims were black, and the reports are so written as to make it appear that the helpless creatures deserved the fate which overtook them.[1]
>
> (Ida B. Wells 1893)

Ida B. Wells, one of the most notable anti-lynching campaigners in the history of the United States, tours England and various parts of continental Europe in 1894 for support for her on her campaigns to end the state-sponsored lynching of black people. In her autobiography *Crusade for Justice*, Wells documents her trips to Liverpool, Manchester, Bristol, Newcastle and London, where she speaks to leadership of various Christian denominations, legislators, journalists and private citizens. She reflects on appealing to the British because it was another great nation that could appeal to the humanity of US leaders, shaming them towards change (Wells-Barnett 1970: 177–178).

In her work, Wells does the work of describing state violence, an invisible aspect of the post-slavery condition, an extension of the formal regime of apartheid in that characterised the United States at the end of the nineteenth century. She campaigns from the decades from the 1880s to the 1920s for legislation to protect black people against being tortured and killed. She documents lynchings and publishes two pamphlets that serve to both archive the murders and to persuade the rest of society to mobilise against the practice. Of course, ultimately, legislation would not remedy state-sanctioned violence altogether, but it promised to reduce the

1 Speech delivered at Tremont Temple in Boston on 13 February 1893. Published in *Our Day* magazine in May, 1893. Ida B. Wells was an outspoken anti-lynching activist in the United States from the 1890s until the 1920s. See Wells 'Lynch law in all its phases (1893)' Black Past website.

frequency of state-sanctioned killings in a time when Black people were in desperate need of relief. Lynchings of Wells' era were heinous because they were carried out under the watchful eye of the state. Authorities, including police and judges, were typically aware that lynchings were taking place, and they sometimes participated in the hangings, cutting and burnings themselves (Allen 2000). The legislation sought by activists like Wells would enjoin the authorities from being complicit in these extrajudicial acts of violence. Theoretically, complicity in such practices had already been illegal, since police were not expected to allow mobs of angry citizens to become renegades and mete out punishment as they saw fit, irrespective of due process considerations for the accused or the strength of the allegations. They were more than an extension of the arm of the criminal justice system, which would have been bad enough; they lifted unspoken racial rules and expectations into the realm of legitimate violence, to be practiced in broad daylight. Given the then recent transition out of slavery and the social chokehold of the Jim Crow era's political and social subordination of black people, the anti-lynching laws were regarded by activists as a necessary step towards securing the administrative and enforcement procedures necessary to curtail immediate and ever-present white supremacist violence. In some ways, the same type of anti-lynching work is being continued today by the Equal Justice Initiative, Black Lives Matter and the African American Policy Forum in the US, the United Friends and Families Campaign and the Institute of Race Relations in the UK and the IOJ, the Campaign for victims of racist police violence (KOP) in Germany, among many other groups and initiatives.

Ida B. Wells' campaigning work in Europe was a coordinated and strategic political move to find influential allies, to connect stories and to mobilise moral and ethical continuities in the service of anti-racism. It certainly is not rare to find contemporary activists making the same journey for solidarity, community building and strategic support. Wells and her collaborators in Europe recognised the structural continuities between state violence in the US and the UK. They also recognised the slight differences in social discourse around the issue of racism that would allow for shifts in strategy – an opportunity to think outside the box. The work that Wells did to build a bridge of anti-racism activism across the Atlantic is highly relevant today. In 2012 in London, Doreen Lawrence, mother of Stephen Lawrence, met Sybrina Fulton, mother of Trayvon Martin, when Martin's family visited the UK to meet campaigners and thank the British public for its support. The meeting was important for advocacy in both places, as it connected the stories of racism and police violence between Europe and the US. The meeting was also symbolically significant, demonstrating the solidarity of the families. Such meetings have been mirrored by activist solidarity campaigns in Europe and the US in recent years, including by German protests of the killing of Martin[2] and the London protests in solidarity with US Black Lives Matter protestors following the killing of Eric Garner in New York[3] and more recently the killings of Philando Castile in Minnesota and Alston Sterling in Louisiana.[4] In the autumn of 2015, UK-based activists, including relatives of people killed by police, travelled to the US to connect with activists similarly campaigning against racism, police brutality and state violence.[5] This exchange was particularly significant because, given the relative intensity of media coverage of police brutality in the US, people in the UK and the rest of Europe know the names of some of those who have died in the US, but people in the US generally do not know the names of those who have died in Europe. Exchanging these stories in detail is important for trans-Atlantic solidarity work.

Also particularly vital in these exchanges is to remember the names and stories of those women who have died in policing encounters, since their names and stories are not as visible in the media and, as Kimberlé Crenshaw and the African American Policy Forum have argued under the banner of #sayhername, the narrative that only men are vulnerable in these encounters is incorrect and indeed harmful for understanding the intersection of racism and sexism in policing violence (Crenshaw and Ritchie 2015).

Rights and anti-racism

Present-day police brutality in the US and Europe shares an important aspect of lynchings from the Jim Crow Era.[6] The most important feature of past and contemporary forms of state violence in this respect is the complicity of the state and the consequent frustration with employing a legal rights-based remedy. Afro-German poet May Ayim seldom described law in her litany of material on racism, but she did discuss power. A line from her poem *die farbe der macht*[7] echoes Wells: 'not the colour of skin/ the colour of power/ decides/ for or against life' (Ayim 1997). Ayim, like Wells, notes that racism is an instrument of power, and those who are racialised into positions of authority have the ability to 'decide': to narrate the order of things, to decide who is worthy of living at all. This decision, regarding

2 See Chapter 2.
3 'Eric Garner Death: 76 arrested at London Westfield demo' 2014.
4 BBC (8 July 2016).
5 Segalov 2015.
6 The similarity in the quality and characteristics of lynchings with contemporary forms of police brutality and institutional racism has been made explicit in the work of the Equal Justice Initiative's 2015 report, *Lynching in America: Confronting the Legacy of Racial Terror.* A summary of the report is available online at www.eji.org/lynchinginamerica accessed 30 May 2016.
7 Translation: 'the colour of power'.

who is who, is centrally important to Wells and Ayim, beyond simply the identity of the executioner.

The decolonial notion of power threaded through the observations of Wells, Ayim and others who have worked to describe anti-racism and state violence certainly does not consider the law, on its own, to be capable of solving the problem of racism. This would, after all, leave legal principles and institutions free from the critique of CRT and critical race feminism that regard law a constituent part of the problem of racism and state violence. The notion, instead, focuses on power in its various incarnations. Considering this, combating racism and state violence in Europe must not be imagined as achievable solely by way of a rights-based approach. That is to say, one can insist on one's freedom from arbitrary violence and right to be treated equally by state institutions, but if the violence or discrimination itself is obscured or justified by those institutions, then the *system* of rights surely must change if those rights are to be meaningful. From a different but related perspective, rights tend to exclude certain aspects of justice, as they are generally limited and conditional in principle or implementation, and their very formulation re-entrenches hegemonic and potentially harmful ideas about difference, justice and the relationship between the state and those living under its rule.

Two important critiques of rights-based approaches as a sole method of achieving justice around racism and state violence in Europe should be considered going forward in anti-racism work in Europe. The first has to do with the elaborating and defining racism, identity categories and corresponding access to protection in a way that takes on the veneer of being static (Brown and Haley 2002). The second is that rights-based claims, and more broadly, any legal claims are complicit in racism and state violence to the extent that they legitimise broader racial power relations by focusing on adjustments rather than complete transformation of the system of law and state power.

Wendy Brown, in *Left Legalism/Left Critique,* discusses what she terms 'suffering the paradoxes of rights.' She contends that rights are not only benevolent or liberating, but in fact, when one claims rights *as* part of a group, they reinforce potentially harmful social ideas about the group's identity and victim status, underscoring a horizon of social change limited to the realisation of the rights themselves (Brown 2002: 422–423). While Brown, like Patricia Williams (1991), also contends that rights approaches are helpful in certain contexts, for advancing social discourse and creating the conditions for negotiating more lasting change, she acknowledges that this is not without a cost. The cost is the strengthening of identity-based rights thinking, and this dynamic is a source of an uncomfortable paradox, which Brown views as an inevitability of social change work.

Second, and perhaps more fundamentally, there is a concern that the pursuit of legal rights falsely promises to deliver incremental improvements towards profound social change and is really only capable of relatively superficial reforms. This promise, then, distracts social movement advocacy from focusing on deeper structural change, allowing the legal and political economy to continue to coerce, target, imprison, exploit and exclude those at the margins of power (Crenshaw 1995, Conrad 2012).

However frustrating it may be to try to address and curtail institutional racism in legal policy and policing institutions, it is equally difficult to make a convincing argument that now is the time to abandon legal change initiatives. The point of these two particular critiques of rights-based approaches is not to disavow the pursuit of rights enforcement altogether. Rather, the objective is to position rights-based approaches more carefully within a larger strategy of social justice work that includes more profound change in the ways we conceptualise of difference, rights and power.

A pedagogy of dissent

Alongside the legal rights approach, which remains a central element of campaigns around policing-related deaths, racial profiling and institutional racism in Europe, there is a deliberate focus on social narratives that legitimatise state violence. The intense scrutiny of these narratives and their foundational assumptions serves the vital purpose of public education. This type of public education attempts to capture the complex practices of state violence, highlighting the importance of the narratives in mobilising the institutional structures that constitute the machinery of state violence. This type of pedagogical praxis prepares future activism with a mode of engaging with empirical patterns and makes this engagement visible for contemporaries in similar struggles abroad. It maps out the contours of invisibilised structural violence and communicates them to society more broadly.

To be an activist is a broad claim, a certain badge of political commitment. As a self-description, it is unabashed, unapologetic. The term does not imply a given strategy. For some, the term implies not only a way of being in the world, but also a foreclosure; can a judge be an activist in the same way as a community organiser can? What about a lawyer, an artist or a teacher? How does one participate in anti-racism activism in one's daily work?

In the course of this research, it has become evident that rejecting or embracing an explicit political orientation towards the project of anti-racism is not only a form of political praxis, but it also a form of pedagogy (Lawrence 1995). Positioning oneself publically and within the context of a movement teaches, conditions and contests. In his essay 'The Word and the River: Pedagogy as Scholarship as Struggle', in the influential foundational CRT text *Critical Race Theory: Key Writings that Formed the Movement*, Charles Lawrence argues that there is a practice of spreading 'the Word', which he describes as 'an articulation and validation of our common experience' (Lawrence 1995: 336). He argues that within this paradigmatic Black tradition of storytelling in the Americas, distinctions between pedagogy and struggle has historically been unhelpful, as are contemporary distinctions between the scholarly, the personal and political. I contend that Lawrence's observation is true not only in the Americas, but in Europe as well, given the modes that Black people have used to establish transnational solidarity with one another and to establish a prominent space for experience-based knowledge about racism to be taken seriously.

This project has become one that explores the modalities of a pedagogy of dissent, albeit indirectly. The term 'pedagogy of dissent' is borrowed from Chandra Mohanty, who discusses the phrase in *Feminism Without Borders* in the context of the US academy (2003). However, I would like to suggest that the phrase, while it refers to pedagogy and makes reference to the classroom setting, is best understood in a far broader context; public engagement and social education is the primary mode of the anti-racism work against the state violence examined in the current project. The expansive libratory notion of pedagogy in this regard is owed in large part to the central focus given to pedagogy as a mode of social struggle in Paulo Freire's *Pedagogy of the Oppressed* (Freire 1970).

The campaigns lodged by the families of those who have lost their lives to racial violence in London and the type of public education that those in similar positions in Germany have engaged in have served to bring the issues of police brutality and racial profiling to the forefront of social movement thinking. Using litigation as an approach has had the clear motivating factor of achieving a certain tangible legal result. However, the legal claim is advanced within the context of a broader social pedagogic engagement around racism, colonial logics and state violence.

There are clear features of a type of pedagogy of dissent in the context of European anti-racism work. First, there is a rejection of single-issue politics and a simultaneous insistence that racism is a central feature of state violence. This is not to imply that the positions taken by activists can ever be all-inclusive or perfectly equitable, but rather, it is to suggest that there is a conscious effort made to connect racial violence to other forms of violence and exclusion in the European context. This includes, for example, the integrated analysis of race and national belonging, and the care taken not to conflate race and foreignness, further reinforcing the hegemonic ethno-national discourse of white European-ness. Anti-racism work is paired with movements against police violence, anti-immigration sentiment and the suppression of protest in an attempt to describe racism as part of a complex system of conceiving of Europe and the regulation of its inhabitants, resources and claims to its space. This description is a form of teaching, highlighting the interconnectedness of systemic practices of exclusion over time.

The second aspect is the dual strategy that such pedagogic practice takes towards change. The first part of the strategy can be described as a reformist approach that insists on certain rights being honoured or certain legal or political claims being realised. The second part of the strategy is a deep critique of systemic oppression, a making visible of power relations such that the current system of regulation risks being debunked. Critical for the pedagogic practice of dissent here is not only that both strategies are advanced in isolation, but rather that they are taken forward together. Despite the seeming mutual exclusivity of reform and transformation, the simultaneous use and critique of rights-based formulas for change is useful in a number of ways. It satisfies, if only partially, various competing notions of justice that give various constituencies within communities of care room to breathe and reformulate the terms of cooperation and political priorities. For instance, the role of assigning individual liability to someone who has been the proximate cause of racial violence is a different strategy from publically revealing and describing the structures and processes associated with such violence. The former is a question of legal accountability (or lack thereof), while the latter is a question of the content of racist ideology, techniques that prevent certain groups of people from speaking, and the entrenched narratives of contemporary and historical institutional power. The uniqueness of the dual strategy is that it demands constant internal critique, is insatiable, and recognises both the limits and possibilities of current constellations of power and institutions as well as the possibility of something different. A pedagogy of dissent (un)comfortably undulates between these aspects of the dual strategy, in much the same way as Wendy Brown describes the political condition of 'suffering [of] the paradoxes of rights'; rights articulate needs while obscuring and depoliticising the conditions that produce such needs and 'yet within existing political discourse [condition of lack or injury] can be signified in no other way' (Brown and Haley 2002: 420 (from title); 431).

The third aspect is the firm temporal-spatial declaration that the ideas and issues being advanced, while deeply European and contemporary, are looped through the transnational and historical flows of ideas, capital, people and influence. This part of anti-racism work, and its pedagogical function, insists that Europe is not an exceptional context and that it has a very deep and important relationship to the development of racialising discourses. It teaches that colonial history is not a brief aberration relegated to the margins of times past, but rather an important formative aspect of the way in which Europe is positioned in the world, as well as the ways that people of the world are positioned within Europe. Foregrounding colonial structures and logics in critiques of contemporary European societies is one facet of a diasporic politic – of learning from the diversity of racialising structures from other contexts in order to test and assess strategic local interventions.

The ways in which activists are able to get these interventions heard varies, but an important aspect, which is also a form of pedagogic practice, is the use of fora over which they have more input and control. Part of what makes Wells' comment so compelling is her observation that 'those who commit the murders write the reports', by which she meant not only the police, but also mainstream media and everyone who was complicit in the violence. Indeed, the very act of speaking out against lynchings was dangerous (Wells-Barnett 1970, Allen 2000). So the form of communication that activists take, including but not limited to social media and other self-organised web-based channels, via sympathetic organisations, universities and artists, is important to reaching wide audiences without seeming only to legitimise forms of and fora for speech that already occupy a central hegemonic social position. This is a deliberate occupation of the margins of a critical and creative space for struggle (Hooks 1984, Kilomba 2008).

Epilogue

Living with the dead

The spectacle of death

Oury Jalloh was found in a fencer's pose. The skin of a burning body tightens and its soft tissue shrinks around the skeletal frame, tugging the limbs into an asymmetrical posture, one arm inevitably bending more than the other.[1] According to forensic evidence, it is likely that Jalloh was not excited, perhaps not even breathing, when the heat clenched his body into the familiar twists of a lynching. The photos of his charred and reddened flesh on the tatters of his jailhouse mattress are gruesome, and extremely important.

The spectacle of death, if it is to serve a purpose, has affective power not only because of the suffering of the human being, but also because of the context of the suffering – and in cases comparable to the Jalloh case, the context is heavily determined by the state. Some of the most powerful memorialisations of the Holocaust are, for many, not suffering human bodies, but rather piles of personal effects, such as thousands of shoes left behind by those killed in gas chambers. However, at the time, it was important to package the story of mass murder for empathetic listeners by putting the body into the frame. These images include the emaciated men and women with closely shorn hair in striped jumpsuits, or the scores of dead bodies piled into mass graves. These images are tortured, they reflect the atrocity of murder through the suffering of those killed and, at the same time, they are haunted by the callousness of the executioners. Needless to say, the complex human story behind atrocity, the banality of torture, the meticulously planned systems of culling, processing, killing and depositing of people into the earth, have been explored – but in the moment of recognition, the testimonial of the image provides a different type of value. It acts as both a call to action as well as an artefact of historical significance.

1 This phenomenon is a well-known feature of bodies burned in an intense fire. This fencer's pose is mentioned in the forensics medial report from Prof. Dr Michael Bohnert, 1 December 2015.

Another very important example of the display of gruesome murder has been the collection of lynching photographs from the early twentieth-century United States contained in the volume *Without Sanctuary* (Allen 2000). This volume is extremely graphic. It reproduces photographic images of Black (and some white) men and women hanging from trees, bridges and electricity poles, bleeding, tongues hanging out. Some people had been burned alive first, some decapitated. One might expect these images, bound in a coffee-table-sized art book, to meet with a hostile reception in the United States as a crass and inappropriately voyeuristic representation of history best left for written accounts rather than photographic ones. However, these photographs, as a set of historical records, have been taken up with care and critical reflection, especially among Black scholars and historians, as an invaluable archival testament and an accurate historical account of the Jim Crow era.

There are two important features of these photographs, beyond the spectacle of death, that make this collection an important feature of analysis. First, the pictures depict the social context of political repression. The pictures reveal the numbers of people involved in the lynchings, sometimes crowds of hundreds, many times including women, children, some smiling for the cameras. These people had not been a small group of Ku Klux Klan members wearing masks; these were, rather, large swaths of US-American society who stood by their actions openly, typically with the knowledge and support of local law enforcement. Second, these pictures were, at the time, developed into postcards and were sold as souvenirs to be sent to friends and relatives in other parts of the country. One 1910 postcard sent from Texas to Kentucky, showing a man hanging from a telephone pole being watched by hundreds of people, reads 'this is taken of a great day we had in Dallas'. Another postcard, depicting the still-hanging burned corpse of William Stanley in 1915 reads, 'This is the Barbecue we had last night. My picture is to the left with a cross over it. Your son, Joe'.[2]

We constantly participate in an economy of death spectacle, particularly now, in the age of digital photography and social media. From men and women leaping from the Twin Towers to Palestinian children trapped under rubble, these images are in no short supply. What is sacred about these images? On the one hand, depicting death seems the one step too far in indulging the voyeuristic pleasures of the human heart, not to mention compromising the privacy and emotional stability of friends and family of the dead. On the other hand, depending on the circumstances, it could be argued that the best way to honour the person is to obliterate the circumstances that led to her death, which may involve strategic deployment of her death's most crucial moment. That decision can be a torture of its own,

2 Both of these postcards can be found in Allen 2000.

where both roads are devastatingly painful. An important aspect of the visualisation of deaths of these sorts is that some images of death simply do not exist. Some deaths go unrecorded, unnoticed and are left to the obscurity of the shadows of everyday life, in Europe and elsewhere. The control of images, and the evidence of such deaths, is a crucial feature of the state's regulation of violence.

The choice to publicly show a photographic image of the tortured body of Oury Jalloh in campaigning work came after lengthy deliberation on the part of the Jalloh family and activists engaged in his legal case against police. This decision came after years of campaigning, and ultimately was not taken until the case was on appeal. Activists, friends and family found that the circumstances, the lack of media attention and social concern for the importance of the case, warranted establishing with the public a more intimate connection with the physical violence that those left behind had been grappling with since 2005. As painful as it was for loved ones to relive Jalloh's torture, they distributed flyers featuring a snapshot of his charred body around the neighbourhood of Kreuzberg in Berlin.

Dressing the pig: a flashback

In the last days of the Oury Jalloh appeal trial in 2012, the lawyers for Jalloh's family had suggested two things – that accelerant may have been used to light the fire that killed Jalloh, which would rule out suicide (since Jalloh was cuffed by his hands and feet to the holding cell wall and floor when he was discovered), and that the presiding judge should allow a test-burn, with and without accelerant, to be conducted on a dead pig. The tests were not ordered by the judiciary during the trial, and the verdict was announced at the end of the year: the police officers were guilty of negligence, no more than that. They were fined. But the issue for activists and family members had never been about solving the prosecutor's question, framed around the suicide thesis. It had always been about finding out how Oury Jalloh died. So the activists had no choice but to commission the tests independently.

There is something deeply humiliating about dressing a pig carcass in a T-shirt and trousers and laying it on a bed to burn it. The pig is already cut in half lengthwise and its severed head placed in the anatomically correct position at the top of the body – morose details but important for assessing the damage to the animal's flesh. The pig is meant to serve as the flesh-and-bone stand-in for Jalloh, who burned to death in the custody of police in a small former-East German city. Until this point, officially commissioned tests have been executed, mainly by the defence in the trial against police officers, to prove the physical possibility of using a lighter to set such a mattress alight. The current tests presuppose that lighting the mattress is possible if one manages to rip it open at the seam with one hand. It attempts to test the other key assumption upon which the defence based its case – that a man lying on such a flame-resistant mattress can, using only a lighter and no accelerant, create and sustain a fire capable of burning his entire body, much of it to the level of muscles and bone, and entirely carbonise the mattress. Both assumptions must be true to negate the possibility of third-party involvement in the current instance of custodial death.

Test A. Ripped mattress and no accelerant

We light a fire in an opening in the mattress the area of two hands, fingers outstretched. The foam does not ignite easily, and even small movements on the surface of the mattress extinguish the fire. The fire expert needs to be persistent and keeps trying to ignite the stubborn foam, until it takes. The flames are around 30 cm high when we finally get a good base established by lighting a few small fires close together. Leaving the cell, closing the door, we watch the grey smoke force its way out of the crack in the door. Thirty minutes pass and, as wisps of smoke signal the fire's end, we open the door and see that one quarter of the mattress's surface is burned – the area from the forearm and down the left side of the body, across the T-shirt and around the left leg. Three quarters of the mattress is left intact and still pale blue, what is left of the T-shirt is bright yellow, the trousers olive greenish brown. The colour is shocking to us who are familiar with the bleak photos of Oury Jalloh's remains, charred skin and red flesh on a bed of ashen tatters.

Test B. Intact mattress and 100 ml of pure alcohol

The pig is barely burned, save a few sooty marks on the skin and a blackened hoof. So a new mattress is procured and we dress the pig in new clothing, brown trousers and a white T-shirt, to test an alternative scenario – one in which accelerant is used. The fire expert opens a bottle of alcohol and pours all 100 ml of it over the clothing of the pig. After explaining the test to the rolling camera, he uses a lighter to ignite the clothing of the pig at the shoulder and the waist. Once the fire ignites we watch it burn for about 60 seconds. One of us lights the T-shirt in a third spot, reaching around the flames to the left shoulder. We leave the cell and shut the door, and after ten minutes, the smoke stops and we take a look inside. The pig has barely been burned, the mattress has not been affected. The white T-shirt is burned away in the front and the trousers have been slightly damaged. This accelerant has not kept the fire going or produced an intensity that would have significantly burned the animal's carcass, let alone incinerate it.

Test C. Ripped mattress and 200 ml of pure alcohol

This time, we decide to open the mattress *and* use accelerant – and more of it. The fire expert uses a knife to cut two half-metre oblong lengths in the mattress covering on either side of the pig, folds back the cover over these new openings, rips at the foam underneath to create ragged edges, and soaks the foam in each opening with 200 ml of pure alcohol, using the last droplets to douse the pig again. We nod at one another, sure that this is to create enough burn to incinerate everything properly. The fire expert lights the mattress on both sides of the pig and within moments, we leave the cell and back away from it. We sit outside the specially built cell that resembles a shed from the outside, counting down the 30 minutes, smoking cigarettes and eating tangerines. 'Now, when that doesn't burn …', one of us begins, '… then we have a real problem on our hands', another finishes.

After 30 minutes, the fire expert puts on his oxygen mask, readies the oxygen tank and enters the room. There are a few small smouldering bits, but the flames have all gone out. We do not need water or a fire extinguisher. Unable to see through the thick smoke, he exits and re-enters 20 minutes later. As he sees up-close, and we see from a safe distance standing outside the cell, much of the mattress is still intact.

In fact, as we discover, only about 35 per cent of the mattress did burn, and mostly where we had soaked the foam inside the mattress with alcohol. We are shocked for a few minutes, expecting the burns to be much more extensive, the mattress mere tatters of crisp paper-like ash, the pig an unrecognisable chargrilled mess. But there it is, staring back at us with a whole unburned head, beige upper hooves poking out of the intact sleeves of a white T-shirt, a fully uncharred tail, uncooked insides, laying on a bed of blue mattress, save the ashen remnants flanking the length of the pig's body. It looks nothing like the scene found in the police station, a charred and naked man on a thin layer of soot.

Whatever caused the fire, both expert and lay-person alike can be confident that it was not a humble lighter and it was not less than a couple bottles of 100 per cent ethyl-alcohol from the local pharmacy. This is particularly since it was determined already in previous tests by the police authorities that there was likely one point of ignition, of central intensity; it does not seem to be a case where this person lit himself on fire in multiple places, if one assumes he lit himself on fire at all. The pig tests reveal what may otherwise seem too abstract or distant, to me and doubtlessly also to others. A gut feeling becomes a tangible, visceral experience of the material limits of the objects we only imagine we know. After all, most of us are not fire experts; we cannot readily describe the technical details about how a flame behaves on a fire-proof mattress, with or without accelerant, on a human being, or indeed a pig.

The Oury Jalloh case: a European human rights challenge?

The death of Oury Jalloh has provoked a social debate much broader than the legal case itself, as discussed in the previous chapter. It has brought much needed attention not only to the issues of police brutality and deaths-in-custody, but also to the concepts of institutional and structural racism. Indeed *Tatort*, a popular crime series watched by millions in Germany, based an episode in 2015 on Jalloh's death and brought the issue of 'institutional racism' (*institutioneller Rassismus*) to a national, prime-time forum.[3] Of course, this is a decade after the event actually transpired, and such attention to the case and the issues would be unthinkable if not for activists, most notably members of the IOJ. So the legal case is clearly important for the public discussion that it has prompted. However, the legal case is not unimportant in legal terms, as the outcome could affect policies regarding human rights protection, policing and race in Germany and Europe, more broadly. Since the 2014 German Supreme Court confirmation of the ruling of the Madgeburg Regional Court, the state prosecutorial service has been running a special investigation on the case. This investigation, however, has not been transparent and it is unclear as to what is being investigated. The other option for furthering the case would be to go to the European Court of Human Rights, arguing that that failure to investigate the many questions left open in the case constitutes a violation of Jalloh's human rights under Article 2 ECHR. The result of a decision of the European Court of Human Rights would be binding on Germany and would set a precedent for the rest of Europe. Additionally, a petition can be made to the UN Human Rights Committee on a similar basis, and the result of any UN Committee determination would be a non-binding judgment.

Moving forward in the Jalloh trial is always for the purpose of moving forward in terms of social understanding of structural forms of state violence and racism. The conclusion of this or similar formal legal trials does not foreclose further social change, and critical work is not reliant only on legal recognition, but rather such critique yearns for openness to change in the discursive landscape of race and law.

Future ghosts

In the context of policing, and particularly given the racially disparate effects of policing in European society, death provides a central point of departure for analysis about state violence. Though death may be in some ways a misleading focus for viewing state violence, for example because it suggests that death is the only or most important manifestation of violence

3 Ebbinghaus, 'Gibt es 'institutionellen Rassismus' in Deutschland?' 2015.

worthy of analysis, death is perhaps the metaphoric tip of an iceberg that reveals a greater depth of systemic failure. Admittedly, such problems can also be viewed without a focus on death. However, if one is to seriously consider Ruthie Gilmore's definition of racism, as a type of 'premature death' (Gilmore 2007), one might consider the finality of death to be an important constituent part of an ongoing process closely related to a life lived in close and constant proximity to structural violence.

To acknowledge that the loss of a life in a policing encounter could have been prevented can prompt us all, as a society, to critically engage with our own complicity in that loss. Equally, to acknowledge that racism plays a role in violent encounters with law underscores the urgency of general anti-racism work. Constantly having to clean up the mess of state violence distracts us fundamentally from doing the work of imagining the world in which we really want to live. In the tension between reformative and transformative thinking, we may find pockets of creative space for claiming the centrality of our knowledge about society and the ways forward in changing what that society looks and feels like. This tension makes archiving, protesting and teaching about policing-related deaths, and state violence more generally, so urgent. We have got to be fluent in the language and techniques of structural violence and institutional racism, and we need to record and remember the ways that we are made to respond to state violence so that we can maintain the breathing space to cultivate the creativity and vision within our struggles.

Bibliography

AG gegen Rassismus in den Lebenswissenschaften, ed. *Gemachte Differenz. Kontinuitäten Biologischer »Rasse« Konzepte.* 1. ed. Münster: Unrast, 2009.

Agamben, Giorgio. *Homo Sacer: Sovereign Power and Bare Life.* Edited by Daniel Heller-Roazen. Stanford, CA: Stanford University Press, 1998.

Aino Schleusener, Jens Suckow, & Burkhard Voigt, eds. *AGG. Kommentar Zum Allgemeinen Gleichbehandlungsgesetz.* 3. ed. Berlin: Luchterhand, 2011.

Aikins, Joshua Kwesi, & Hoppe, Rosa. 'Straßennamen als Wegweiser für eine postkoloniale Erinnerung in Deutschland', in Arndt, Susan, & Nadja Ofuatey-Alazard, eds. *Wie Rassismus Aus Wortern Spricht: (K)Erben Des Kolonialismus Im Wissensarchiv Deutsche Sprache: Ein Kritisches Nachschlagewerk.* 1. Aufl. ed. Munster: Unrast, 2011.

Allen, James. *Without Sanctuary: Lynching Photography in America.* Santa Fe, NM: Twin Palms, 2000.

Althusser, Louis. *Lenin and Philosophy, and Other Essays.* New York: Monthly Review Press, 2001.

American Anthropological Association. 'Call for Papers, 108th Annual Meeting, American Anthropological Association: The End/S of Anthropology'. *Anthropolgy News* 50, no. 1 (2009): 16–18.

American Anthropological Association Executive Board. 'Statement on Human Rights.' *American Anthropologist* 49 (1947): 539-43.

Anderson, Benedict R. *Imagined Communities: Reflections on the Origin and Spread of Nationalism.* Rev. ed. London; New York: Verso, 2006.

Anderson, Rachel J. 'Redressing Colonial Genocide: The Hereros' Cause of Action against Germany'. *California Law Review* 93 (2005): 1155–71.

Appadurai, Arjun. *Modernity at Large: Cultural Dimensions of Globalization.* Public Worlds. Minneapolis, MN: University of Minnesota Press, 1996.

Arendt, Hannah. *The Origins of Totalitarianism.* A Harvest Book, New ed. New York: Harcourt Brace Jovanovich, 1973.

Arndt, Susan, & Nadja Ofuatey-Alazard, eds. *Wie Rassismus Aus Wortern Spricht: (K)Erben Des Kolonialismus Im Wissensarchiv Deutsche Sprache: Ein Kritisches Nachschlagewerk.* 1. Aufl. ed. Munster: Unrast, 2011.

Arndt, Susan, Antje Hornscheidt, & Marlene Bauer. *Afrika Und Die Deutsche Sprache: Ein Kritisches Nachschlagewerk.* 1. Aufl. ed. Mumlunster: Unrast, 2004.

Ayim, May. *Nachtgesang.* Berlin: Orlanda Frauenverlag, 1997.

Ayim, May, Katharina Oguntoye, & Dagmar Schultz. *Showing Our Colors: Afro-German Women Speak Out.* Amherst: University of Massachusetts Press, 1992.

Balibar, Etienne. 'Outlines of a Topography of Cruelty: Citizenship and Civility in the Era of Global Violence'. *Constellations* 8, no. 1 (2001): 15–29.

Balibar, Etienne. *We, the People of Europe?: Reflections on Transnational Citizenship.* Translation/Transnation. Princeton NJ; Oxford: Princeton University Press, 2004.

Baraka, Imamu Amiri. *Blues People: Negro Music in White America.* New York: W. Morrow, 1968.

Barskanmaz, Cengiz. 'Rasse – Unwort Des Antidiskriminierungsrechts?'. *Kritische Justiz* (2011): 382–89.

Barskanmaz, Cengiz. Rassismus und Recht. Eine rassismusanalytische Würdigung menschenrechtlicher Instrumente. PhD Dissertation. Berlin: Humboldt University of Berlin, 2015.

Bausch, Stephanie. *The Use of Emetics to Obtain Internally Concealed Drugs as Evidence – an International Law Comparison with Global, Regional and National Aspects.* Norderstedt: Grin Verlag, 2005.

Becker, Frank. 'Hybridity and Race Relations', in Poddar, Prem, Rajeev S. Patke, and Lars Jensen, eds. *A Historical Companion to Postcolonial Literatures: Continental Europe and its Empires.* Edinburgh: Edinburgh University Press, 2008.

Beriss, David. *Black Skins, French Voices: Caribbean Ethnicity and Activism in Urban France.* Westview Case Studies in Anthropology. Boulder, CO: Westview Press, 2004.

Berlant, Lauren. 'The Subject of True Feeling: Pain, Privacy and Politics', in Sarat, Austin and Thomas R. Kearns, eds. *Cultural Pluralism, Identity Politics, and the Law, Amherst Series in Law, Jurisprudence, and Social Thought.* Ann Arbor: University of Michigan Press, 1999.

Bleich, Erik. 'Anti-racism without races: Politics and policy in a "color-blind" state' in Herrick Chapman and Laura Frader, eds. *Race in France: Interdisciplinary Perspectives on the Politics of Difference.* New York: Berghahn Books, 2004.

Bleich, Erik. 'Where Do Muslims Stand on Ethno-Racial Hierarchies in Britain and France? Evidence from Public Opinion Surveys, 1988–2008'. *Patterns of Prejudice* 43, no. 3–4 (2009): 379–400.

Bowersox, Jeff. *Raising Germans in the Age of Empire: Youth and Colonial Culture, 1871–1914.* Oxford: Oxford University Press, 2013.

Bowling, Benjamin. *Violent Racism: Victimization, Policing and Social Context.* Clarendon Studies in Criminology. Rev. ed. Oxford: Clarendon Press, 1998.

Bowser, Benjamin P. *Racism and Anti-Racism in World Perspective.* Sage Series on Race and Ethnic Relations. Thousand Oaks, CA: Sage Publications, 1995.

Brown, Donathan L. 'An Invitation to Profile: Arizona V. United States'. *International Journal of Discrimination and the Law* 12, no. 2 (2012): 117–27.

Brown, Wendy. 'Suffering the Paradoxes of Rights', in Brown, Wendy and Janet E. Halley. *Left Legalism/Left Critique.* Durham: Duke University Press, 2002.

Brown, Wendy and Janet E. Halley. *Left Legalism/Left Critique.* Durham: Duke University Press, 2002.

Bruce-Jones, Eddie. 'Anthropology as Critical Legal Intervention? Instrumentalization, Co-Construction and Critical Reformulation in the Relationship between Anthropology and International Law'. *UCLA Journal of International Law and Foreign Affairs* 14, no. 2 (2009): 331–65.

Bruce-Jones, Eddie. 'Race, Space and the Nation-State: Racial Recognition and the

Prospects for Substantive Equality under Anti-Discrimination Law in France and Germany'. *Columbia Human Rights Law Review* 39, no. 2 (2008): 421–70.

Bruce-Jones, Eddie. 'Germany's Stephen Lawrence'. *Race & Class* 54, no. 2 (Oct–Dec 2012): 82–87.

Bruce-Jones, Eddie. 'German Policing at the Intersection: Race, Gender, Migrant Status and Mental Health'. *Race & Class* 56, no. 3 (2015): 36–49.

Butler, Judith. *Precarious Life: The Powers of Mourning and Violence.* London: Verso, 2006.

Butler, Judith, & Gayatri Chakravorty. *Who Sings the Nation-State? Language, Politics, Belonging.* Oxford: Seagull, 2007.

Campbell, Patrick, & Adrian Kear, eds. *Psychoanalysis and Performance.* London: Routledge, 2001.

Campt, Tina. *Other Germans: Black Germans and the Politics of Race, Gender, and Memory in the Third Reich.* Social History, Popular Culture, and Politics in Germany. Ann Arbor: University of Michigan, 2004.

Case, Rhonda Evans. 'Re-Engineering Legal Opportunity Structures in the European Union?'. *Journal of Common Market Studies* 48, no. 2 (2010): 221–41.

Cesaire, Aime, & Robin D. G. Kelley. *Discourse on Colonialism.* New York: Monthly Review Press, 2000.

Cheah, Pheng, & Bruce Robbins, eds. *Cosmopolitics: Thinking and Feeling Beyond the Nation.* Cultural Politics. Minneapolis, MN: University of Minnesota, 1998.

Clifford, James. *Routes: Travel and Translation in the Late Twentieth Century.* Cambridge, MA: Harvard University Press, 1997.

Cohen, Robin. *Global Diasporas: An Introduction.* Global Diasporas. Second Edition ed. London: Routledge, 2008.

Collins, Patricia Hill. *Black Feminist Thought : Knowledge, Consciousness, and the Politics of Empowerment.* Perspectives on Gender. New York: Routledge, 1991.

Conrad, Ryan, ed. *Against Equality: Prisons Will Not Protect You.* AK Press, 2012.

Cremer, Hendrik. 'Das Verbot rassistischer discriminierung nach Art 3 Abs 3 GG', *Anwaltsblatt* 22 (2013): 896–99.

Crenshaw, Kimberle. 'Mapping the Margins: Intersectionality, Identity Politics and Violence against Women of Color'. *Stanford Law Review* 43, no. 6 (1991): 1241–99.

Crenshaw, Kimberle. *Critical Race Theory : The Key Writings That Formed the Movement.* New York: New Press; Distributed by W.W. Norton & Co., 1995.

Crenshaw, Kimberlé, & Andrea Ritchie. 'Say Her Name: Resisting Police Brutality Against Black Women', African American Policy Forum and the Center for Intersectionality and Social Policy Studies: New York, July 2015 (online: www.aapf.org).

Delathuy, A. M. *De Kongostaat Van Leopold II: Het Verloren Paradijs, 1876–1900.* Antwerpen: Standaard, 1989.

de Mol, Mirjam. 'The Novel Approach of the CJEU on the Horizontal Direct Effect of the EU Principle of Non-discrimination: (Unbridled) Expansionism of EU Law?' *Maastricht Journal* 18 (2011), no. 1–2, 109–135.

Denzin, Norman K. *Interpretive Ethnography: Ethnographic Practices for the 21st Century.* Thousand Oaks, CA: Sage Publications, 1997.

Diamond, Elin, ed. *Performance and Cultural Politics.* London: Routledge, 1996.

Du Bois, W. E. B. *The Souls of Black Folk.* A Signet Classics. New York: New American Library, 1969.

Eggers, Maureen Maisha. 'Schwarzes Wissensarchiv', in Piesche, Peggy, ed. *Euer Schweigen Schützt Euch Nicht. Audre Lorde Und Die Schwarze Frauenbewegung in Deutschland.* Berlin: Orlanda Frauenverlag, 2012.

Eggers, Maureen Maisha, Grada Kilomba, Peggy Piesche, & Susan Arndt, eds. *Mythen, Masken Und Subjekte: Kritische Weissseinsforschung in Deutschland* 1. Aufl. ed. Munster: Unrast, 2005.

El-Tayeb, Fatima. *European Others: Queering Ethnicity in Postnational Europe.* Difference Incorporated. Minneapolis: University of Minnesota Press, 2011.

El-Tayeb, Fatima. *Schwarze Deutsche: Der Diskurs Um „Rasse' Und Nationale Identitat 1890–1933.* Frankfurt/Main; New York: Campus, 2001.

Engelke, Matthew Eric. *The Objects of Evidence: Anthropological Approaches to the Production of Knowledge.* Chichester, UK; Malden, MA: Wiley-Blackwell, 2009.

Engle, Karen. 'From Skepticism to Embrace: Human Rights and the American Anthropological Association from 1947–1999'. *Human Rights Quarterly* 23 (2001): 536–59.

Essed, Philomena. *Understanding Everyday Racism: An Interdisciplinary Theory.* Sage Series on Race and Ethnic Relations. Newbury Park, CA: Sage Publications, 1991.

Essed, Philomena and Sandra Trienekens. '"Who Wants to Feel White?" Race, Dutch Culture and Contested Identities'. *Ethnic and Racial Studies* 31, no. 1 (2008): 52–72.

Fanon, Frantz. *Black Skin, White Masks.* Translated by Charles Lam Markmann. New York: Grove Press, 1967. Peau Noire, Masques Blancs.

Fanon, Frantz. *The Wretched of the Earth.* Translated by Constance Farrington. London: Penguin Books, 1963.

Fanon, Frantz, & Azzedine Haddour. *The Fanon Reader.* London: Pluto Press, 2006.

Fekete, Liz. 'How the German Press Stoked the Lübeck Fires'. *Race & Class* 41, no. 4 (2000): 19–41.

Fekete, Liz. 'Why the NSU case matters: Structural racism and covert policing in Europe', in Sebastian Friedgrich et al., eds. *Der NSU in bester Gesellschaft: Zwischen Neonazismus, Rassismus und Staat.* Munster: Unrast Verlag, 2015.

Fischer-Lichte, Erika. *The Transformative Power of Performance: A New Aesthetics.* New York: Routledge, 2008.

Fischer-Lichte, Erika. *History of European Drama and Theatre.* Edited by Jo Riley Routledge: London, 2004.

Fischer-Lichte, Erika. *The Semiotics of Theater (Advances in Semiotics).* Edited by Jeremy Gaines and Doris Jones Bloomington: Indiana University Press, 1992.

Foucault, Michel. *The History of Sexuality Volume 1: An Introduction.* 1st Vintage Books ed. New York: Vintage Books, 1990.

Fredman, Sandra. *Discrimination Law.* Clarendon Law Series. 2nd ed. Oxford; New York: Oxford University Press, 2011.

Freeman, Michael D. A., & A. David Napier. *Law and Anthropology.* Current Legal Issues Vol 12. Oxford; New York: Oxford University Press, 2009.

Friedrichsmeyer, Sara, Sara Lennox, & Susanne Zantop. *The Imperialist Imagination: German Colonialism and its Legacy.* Social History, Popular Culture, and Politics in Germany. Ann Arbor: University of Michigan Press, 1998.

Freire, Paulo. *Pedagogy of the Oppressed.* New York: Herder and Herder, 1970.

Frindte, Wolfgang, Friedrich Funke, & Sven Waldzus. 'Xenophobia and Right-Wing-Extremism in German Youth Groups: Some Evidence against

Unidimensional Misinterpretations'. *Prejudice, Discrimination and Conflict* 20, no. 3–4 (1996): 463–78.

Fuchs, Anne, Kathleen James, & Linda Shortt, eds. *Debating German Cultural Identity since 1989.* Studies in German Literature, Linguistics, and Culture. Rochester, NY: Camden House, 2011.

Geertz, Clifford. 'Distinguished Lecture: Anti-anti Relativism'. American Anthropologist 86, no. 2 (1984): 263–78.

Gilmore, Ruth Wilson. *Golden Gulag. Prisons, Surplus, Crisis and Opposition in Globalizing California.* Los Angeles: Univeristy of California Press, 2007.

Gilroy, Paul. *Between Camps: Race, Identity and Nationalism at the End of the Colour Line.* London: Allen Lane, 2000.

Goertz, Karein. 'Showing Her Colors: An Afro-German Writes the Blues in Black and White', *Callaloo* 26, no. 2 (Spring 2003): 306–19.

Göktürk, Deniz. 'Interrupting unity: The Berlin Wall's second life on screen – A transnational perspective', in Anne Fuchs, Kathleen James, & Linda Short, eds. *Debating German Cultural Identity since 1989.* Studies in German Literature, Linguistics, and Culture. Rochester, NY: Camden House, 2011.

Good, Anthony. 'Cultural evidence in courts of law', in Matthew Eric Engelke, ed. *The Objects of Evidence: Anthropological Approaches to the Production of Knowledge.* Chichester, UK; Malden, MA: Wiley-Blackwell, 2009.

Gordon, Lewis R. *What Fanon Said: A Philosophical Introduction to His Life and Thought.* First edition. ed, Just Ideas. London: Hurst & Company, 2015.

Grillo, Ralph D. *Social Anthropology and the Politics of Language.* Sociological Review Monograph. Routledge: London, 1989.

Grosfoguel, Ramon. 'World-System Analysis and Postcolonial Studies: A Call for a Dialogue from the "Coloniality of Power" Approach', in Grosfoguel, Ramon, *The Postcolonial and the Global,* Minneapolis: University of Minnesota Press, 2008.

Grosfoguel, Ramon. 'The Epistemic Decolonial Turn'. *Cultural Studies* 21, no. 2–3 (2007): 211–23.

Hamman, Philippe, & Frank, Cécile. 'The EU's Racial Equality Directive and the Evolution of Discourse in the Field of the Fight Against Discrimination. A Comparison Between France, the UK and Spain'. *Sociological Research Online* 20, vol. 2, 1 (2015) (online: www.socresonline.org.uk/20/2/1.html).

Haney-Lopez, Ian. *White by Law: The Legal Construction of Race.* Critical America. Rev. and updated, 10th anniversary ed. New York: New York University Press, 2006.

Hargreaves, Alec. 'Half-measures: Anti-discrimination policy in France', in Herrick Chapman and Laura Frader, eds. *Race in France: Interdisciplinary Perspectives on the Politics of Difference.* New York: Berghahn Books, 2004.

Hine, Darlene Clark, Trica Danielle Keaton, & Stephen Small, eds. *Black Europe and the African Diaspora.* Urbana Champaign: University of Illinois Press, 2009.

Hitler, Adolf. *Mein Kampf.* xxviii Auflage. Munchen: Ed. Franz Eher Nachfolger, 1933.

Hochschild, Adam. *King Leopold's Ghost: A Story of Greed, Terror, and Heroism in Colonial Africa.* Boston, MA: Houghton Mifflin, 1998.

hooks, bell. *Feminist Theory from Margin to Center.* Boston, MA: South End Press, 1984.

Hügel-Marshall, Ika. *Daheim Unterwegs. Ein Deutsches Leben.* Berlin: Orlanda Frauenverlag, 1998.

Hügel, Ika, Chris Lange, May Ayim, Ilona Bubeck, Gül en Akta , & Dagmar Schultz, eds. *Entfernte Verbindungen. Rassismus, Antisemitismus, Klassenunterdrückung.* 2nd ed. Berlin: Orlanda Frauenverlag, 1999.

Initiative Schwarze Menschen in Deutschland, e.V. *Homestory Deutschland. Schwarze Biografien in Geschichte Und Gegenwart (Ausstellungskatalog).* Berlin: Bundeszentrale für politische Bildung, 2011.

Johnson-Reagon, Bernice. 'Coalition politics: Turning the century', in Barbara Smith, ed. *Home Girls: A Black Feminist Anthology.* New Brunswick, NJ: Rutgers University Press, 2000.

Kennedy, Duncan. 'A Cultural Pluralist Case for Affirmative Action in Legal Academia', in Crenshaw, Kimberle, ed. *Critical Race Theory: The Key Writings That Formed the Movement.* New York: New Press : Distributed by W.W. Norton & Co., 1995.

Kilomba, Grada. *Plantation Memories: Episodes of Everyday Racism.* 1. Aufl. ed. Munster: Unrast, 2008.

Kimmel, Michael S., & Abby L. Ferber. *Privilege: A Reader.* 2nd ed. Boulder, CO: Westview Press, 2010.

Kosnick, Kira. 'Selecta at the Door: Queer "Oriental" Space and the Problem of Getting the Mix Right at Gayhane Homoriental Clubnights'. *Berliner Blätter* 37 (2005): 126–31.

Krishnaswamy, Revathi, &John C. Hawley, eds. *The Post-Colonial and the Global.* Minneapolis: University of Minnesota Press, 2008.

Lawrence, Charles R. 'The Word and the River: Pedagogy as Scholarship as Struggle', in Crenshaw, Kimberle, ed. *Critical Race Theory: The Key Writings That Formed the Movement.* New York: New Press: Distributed by W.W. Norton & Co., 1995.

Leonard, Neil. *Jazz and the White Americans; the Acceptance of a New Art Form.* Chicago: University of Chicago Press, 1962.

Linke, Uli. *German Bodies: Race and Representation after Hitler.* New York: Routledge, 1999.

Lorde, Audre. *Sister Outsider: Essays and Speeches.* The Crossing Press Feminist Series. Trumansburg, NY: Crossing Press, 1984.

Mandel, Ruth Ellen. *Cosmopolitan Anxieties: Turkish Challenges to Citizenship and Belonging in Germany.* Durham: Duke University Press, 2008.

Martin, Peter. *Schwarze Teufel, Edle Mohren.* 1. Aufl. ed. Hamburg: Junius, 1993.

Massaquoi, Hans-Jürgen. *'Neger, Neger, Schornsteinfeger!' Meine Kindheit in Deutschland.* München: Knaur, 1999.

Mecheril, Paul. 'Besehen, Beschrieben, Besprochen. Die Blasse Uneigentlichkeit Rassifizierter Anderer'. In Nghi Ha, Kien, Nicola Lauré al-Samarai, Sheila Mysorekar, eds. *Re/Visionen. Postkoloniale Perspektiven Von People of Color Auf Rassismus, Kulturpolitik Und Widerstand in Deutschland.* First ed. Münster: Unrast, 2007.

Merry, Sally Engle. 'Human Rights Law and the Demonization of Culture'. *PoLAR: Political and Legal Anthropology Review* 26, no. 1 (2003): 55–76.

Mohanty, Chandra Talpade. *Feminism Without Borders: Decolonizing Theory, Practicing Solidarity.* Durham London: Duke University Press, 2003.

Moore, Sally Falk. *Law and Anthropology: A Reader.* Blackwell Anthologies in Social and Cultural Anthropology. Malden, MA: Blackwell Pub., 2005.

Morrison, Toni. *Jazz.* 1st trade ed. New York: Knopf: Distributed by Random House, 1992.

Möschel, Mathias. 'Color Blindness or Total Blindness? The Absence of Critical Race Theory in Europe'. *Rutgers Race & the Law Review* 9, no. 1 (2007): 57–127.

Mundy, Martha. *Law and Anthropology.* The International Library of Essays in Law and Legal Theory Second Series. Aldershot, Hants, England; Burlington, VT: Ashgate/Dartmouth, 2002.

Narr, Wolf-Dieter, & Dirk Vogelskamp. *Der Mord in Dessau Im Schoß Der Polizei – Mit Gerichtlichen Nachspielen.* Köln: Komitee für Grundrechte und Demokratie e.V., 2010.

Nghi Ha, Kien. *Ethnizität Und Migration Reloaded. Kulturelle Identität, Differenz Und Hybridität Im Postkolonialen Diskurs.* Berlin: Wissenschaftlicher Verlag Berlin, 2004.

Nghi Ha, Kien, Nicola Lauré al-Samarai, & Sheila Mysorekar, eds. *Re/Visionen. Postkoloniale Perspektiven Von People of Color Auf Rassismus, Kulturpolitik Und Widerstand in Deutschland.* 1st ed. Münster: Unrast, 2007.

Nghi Ha, Kien. *Unrein Und Vermischt: Postkoloniale Grenzgänge Durch Die Kulturgeschichte Der Hybridität Und Der Kolonialen »Rassenbastarde«.* Bielefeld: Transcript Verlag, 2010.

Oguntoye, Katharina. *Eine Afro-Deutsche Geschichte: Zur Lebenssituation Von Afrikanern Und Afro-Deutschen in Deutschland Von 1884 Bis 1950.* Berlin: Hoho Verlag Christina Hoffman, 1997.

Oguntoye, Katharina, May Ayim, & Dagmar Schultz. *Farbe Bekennen: Afro-Deutsche Frauen Auf Den Spuren Ihrer Geschichte.* 1. Aufl. ed. Berlin: Orlanda Frauenverlag, 1986.

Olusoga, David, & Casper W. Erichsen. *The Kaiser's Holocaust : Germany's Forgotten Genocide and the Colonial Roots of Nazism.* London: Faber and Faber, 2010.

Open Society Institute. *Racial Profiling in the European Union: Pervasive, Ineffective and Discriminatory.* New York: Open Society Institute, 2009

Partridge, Damani J. *Hypersexuality and Headscarves: Race, Sex, and Citizenship in the New Germany.* New Anthropologies of Europe. Bloomington: Indiana University Press, 2012.

Patterson, Orlando. *Slavery and Social Death: A Comparative Study.* Cambridge, MA: Harvard University Press, 1982.

Peretti, Burton W. *The Creation of Jazz: Music, Race, and Culture in Urban America.* Music in American Life. Urbana: University of Illinois Press, 1992.

Piesche, Peggy, ed. *Euer Schweigen Schützt Euch Nicht. Audre Lorde Und Die Schwarze Frauenbewegung in Deutschland.* Berlin: Orlanda Frauenverlag, 2012.

Pieche, Peggy, Michael Küppers, Ekpenyong Ani, & Angela Alagiyawanna-Kadalie, eds. *May Ayim Award. Erster Internatinoaler Schwarzer Deutscher Literaturpreis 2004.* Berlin: Orlanda Frauenverlag, 2004.

Poddar, Prem, Rajeev S. Patke, & Lars Jensen, eds. *A Historical Companion to Postcolonial Literatures: Continental Europe and Its Empires.* Edinburgh: Edinburgh University Press, 2008.

Poiger, Uta G. *Jazz, Rock, and Rebels: Cold War Politics and American Culture in a Divided Germany.* Studies on the History of Society and Culture. Berkeley, CA: University of California Press, 2000.

Pommerin, Reiner. *Sterilisierung Der Rheinlandbastarde: Der Schicksal einer farbigen deutschen Minderheit 1918–1937.* Dusseldorf: Droste, 1979.

Razack, Sherene H. 'Timely Deaths: Medicalizing the Deaths of Aboriginal People in Police Custody'. *Law, Culture and the Humanities* 33 (June 30, 2011): 67–83.

Reddy, Maureen. 'Invisibility/hypervisibility: The paradox of normative whiteness', in Michael S. Kimmel, & A. L. Ferber, eds. *Privilege: A Reader*. Boulder, CO: Westview Press, 2010.

Reed-Anderson, Paulette. *Rewriting the Footnotes: Berlin and the African Diaspora /Berlin Und Die Afrikanische Diaspora*. Miteinander Leben in Berlin. uberarbeitete und erw. Ausg. ed. Berlin: Auslanderbeauftragte des Senats, 2000.

Rich, Adrienne. *Blood, Bread and Poetry*. London: Virgo, 1978.

Rich, Adrienne. *Blood, Bread, and Poetry: Selected Prose, 1979–1985*. 1st ed. New York: Norton, 1986.

Riles, Annelise. *Documents: Artifacts of Modern Knowledge*. Ann Arbor: University of Michigan Press, 2006.

Riles, Annelise. *Collateral Knowledge: Legal Reasoning in the Global Financial Markets*. Chicago Series in Law and Society. Chicago; London: University of Chicago Press, 2011.

Sack, Peter G., & Jonathan Aleck. *Law and Anthropology*. The International Library of Essays in Law and Legal Theory Legal Cultures. New York, NY: New York University Press, 1992.

Sacksofsky, Ute. *Mittelbare Diskriminierung Und Das Allgemeine Gleichbehandlungsgesetz*. Berlin: Antidiskriminierungsstelle des Bundes, 2010.

Sarat, Austin, and Thomas R. Kearns. *Cultural Pluralism, Identity Politics, and the Law*. Amherst Series in Law, Jurisprudence, and Social Thought. Ann Arbor: University of Michigan Press, 1999.

Sarat, Austin, and Thomas R. Kearns. *Law's Violence*. The Amherst Series in Law, Jurisprudence, and Social Thought. Ann Arbor: University of Michigan Press, 1992.

Schöbener, Burkhard, & Stork, Florian. 'Anti-Diskriminierungsregeleungen der Europäischen Union im Zivilrecht – zur Bedeutung der Vertragsfreiheit und des Rechts auf Privatleben'. *Zeitschrift für europarechtliche Studien* Heft 1: 43–82.

Shakespeare, William. *Hamlet*. The World's Classics. Oxford: ed. G.R. Hibbard Clarendon, 1987.

Smith, Barbara. *Home Girls: A Black Feminist Anthology*. New Brunswick, NJ: Rutgers University Press, 2000.

Solanke, Iyiola. 'Where are the Black lawyers in Germany?', in Arndt, Susan, Antje Hornscheidt, & Marlene Bauer, eds. *Afrika Und Die Deutsche Sprache: Ein Kritisches Nachschlagewerk*. 1. Aufl. ed. Mumlunster: Unrast, 2004.

Solanke, Iyiola. *Making Anti-Racial Discrimination Law: A Comparative History of Social Action and Anti-Racial Discrimination Law*. London; New York: Routledge, 2009.

Sow, Noah. *Deutschland Schwarz Weiss. Der Alltägliche Rassismus* C. Bertelsmann Verlag, 2008.

Sow, Noah. 'Ist deutscher Rassismus Geschichte', in Susan Arndt, & Nadja Ofuatey-Alazard, eds. *Wie Rassismus Aus Wortern Spricht : (K)Erben Des Kolonialismus Im Wissensarchiv Deutsche Sprache: Ein Kritisches Nachschlagewerk*. 1. Aufl. ed. Munster: Unrast, 2011.

Spade, Dean. *Normal Life: Administrative Violence, Critical Trans Politics, and the Limits of Law*. Brooklyn, NY: South End Press, 2011.

Stork, Florian and Schöbener, Burkhard. 'Anti-Diskriminierungsregelungen Der

Europäischen Union Im Zivilrecht – Zur Bedeutung Der Vertragsfreiheit Und Des Rechts Auf Privatleben'. *Zeitschrift für europarechtliche Studien* Heft 1 (2004): 43–82.

Thomson, Michael. *Reproducing Narrative: Gender, Reproduction, and Law.* Brookfield, VT: Ashgate/Dartmouth, 1998.

Tischbirek, Alexander, & Timo Wihl. 'Verfassungswidrigkeit Des "Racial Profiling": Zugleich Ein Beitrag Zur Systematik Des Art. 3 Gg'. *JuristenZeitung* 68, no. 5 (2013): 219–24.

Townsend, Peter. *Jazz in American Culture.* Edinburgh: Edinburgh University Press, 2000.

Trinh, T. Minh-Ha. *Woman, Native, Other: Writing Postcoloniality and Feminism.* Bloomington: Indiana University Press, 1989.

Utlu, Deniz. 'Migrationshintergrund. Ein metaphernkritischer Kommentar', in Arndt, Susan, & Nadja Ofuatey-Alazard, eds. *Wie Rassismus Aus Wortern Spricht: (K)Erben Des Kolonialismus Im Wissensarchiv Deutsche Sprache: Ein Kritisches Nachschlagewerk.* 1. Aufl. ed. Munster: Unrast, 2011.

Wacquant, Pierre Bourdieu, & Loïc. 'On the Cunning of Imperialist Reason'. *Theory, Culture & Society* 16, no. 1 (1999): 41–58.

Weheliye, Alexander. *Habeas Viscus: Racializing Assemblages, Biopolitics, and Black Feminist Theories of the Human.* Durham, NC: Duke Univeristy Press, 2014.

Wells-Barnett, Ida B. *Crusade for Justice; the Autobiography of Ida B. Wells, Negro American Biographies and Autobiographies.* Chicago: University of Chicago Press, 1970.

Widenroth-Coulibaly, Eleonore. 'Zwanzig Jahre Schwarzer Widerstand in bewegten Räumen. Was sich im Kleinen abspielt und aus dem Verborgenen erwächst', in Nghi Ha, Kien, Nicola Lauré al-Samarai, & Sheila Mysorekar, eds. *Re/Visionen. Postkoloniale Perspektiven Von People of Color Auf Rassismus, Kulturpolitik Und Widerstand in Deutschland.* 1st ed. Münster: Unrast, 2007.

Williams, Patricia J. *The Alchemy of Race and Rights.* Cambridge, MA: Harvard University Press, 1991.

Williams, Patricia J. *Seeing a Color-Blind Future: The Paradox of Race.* The 1997 BBC Reith Lectures. 1st American ed. New York: Noonday Press, 1998.

Wright, Michelle M. *Becoming Black: Creating Identity in the African Diaspora.* Durham: Duke University Press, 2004.

Zimmerman, Andrew. *Alabama in Africa: Booker T. Washington, the German Empire, and the Globalization of the New South.* America in the World. Princeton, NJ: Princeton University Press, 2010.

Legislation

France

Law Against Racism 1972.

Germany

Allgemeines Gleichbehandlungsgesetz [AGG] (German General Equal Treatment Law) 14.08.2006.

Asylbewerberleistungsgesetz [AsylbLG] (Asylum Seekers Benefit Law) 5.8.1997.
Bundesvertriebenengesetz [BVFG] (Federal Refugees Act) 2.6.1993.
Deutsches Ausländerrecht (German Aliens Law). AuslR. 1 § 60a. 2005.
Gesetze zur Verhütung erbdranken Nachwuchses, GVeN, 14.7.1933
Grundgesetz [GG] (German Basic Law) 23. Mai 1949 (BGBl. S. 1).
Staatsangehörigkeitsgesetz [StAG] (Citizenship Law) 22.7.1913, amended on 21.8.2005.
Strafgestzbuch [StGB] (German Criminal Code) 13.11.1998.

European Union and Council of Europe

Charter of Fundamental Rights of the European Union C326/391 26.10.2012.
Council of Europe Framework Convention for the Protection of National Minorities 1.2.1995.
European Convention on Human Rights 4.11.1950.
European Union Race Directive, 2000/43/EC.
Treaty on the Functioning of the European Union, C/326 26.10.2012.

Government reports

United Kingdom

The Scarman Report: The Brixton Disorders 10–12 April 1981, Her Majesty's Stationary Office, London, November 1982.
The Macpherson Report: The Stephen Lawrence Inquiry Report 1999, Secretary of State for the Home Department, London, February 1999.

European Union

Fundamental Rights Agency 'Making hate crime visible in the European Union: acknowledging victims' rights'. Luxembourg: Publications Office of the European Union, 2012.

Cases

Germany

Beschl. v. 31.03.2006, Az. 2 M 156/06 (Oberverwaltungsgericht Magdeburg 2006).
Beschluss v. 31.11.2011 – 4 K 1163/11.KS (Verwaltungsgericht Kassel 2011).
Beschluss v. 27.3.2012 – 2 Ss 329/11 (Oberlandesgericht Frankfurt 2012).
Beschluss v. 29.10.2012 – 7 a 10532/ 12 (Oberverwaltungsgericht Rheinland-Pfalz 2012).
Application for Appeal in the case against ./. Schubert (in der Strafsache ./. Schubert) – 6 Ks 4/05.
Urteil v. 07.01.2010 – 4 Str 413/09 (Bundesgerichtshof 2010).
Urteil v. 12.12.2011 – 10U 106/11 (Oberlandesgericht Stuttgart 2011).

Urteil v. 16.12.2008 – 6 Ks 4/05 (Landgericht Dessau-Rosslau 2008).
Urteil v. 28.2.2012 – 5 K 1026/11.KO (Verwaltungsgericht Koblenz 2012).
Urteil v. 13.12.2012 – 21 Ks 141 Js 13260/10 (8/10) (Landgericht Magdeburg 2012).
Urteil v. 21.04.2016, 7 A 11108/14 (Oberverwaltungsgericht Rheinland-Pfalz 2016).

United States of America

The Herero People's Reparations Corporation, Et. Al. V. Deutsche Bank A.G. and Woermann Line, D/B/a Deutsche Afrika-Linien Gmblt & Company, U.S.App.D.C. Reports. Decided 11 June 2004.

European judgments

Borbola Kiss v. Hungary 26 Sept 2012 (ECtHR 2012).
Eduard Popa v. Maldova 12 May 2013 (ECtHR 2013).
Mangold v. Helm, C144/04 (ECJ 2005).
Nachova and others v. Bulgaria (Grand Chamber) 6 July 2005 (European Court of Human Rights 2005).
Ribbitsch v. Austria 4 Dec 1995 (ECtHR 1995).

International

Communication No. 1493/2006, *Williams V. Spain.* UN Human Rights Committee. 17 August 2009.

Internet resources

News articles

'Affe, Bimbo, Nigger' – Interview mit Adebowale Ogungbure', Bundeszentrale für politische Bildung (15 February 2007) www.bpb.de/politik/extremismus/rechtsextremismus/41781/affe-bimbo-nigger-interview-mit-adebowale-ogungbure accessed 30 May 2016.
'Affidavit Says Zimmerman "Profiled" Martin', *CNN* (13 April 2012) http://edition.cnn.com/2012/04/12/justice/florida-teen-shooting/index.html?_s=PM:JUSTICE accessed 30 May 2016.
'Ausschreitungen: Fußballer Reagiert Auf Schmähungen Mit Hitlergruß', *Frankfurter Allgemeine Zeitung* (28 March 2006) www.faz.net/aktuell/sport/fussball/ausschreitungen-fussballer-reagiert-auf-schmaehungen-mit-hitlergruss-1305403.html accessed 30 May 2016.
Batty, David. 'Prevent Strategy "sowing mistrust and fear in Muslim communities"', *The Guardian* (3 Febrary 2015) www.theguardian.com/uk-news/2016/feb/03/prevent-strategy-sowing-mistrust-fear-muslim-communities accessed 30 May 2016.
Bause, Tanja. 'Horseback Demo against Germany's Un Ambitions', *The Namibian* (25 August 2005) www.namibian.com.na/index.php?id=28&tx_ttnews[tt_news]=12591&no_cache=1 accessed 30 May 2016.

BBC. 'Hundreds join Black Lives Matter march through London', (8 July 2016) www.bbc.co.uk/news/uk-england-london-36750533 accessed 10 July 2016.

BBC News. 'Germany returns Namibian skulls taken in colonial era', (30 September 2011) www.bbc.co.uk/news/world-europe-15127992 accessed 30 May 2016.

BBC News. 'EU Referendum Results', (24 June 2016) www.bbc.co.uk/news/politics/eu_referendum/results accessed 1 July 2016.

'Bremer Brechmittel-Prozess: Am Ende kein Urteil', *Taz.de* (2 November 2013) www.taz.de/!5055796/ accessed 11 July 2016.

Broomby, Ray. 'Race Hate in Germany', *BBC News* (3 September 2000) http://news.bbc.co.uk/1/hi/programmes/from_our_own_correspondent/908592.stm accessed 30 May 2016.

Buhe, Diana. '"Ihre Papiere Bitte!" Racial Profiling in Deutschland', *Mut Gegen Rechte Gewalt* (7 January 2013) www.mut-gegen-rechte-gewalt.de/projekte/aktuelle-aktionen/ihre-papiere-bitte-racial-profiling-deutschland-2013-01 accessed 30 May 2016.

'Defying Racial Profiling in Germany: "I Didn't Want to Be Treated Differently Any Longer"', *Spiegel Online* (2 November 2012) www.spiegel.de/international/germany/interview-with-plaintiff-of-racial-profiling-case-in-germany-a-864932.html accessed 30 May 2016.

Denso, Christian. 'Der Tod Des Dealers Achidi John', *Hamburger Abendblatt*, (13 July 2006) www.abendblatt.de/hamburg/article107135246/Der-Tod-des-Dealers-Achidi-John.html accessed 30 May 2016.

Der Spiegel. 'Polizeikontrolle wegen der Hautfarbe: "Der schlimmste Tag meines Lebens"', (1 November 2012), www.spiegel.de/unispiegel/wunderbar/schwarzer-student-gewinnt-prozess-um-widerrechtliche-polizei-kontrolle-a-864589.html accessed 26 April 2013.

Der Spiegel. 'Defying Racial Profiling in Germany: "I Didn't Want to Be Treated Differently Any Longer"', (2 November 2012), www.spiegel.de/international/germany/interview-with-plaintiff-of-racial-profiling-case-in-germany-a-864932.html accessed 26 April 2013.

Dieckmann, Christoph. 'Kristallnacht Im August. "Deutschland Den Deutschen": Im Sommer 1992 Wütete Ein Entfesselter Mob in Rostock-Lichtenhagen Drei Abende Lang Gegen "Ausländer" Und "Asylanten"', *Zeit Online* (22 August 2012) www.zeit.de/2012/34/Rostock-Lichtenhagen-Rechtsextremismus accessed 30 May 2016.

Diehl, Jörg. 'Ermyas-Mulugeta-Prozess: Kein Täter – Nur Opfer', *Spiegel Online* (15 June 2007) www.spiegel.de/panorama/justiz/ermyas-mulugeta-prozess-kein-taeter-nur-opfer-a-488791.html accessed 30 May 2016.

Ebbinghaus, Uwe. 'Gibt es 'institutionellen Rassismus' in Deutschland?', *Frankfurter Allgemeine Zeitung* (11 October 2015) www.faz.net/aktuell/feuilleton/medien/tatortsicherung/faz-net-tatortsicherung-gibt-es-institutionellen-rassismus-in-deutschland-13847665.html accessed 30 May 2016.

'Eric Garner Death: 76 arrested at London Westfield demo', *BBC* (11 December 2014) www.bbc.co.uk/news/uk-england-london-30424338 accessed 30 May 2016.

'Flüchtlinge Verlängern Protest Am Brandenburger Tor', *Zeit Online* (5 November 2012) www.zeit.de/gesellschaft/zeitgeschehen/2012-11/fluechtlinge-brandenburger-hungerstreik 30 May 2016.

France24. 'French minorities accuse state of racial profiling', (13 April 2012), www.france24.com/en/20120412-france-racial-profiling-arab-black-police-foreign-ministry accessed 26 April 2013.

'French Minorities Accuse State of Racial Profiling', *France 24 International News* (13 April 2012) www.france24.com/en/20120412-france-racial-profiling-arab-black-police-foreign-ministry accessed 30 May 2016.

Frank Jansen, Johannes Radke, Heike Kleffner, & Toralf Staud. 'Tödlicher Hass: 149 Opfer Rechte Gewalt', *Der Tagesspiegel* (31 May 2012) www.tagesspiegel.de/politik/rechtsextremismus/toedlicher-hass-149-todesopfer-rechter-gewalt-seite-3/1934424-3.html accessed 30 May 2016.

Friedrichsen, Gisela. 'Ermyas-Prozess: Pieps Und Die Wahrscheinlichkeiten', *Der Spiegel* (4 May 2007) www.spiegel.de/panorama/justiz/ermyas-prozess-pieps-und-die-wahrscheinlichkeiten-a-481105.html accessed 30 May 2016.

'Germany's Schlosspark Theatre Defends "Blackface" Actor', *BBC* (10 January 2012) www.bbc.co.uk/news/world-europe-16492222 accessed 30 May 2016.

'Germany Asks for Namibians' "Forgiveness"', *Deutsche Welle* (14 August 2004) www.dw.de/germany-asks-for-namibians-forgiveness/a-1298060 accessed 30 May 2016.

Greiner, Lena. 'Diskriminierung an Der Discotür: "Guck Mal, Wie Du Aussiehst"', *Spiegel Online* (4 February 2013), www.spiegel.de/unispiegel/wunderbar/studenten-klagen-gegen-diskriminierung-an-der-discotuer-a-878459.html accessed 30 May 2016.

Guyton, Patrick. 'Der Lange Marsch Der Flüchtlinge', *Der Tagesspiegel* (24 September 2012) www.tagesspiegel.de/politik/asylpolitik-der-lange-marsch-der-fluechtlinge/7173520.html accessed 30 May 2016.

'Herero Massacre: General's Descendants Apologize for "Germany's First Genocide"', *Spiegel Online* (8 October 2007) www.spiegel.de/international/world/herero-massacre-general-s-descendants-apologize-for-germany-s-first-genocide-a-510163.html accessed 30 May 2016.

Izoya, Isaac. 'German Policewoman: Shot and Killed a (Benin) Nigerian Woman', *Modern Ghana*, (28 May 2011) www.modernghana.com/newsp/331132/1/pagenum2/german-policewoman-shot-and-killed-a-benin-nigeria.html accessed 30 May 2016.

'Kein Vergeben, Kein Vergessen: Alberto Adriano', *Indy Media* (31 May 2010) http://de.indymedia.org/2010/05/282575.shtml accessed 30 May 2016.

'Kolonial-Rassistischer Sprachgebrauch in Einem Theaterstück an Der Volksbühne Berlin (Interview mit Mitglieder der ISD)', *Freie-Radios* (3 January 2004) www.freie-radios.net/5812 accessed 30 May 2016.

Kuhn, Philip. 'Erneut Hetze Gegen Farbige in Polizei-Kalender', *Die Welt* (2 May 2012) http://de.nachrichten.yahoo.com/erneut-hetze-gegen-farbige-in-polizei-kalender-155136012.html accessed 30 May 2016.

Lamar, Jake. 'How Do You Say the N-Word in French?', *The Root* (28 October 2010) www.theroot.com/views/how-do-you-say-n-word-french-0 accessed 30 May 2016.

Leiß, Birgit. 'Antidiskriminierungsgesetz. Beschränkte Gleichbehandlung', *Berliner Mietverein MieterMagazin* (1 September 2006) www.berliner-mieterverein.de/magazin/online/mm0906/090620.htm accessed 30 May 2016.

'Özdemir: No-Go-Areas Für Schwarze in Deutschland Realität', *Die Welt* (19 May 2006) www.welt.de/politik/article218145/Oezdemir-No-Go-Areas-fuer-Schwarze-in-Deutschland-Realitaet.html accessed 30 May 2016.

'Police Doctor Acquitted over Forced Vomiting Death', *The Local* (14 June 2011) www.thelocal.de/national/20110614-35643.html#.UW6Z6UpWL4o accessed 30 May 2016.

'Polizeikontrolle Wegen Der Hautfarbe: "Der Schlimmste Tag Meines Lebens"', *Spiegel Online* (1 November 2012) www.spiegel.de/unispiegel/wunderbar/schwarzer-student-gewinnt-prozess-um-widerrechtliche-polizei-kontrolle-a-864589.html accessed 30 May 2016.

Pollähne, Dr. iur. habil. Helmut. 'Bgh Hebt Freispruch Um Brechmitteltod Erneut Auf: Bremen – "Hauptstadt Des Erbrechens"', *The Legal Tribune Online* (21 June 2012) www.lto.de/recht/hintergruende/h/bgh-hebt-freispruch-um-brechmitteltod-erneut-auf-arzt-polizei/ accessed 30 May 2016.

Privot, Michael. 'Racial profiling at borders will not help counter terrorism', *ESharp Magazine* (16 February 2016) http://esharp.eu/debates/external-action/racial-profiling-at-borders-will-not-help-counter-terrorism accessed 30 May 2015.

Ragazzi, Francesco. 'Trust and suspiscion under "policed multiculturalism"', *Open Democracy* (10 February 2016) www.opendemocracy.net/digitaliberties/francesco-ragazzi/trust-and-suspicion-under-policed-multiculturalism accessed 30 May 2016.

Rassismus aus Selbstschutz. 'Ladenbesitzerin erteilt allen Roma Hausverbot', *Märkische Allgemeine.* Berlin 2016.

'Rassistische Attacke Beim Fußball Nigerianer Wehrt Sich Und Zeigt Hitlergruß', *Der Tagesspiegel* (28 March 2006) www.tagesspiegel.de/sport/rassistische-attacke-beim-fussball-nigerianer-wehrt-sich-und-zeigt-hitlergruss/697172.html accessed 30 May 2016.

Schauka, Frank. 'Fall Ermyas Mulugeta: Rassismus Vergeblich Gesucht', *Frakfurter Allgemeine Zeitung* (15 June 2007) www.faz.net/aktuell/politik/fall-ermyas-mulugeta-rassismus-vergeblich-gesucht-1435472.html accessed 30 May 2016.

Schearer, T. D. a. J. 'Stop Racial Profiling in Germany' (Fall 2012) www.theafrican-courier.de/index.php?option=com_content&view=article&id=526 accessed 26 April 2013.

Schearer, Jamie, & Tahir Della. 'Stop Racial Profiling in Germany'. *African Courier* (Fall 2012) www.theafricancourier.de/index.php?option=com_content&view=article&id=526 accessed 30 May 2016.

Schmeller, Johanna. 'Germany Refuses to Acknowledge Herero Massacres as Genocide'. *Deutsche Welle* (23 March 2012) www.dw.de/germany-refuses-to-acknowledge-herero-massacres-as-genocide/a-15830118 accessed 30 May 2016.

Segalov, Michael. 'Justice activists join hands across the Atlantic to end police killings: Black Lives Matter across the pond', *Huck Magazine* (12 December 2015) www.huckmagazine.com/perspectives/activism-2/black-lives-matter/ accessed 30 May 2016.

Seidler, Ulrich. 'Das Deutsche Theater Berlin Schminkt Sich Um', *Berliner Zeitung* (23 March 2012) www.berliner-zeitung.de/kultur/debatte-das-deutsche-theater-berlin-schminkt-sich-um,10809150,11953918.html accessed 30 May 2016.

Spiegelberger, William. 'Can a Claim under Customary International Law Succeed in the United States?', *Bloomberg News* (17 September 2003) www.whitecase.com/Publications/Detail.aspx?publication=682#.UXa5pEpWL4o accessed 30 May 2016.

'Strafbar Oder Nicht?', *Mitteldeutsche Zeitung* (9 January 2012) www.mzweb.de/mitteldeutschland/recht-strafbar-oder-nicht-,20641266,17361856.html accessed 30 May 2016.

'Tod Von Trayvon Martin: Weiß Gegen Schwarz', *Stuttgarter Zeitung*, (24 March 2012) www.stuttgarter-zeitung.de/inhalt.tod-von-trayvon-martin-weiss-gegen-schwarz.44d95ca8-1451-4d89-bab4-fd2142886889.html accessed 30 May 2016.

Topcu, Özlem. 'Kinderbuch-Debatte: Stellt Euch Nicht So An', *Zeit Online* (24 January 2013) www.zeit.de/2013/05/Kinderbuch-Debatte-Neger-Rassismus accessed 30 May 2016.

Wirner, Stefan. 'Bei Ankunft Todesschuss', *Jungle World* (5 September 2001) http://jungle-world.com/artikel/2001/36/25246.html accessed 30 May 2016.

Zöllner, Abini. 'Don't Call Me Neger. Ein Wort Hat Seine Unschuld Verloren, Das Erfuhr Jetzt Auch Die Volksbühne', *Berliner Zeitung* (12 December 2003) www.berliner-zeitung.de/archiv/ein-wort-hat-seine-unschuld-verloren—das-erfuhr-jetzt-auch-die-volksbuehne-don-t-call-me-neger,10810590,10136124.html accessed 30 May 2016.

Press releases

'Aufruf: Tribunal in Gedenken an Dominique Koumadio, Oury Jalloh Und Alle Anderen Opfer Rassistischer Staatsgewalt', The Caravan (4 June 2008) www.thecaravan.org/node/1528 accessed 30 May 2016.

'Justice for Mouctar Bah – Fax Campaign against the City of Dessau-Rosslau', The Voice Refugee Forum (15 February 2008) http://thevoiceforum.org/node/698 accessed 30 May 2016.

'Press Release: Die Verfolgung Eines Wortes Und Ein Anruf Zur Aktion', Die Karawane (6 December 2007) http://thecaravan.org/node/1252 accessed 30 May 2016.

'Press Release: The Position of the OCD 1904 on the Genocide Motion in the German Bundestag', Ovaherero/Ovambanderu Council for the Dialogue on the 1904 Genocide (OCD-1904) (29 March 2012) www.flickr.com/photos/77161030@N03/6926520646/ accessed 30 May 2016.

'Press Release: The Persecution of a Word and a Call for Action', The Voice Refugee Forum (15 June 2007) http://initiativeouryjalloh.wordpress.com/2007/06/15/the-persecution-of-a-word-and-a-call-for-action/ 30 May 2016.

'Presseerklärung: Klageerzwingungsverfahren Beantragt', Anwaltsbüro Heinecke Klingner Mücher Töpfer Wittmann (5 February 2003) www.brechmitteleinsatz.de/presse/pe-02-03.html accessed 30 May 2016.

'Pressemitteilung Zum Ende Des Gerichtsprozesses Im Fall Oury Jalloh', Initiative in Gedenken an Oury Jalloh e.V. (4 December 2008) http://initiativeouryjalloh.wordpress.com/2008/12/04/pressemitteilung-zum-ende-des-gerichtsprozesses-im-fall-oury-jalloh/ accessed 30 May 2016.

'Pressemitteilung: Für Eine Gesellschaft Frei Von Mord Und Todschlag', Die Karawane (14 April 2009) http://thecaravan.org/node/1920 accessed 30 May 2016.

'Pressemitteilung: Klage Gegen Diskriminierende Einlasskontrolle Erfolgreich', Das Antidiskriminierungsbüro Freistaat Sachsen (21 May 2012) www.adb-sachsen.de/media/documents/1337680338.pdf accessed 30 May 2016.

'Pressemitteilung: Rassismus, Diskriminierung, Polizeigewalt Müssen Denunziert

Werden!', Initiative in Gedenken an Oury Jalloh e.V. (27 May 2012) http://initiativeouryjalloh.wordpress.com/2012/05/27/rassismus-diskriminierung-polizeigewalt-mussen-denunziert-werden/ accessed 30 May 2016.

'Pressemitteilung: Vorgang Oury Jalloh Aus Polizeijournal Gelöscht. Vom Gericht Auf Die Straßen Berlins Geht Die Initiative in Gedenken an Oury Jalloh e.V. Am 16.7.2011', Initiative in Gedenken an Oury Jalloh e.V. (11 July 2011) http://initiativeouryjalloh.wordpress.com/2011/07/11/pressemitteilung-vorgang-oury-jalloh-aus-polizei-journal-geloscht-vom-gericht-auf-die-strasen-berlins-geht-die-initiative-in-gedenken-an-oury-jalloh-e-v-am-samstag-den-16-07-2011/ accessed 30 May 2016.

'Pressemitteilung: Wir Fordern Die Mordanklage! – Aufruf Der Initiative in Gedenken an Oury Jalloh', Die Karawane (11 August 2012) http://thecaravan.org/node/3522 accessed 30 May 2016.

'Pressemitteilung: First Died Oury Jalloh – Now Mouctar Bah's Telecafé Is to Be Closed', The Voice (31 January 2006) http://thevoiceforum.org/node/352 accessed 30 May 2016.

'Pressemitteilung: Initiative Oury Jalloh out of the Court Back on the Street', Die Karawane (28 July 2008) http://thecaravan.org/node/1623 accessed 30 May 2016.

'Pressemitteilung: Mörderische Verhältnisse Im Polizeirevier Dessau – Roßlau!', Initiative in Gedenken an Oury Jalloh e.V. (7 January 2013) http://initiativeouryjalloh.files.wordpress.com/2013/01/pm7-1-13-1.pdf accessed 30 May 2016.

'Pressemitteilung: The Voice Jena on Oury Jalloh – Prozessfarce Statt Rechtsstaatlichkeit', The Voice Refugee Forum (6 March 2012) http://thevoice-forum.org/node/2463 accessed 30 May 2016.

'Pressemittilung: "Kommen Sie Mit, Wir Kaufen Reinen Alkohol"', Initiative in Gedenkan an Oury Jalloh e.V., (14 November 2012) http://initiativeouryjalloh.files.wordpress.com/2012/11/pm_initiative-oury-jalloh_14-11-20124.pdf accessed 30 May 2016.

'Stellungnahme Der Initiative Vom November', Initiative in Gedenken an Oury Jalloh e.V. (8 December 2012) http://initiativeouryjalloh.wordpress.com/2012/12/08/stellungnahmen-der-initiative-vom-november/ accessed 30 May 2016.

'Stellungnahme Nach Dem Urteil Des Magdeburger Landgerichts – Wie Viele Von Uns Werden Sie Noch Töten?', Initiative in Gedenkan an Oury Jalloh e.V. (13 December 2012) http://initiativeouryjalloh.files.wordpress.com/2012/12/statement_urteil.pdf accessed 30 May 2016.

'Stellungnahme Zum Laufenden Revisionsverfahren Um Den Tod Von Oury Jalloh Vor Dem Magdeburger Landgericht', Initiative in Gedenkan an Oury Jalloh e.V. (12 November 2012) http://initiativeouryjalloh.wordpress.com/2012/11/12/stellungnahme-zum-laufenden-revisionsverfahren/ accessed 30 May 2016.

'Warum Starb Ousman Sey? Mahnwache Am Dienstag!', Initiative Christy Schwundeck (11 July 2011) http://initiative-christy-schwundeck.blogspot.de/2012/07/warum-starb-ousman-sey-mahnwache-am.html accessed 30 May 2016.

Reports

Equal Justice Initiative. *Lynching in America: Confronting the Legacy of Racial Terror* (2005). A summary of the report is available online at www.eji.org/lynchinginamerica accessed 30 May 2016.

United for Intercultural Action. *List of 17,306 documented refugee deaths through Fortress Euorpe* (2012). www.unitedagainstracism.org/pdfs/listofdeaths.pdf accessed 30 May 2016.

Organisational homepages

Afrika-Positiv, e.V. website, www.africa-positive.de/ accessed 30 May 2016.

'Against Black-Face Roles in German Theatre (Petition)', Aavaz website www.avaaz.org/en/petition/Against_BlackFace_Roles_in_German_Theatre/ accessed 30 May 2016.

Aikins, Joshua Kwesi. 'Rede – May Ayim Ufer', Initiative Schwarze Menschen in Deutschland website (14 November 2012) http://isdonline.de/rede-may-ayim-ufer-von-joshua-kwesi-aikins/ accessed 30 May 2016.

Bühnenwatch. 'Erste Intervention/Aktion Gegen Blackface an Deutschen Theaterbühnen' (12 February 2012) http://buehnenwatch.com/erste-interventionaktion-gegen-blackface-an-deutschen-theaterbuhnen/ accessed 30 May 2016

Bundesministerium des Innern website. www.bmi.bund.de/DE/Themen/Gesellschaft-Verfassung/Nationale-Minderheiten/Nationale-Minderheiten-Deutschland/nationale-minderheiten-deutschland_node.html accessed 30 May 2016.

Bruce-Jones, Eddie. 'The Production of an Attacker: Emrah Kara and the Shooting of the Mentally Ill'. *Institute of Race Relations News Comment.* Institute of Race Relations website, 2014.

Der Braune Mob, e.V. website. http://derbraundemob.de accessed 30 May 2016. e.V., ADEFRA. www.adefra.de.

'Dominique – Von Polizei Erschossen', No Racism (15 May 2006) http://no-racism.net/article/1679 accessed 30 May 2016.

Edathy, Sebastian. 'Rede Vor Dem Deutschen Bundestag vom 21. Januar 2005', Sebastian Edathy website (21 January 2005) www.edathy.de/edathy.php/cat/28/aid/636/title/Rede_vor_dem_Deutschen_Bundestag_vom_21._Januar_2005 accessed 10 January 2012.

Fekete, Liz. 'Freedom of Speech on Racism under Threat', Institute for Race Relations (23 February 2010) www.irr.org.uk/news/germany-freedom-to-speak-on-racism-under-threat accessed 30 May 2016.

Initiative Schwarze Menschen in Deutschland website, http://neu.isdonline.de/ accessed 30 May 2016.

Joliba Interkulturelles Netzwerk in Berlin, e.V. website www.joliba-online.de/ accessed 30 May 2016.

Karawane e.V. website http://thecaravan.org/ accessed 30 May 2016.

'Kundgebung in Gedenken an Dominique Koumadio', Flüchtlingsinitiative Berlin-Brandenburg (13 April 2009) http://fibb.wordpress.com/2009/04/13/kundgebung-in-gedenken-an-dominique-koumadio/ accessed 30 May 2016.

'Linksextremistische Medien' ('Left Radical Media'), Bundeszentrale für politische Bildung website (22 December 2014) www.bpb.de/politik/extremismus/linksextremismus/33630/medien accessed 30 May 2016.
'Michael Paul Nwabuisi – Tod Nach Brechmitteleinsatz in Hamburg', No Racism (12 December 2001) http://no-racism.net/article/1082/ accessed 30 May 2016.
Nigerian Community Germany, e.V. website http://nigeriancommunitygermany.com/ accessed 30 May 2016.
'Polizeiaktion Gegen Telecafe Und Mouctar Bah Vor Gerichtstermin Im Fall Oury Jalloh', Die Karawane website (16 December 2009) http://thecaravan.org/node/2232 accessed 30 May 2016.
'Reaction from Kassel Branch: "The German Police at It Again"', No Racism (9 June 2011) http://no-racism.net/article/4050/ accessed 30 May 2016.
'A Shift in Perspective: The May Ayim Ufer', Amadeu Adriano Stiftung (2010), www.amadeu-antonio-stiftung.de/eng/news/the-may-ayim-ufer/ accessed 30 May 2016.
Southall Black Sisters website www.southallblacksisters.org.uk accessed 30 May 2016.
Stop Racial Profiling website www.stoppt-racial-profiling.de. accessed 30 May 2016.
'Trayvon Martin', (Thema) Der Spiegel http://spiegel.de/thema/trayvon_martin/ accessed 30 May 2016.
Wells, Ida B. 'Lynch law in all its phases (1893)', Black Past website, www.blackpast.org/1893-ida-b-wells-lynch-law-all-its-phases accessed 30 May 2016.

Index